STUDIES IN GRAMMAR

BY

MABEL C. HERMANS

JEFFERSON HIGH SCHOOL, LOS ANGELES, CALIFORNIA

NEW YORK
HENRY HOLT AND COMPANY

PREFACE

For years it has been my task and my privilege to teach grammar. This grammar has never been the purely disciplinary subject, but rather the grammar that functions in correctly spoken and written English. My classes have ranged from the fourth grade, where no technical grammar is given, through the twelfth grade, where the necessary technical points are supposed to be mastered. The members of these classes have been boys and girls in day schools, and men and women in night schools; people who have heard no language but English, considerably misused and corrupted, and people who are entirely unfamiliar with our language and at the best know only its incorrect forms. The mentality of the individuals of these classes has ranged from that of the moron to that of the super-bright.

I have used numerous text books and have had varying degrees of success with each. Never have I been able to put a book into the hands of all the pupils of any one class and have it actually function as a guide to their activity unless I supplemented it with much explanation and other work. The reason for this is that no book that I have found was written primarily for all the pupils of such a supposedly homogeneous group as a public school class. Writers of text books have unconsciously considered it the business of the teacher to explain the material put into the hands of the pupils.

This is not an ideal condition. I believe in the maximum of pupil activity. Consequently, I looked for a text book that would be a guide to the student in all his work, one that would stimulate him to teach himself, and one that would set standards so that he could judge himself. I wanted a text book written for the students, not one for the teacher to expound to the pupils. In other words, I tried to find a book that would result in a maximum of student activity and a minimum of teacher activity.

About a year ago I decided to make a set of lessons for my own classes; lessons that could be used by every pupil, lessons so simply written that the slow, as well as the bright, would be able to gain the information that would function in his written and oral expression. Little by little the lessons grew into problems until there came into existence an entire course in grammar, sentence construction, and punctuation, based upon the laws of logic and psychology.

When the lessons were mimeographed and given to the students, a new experience came to me. Students, the slow and the bright, literally " devoured " the problems at their maximum rate; they clamored for more, and were happy over their accomplishments. Pupils who had failed times almost innumerable began to " see light," and the real joy that comes from success was written on their faces. At the end of the term there were fewer failures, greater knowledge, and a keener desire for an education on the part of all.

There is no attempt at erudition in the exercises of *Studies in Grammar*. It is not a book of rhetoric, nor is it a technical grammar. It is not an end in itself; it is merely a guide to an end, correctly spoken and written English. There is nothing new within its pages. I merely hope that the hard has been made interesting and easy, and that it will not be necessary for any teacher to " expound " the information to her students. Finally, it is not written for the purpose of training essayists or writers of fiction; it is written to be a laboratory in which the boys and girls who constitute the average folk will gain the ability to express their thoughts in correct English, a possession that can bring much happiness to the one who possesses it.

M. C. H.

A WORD TO THE PUPIL

Would you like to become your own teacher? Would you like to depend less upon the teacher of the class and become better able to do your work by yourself? Would you like to mark your own papers? Do you want to be sure of knowing your work day by day? Are you really anxious to succeed in your school life? Do you want to accomplish something really fine and splendid? You may if that is a sincere desire. How? Read further.

This is your book. By means of this book you may become your own teacher. You may decide for yourself whether you know your work or not. You can mark and judge your own papers and know definitely just where you stand. If you observe the directions and suggestions that follow, you can be certain of doing satisfactory work. If you are honest with yourself as you work the lessons, you can have success.

First of all, you will want to know what sort of a book this is and what its purpose is. *Studies in Grammar* will help you to speak and write correct English. Do you always use "who" and "whom" correctly? And do you know why you use them? Are you certain that you never use "done" for "did" or "seen" for "saw?" Do you understand when to use "in" and when to use "into?" Do you ever punctuate a sentence incorrectly? If you have difficulty in using words correctly, in forming sentences, or punctuating them, you can learn how to do so by working carefully the exercises that follow.

Now that you know the purpose of the book, you will want to know how to use it. Read all of these directions so that you can have an idea of the entire process.

1. The book is divided into twenty *problems*. A *problem* consists of a group of *exercises* that you yourself plan and work and mark. Open to *Problem I*. Read the *Purpose of Study,* and glance over the exercises to get an idea of what you are going to learn. When you have done this, sit down and write in your own words your reason for working the problem. Do not copy the words of the book. Possibly you wish to be able to recognize sentences, or possibly you want to be able to write sentences. Whatever your reason is, state it very sincerely.

2. Read all of the first exercise and then write the assignment neatly in ink on regular theme paper.

3. Now look on the first page of the " Keys to the Exercises " and you will find a Key to this exercise. Mark your paper correctly, checking any mistakes. If your paper is practically perfect, correct the mistakes; if you made many mistakes, you should rewrite the paper.

4. Have your teacher or some one in the class correct the original part of the exercise. If you choose a member of the class, be sure that he or she is able to help you. You will not gain anything by having some one do this who knows less about the work than you do. If you want the teacher to correct the original work, go to her desk and wait quietly for your turn.

5. Work all exercises in. *Problem I* in this way. First write the assignment given in the exercise and correct it by the key. Then write the original part and have it corrected by the teacher or some excellent student.

6. When you think you have mastered all the exercises of *Problem I,* clip them together and put the purpose, which

you wrote first, on the introductory page. Take these to your teacher at the beginning of the period and tell her that you are ready for a test. She will take the lessons and give you a short test that you must work in one period. Use theme paper and ink. Write neatly and spell carefully, for she will notice these points especially. If you finish before the class is dismissed, hand the paper to her at once.

7. Now proceed to *Problem II,* working it as you did *Problem I.*

8. At her earliest convenience, your teacher will call you to her desk, and you and she will correct your test together. If you pass, you will take the test for *Problem II* as soon as you know the work. If, however, your test proves to you that you do not understand the work of *Problem I,* your teacher will tell you which exercises you need to review. When you are quite certain that you have mastered *Problem I,* you will take your papers to the teacher again, and she will give you another test on *Problem I.* If you have been honest and conscientious in your work, you will not have to take a third test. Of course, you ought not to need a second test if you make the necessary effort.

9. Work all problems in the way outlined. Write the assigned exercise first, and then consult the key. If it is necessary, rewrite it to have it practically perfect. Then work the original part and have it corrected. When you know that you are ready for the test, take your papers to the teacher and she will give you a test.

10. Your success depends entirely upon you. Read the explanation and directions before you work an exercise. Then consult the key so that you can be sure that you understand the work. You hurt no one but yourself if you are careless.

11. Be independent of the teacher. See how seldom you need to go to her for help. All the information that you need in order to work each exercise is in the explanation. You can understand the work if you will read it carefully.

12. Finally, remember that you can succeed if you want to. It will take time and earnest effort, but surely you are willing to give freely of these in order to be successful. You will not fail if you are honest with yourself.

CONTENTS

STUDIES IN GRAMMAR

STUDIES IN GRAMMAR

PROBLEM I

THE SENTENCE

Purpose of Study

In expressing ideas, whether they are oral or written, the sentence is the unit of thought. For that reason we must know what sentences are and how to construct them correctly.

Exercises

1. Recognition of the sentence as the unit of thought
2. Recognition of sentences and completion of incomplete groups into sentences with capitalization
3. Punctuation of sentences
4. Recognition and punctuation of sentences

I. Exercise 1. *Are you able to recognize groups of words that express complete thoughts and groups of words that do not express complete thoughts?*

EXPLANATION. Notice the following groups of words:

    1. When he saw me.
    2. She will open the door for you.
    3. Asking them to go to the play.

1

In the first and third groups we do not know what the thought of the speaker is. There is no difficulty, however, in understanding the second group of words, for it expresses a complete thought. When a group of words expresses a complete thought, the group is called a sentence. People who speak and write well use sentences to express their thoughts.

DIRECTIONS. *A.* Which of the groups of words that follow are sentences? Make a list of the numbers of the groups that are sentences, and opposite on the same paper make a list of the numbers of the groups that are not sentences.

1. He entered the room as she left.
2. When he came to the end of the bridge.
3. Standing with his bag in his hand.
4. He reached out his hand for his bag.
5. Upon the hard, snowy road.
6. And every night prayed long, fervent prayers.
7. The sad girl began to go about with a brighter face and a lighter step.
8. Referring to his book which he carried in his bag.
9. You must protect yourself and your belongings.
10. Which I have told him again and again.
11. He was very cheerful, and as he sat leaning forward.
12. No mention was made of the great master himself.
13. Although she had only a small pension.
14. She wanted to form her own opinion about the matter.
15. Without her noticing it, or being able to prevent it.
16. He was beginning to enjoy his Latin.
17. I have my pockets full of money.

18. Hoping to hear from you soon.
19. He went to the desk and asked for paper and pencil.
20. Seeing a peculiar man come into the office.

B. Select something that you have written and see if it contains any groups of words that are not sentences. If you find any such groups, make them into sentences by adding more words.

I. Exercise 2. *Can you write groups of words that express complete thoughts?*

EXPLANATION. If we wish to express our thoughts so that they can be understood easily, we must state them in sentences. A sentence, we have learned, is a group of words that expresses a complete thought.

In order to let our readers know where a sentence begins, we write the first word of every sentence with a capital.

DIRECTIONS. *A.* Study the following groups of words and make a list of the groups that do not express complete thoughts.

B. Construct sentences by adding to the groups that do not express complete thoughts. Begin each sentence with a capital.

1. upon the rough and lonely road
2. just then he needed help
3. writing several compositions every week
4. watching the poor little woman struggling down the street
5. several men on the other side of the street
6. and when he turned

7. he stood there with a peculiar smile upon his face
8. but when she came into the house
9. which is a very interesting story
10. although she chose her words carefully
11. trying to coax his mother for some money
12. and was happy over his success
13. because he had no one else to see
14. when he went away into a far country
15. they told him the success of the play depended upon him
16. he was a brave man
17. the soldiers having heard the roar of the cannons
18. hoping to hear from you soon
19. although he laughed heartily and seemed happy
20. the teacher smiled and told the boys to close their books

I. Exercise 3. *Do you know how to write and punctuate different kinds of sentences?*

EXPLANATION. If you read the following sentences carefully you will see that each expresses a different thought.

1. The man opened the door. (This sentence states a fact.)
2. Open the door. (This sentence expresses a command.)
3. Will you open the door? (This sentence asks a question.)
4. Oh, the door is open! (This sentence expresses a sudden thought.)

Every sentence that we write belongs to one of these four kinds: it states a fact, gives a command or request, asks a question, or expresses sudden thought or strong feeling.

You have noticed, doubtless, that each of the sentences given above is followed by a mark of punctuation. Just as capital letters show the beginning of sentences, so certain marks of punctuation indicate the end of sentences. All sentences, however, are not followed by the same mark of punctuation. The meaning determines the mark that is used.

1. A sentence that states a fact is followed by a period.

> He ate his breakfast.
>
> They come here every day.

2. A sentence that expresses a command or an entreaty is followed by a period.

> Boys, close your books.
>
> Send the children home.

3. A sentence that asks a question is followed by a question mark.

> When are you coming home?
>
> Was he a great man?

4. A sentence that expresses sudden thought or strong feeling is followed by an exclamation mark.

> Oh, how long have I waited for you!
>
> The man has fallen!

DIRECTIONS. *A*. Write the following sentences correctly. Show the beginning of each sentence by writing the first word with a capital. Let your reader know where the sentence ends by using the correct punctuation mark.

1. where is my book
2. why has he gone away
3. please take me to the party

4. I cannot find my cap
5. open that door for me
6. oh, that man is falling
7. when did you come
8. the children can not go now
9. shall I see you this afternoon at the party
10. where has he gone
11. leave those books in this room
12. goodness, I have lost my necklace
13. sing me a song, John
14. will he come soon
15. be sensible, little boy

B. Write two original sentences to illustrate each way in which thoughts may be expressed.

I. Exercise 4. *How well can you recognize sentences? Are you able to place the end punctuation marks correctly?*

EXPLANATION. Every sentence must express a complete thought and must be followed by a punctuation mark. The meaning of a sentence decides what the end punctuation will be. If the sentence asks a question, it must be followed by a question mark. If it expresses strong feeling or sudden thought, it is followed by an exclamation mark. All other sentences are followed by periods.

The end of a sentence is indicated by a punctuation mark; the beginning is shown by capitalizing the first word.

DIRECTIONS. *A.* Separate the following groups of words into sentences and use the proper end punctuation:

how should you like to have everything you touch turn to gold that is what happened to an ancient king have you never read the story of Midas this is it many years ago there lived in a foreign land a king and his little daughter their home was a beautiful palace built on the shore of the ocean where the king and his daughter could see the wonderful sunsets about the palace was a beautiful garden in which there were all kinds of lovely flowers the king had many servants who worked continually to keep his palace and gardens beautiful king Midas was very rich he owned a great city and a magnificent palace filled with costly furniture he also had countless bags filled with gold coins and gold dust did he enjoy all this wealth and beauty he did not he rarely looked at the ocean and the gorgeous sunsets seldom did he go into his gardens and enjoy the beauty of the flowers there was only one thing that he really enjoyed that was to count his coins and run the gold dust through his greedy fingers he had only one desire that was to gain more gold to give to his daughter sometimes the little girl would beg her father to look at a sunset every time he did this he wished he could turn the gold of the clouds into coins occasionally he would go into the garden with his child then he would wish that he could turn the roses into gold how foolish he was not to enjoy the beauty of nature one day his wish to have more gold was granted everything he touched turned to gold did that bring happiness it did not it brought only misery and suffering do you wish to know the rest of the story of King Midas ask the librarian for it you will find that it is very interesting

B. 1. State what you have learned about sentences by working *Problem I.*

2. Of what value should these facts be to you in all of your written work?

PARTS OF A SENTENCE

Purpose of Study

Every sentence has two parts: a subject and a predicate. Since it is our purpose to write and speak correctly at all times, we must know what the subject and the predicate of a sentence are. Furthermore, we must be sure that every sentence we use has a subject and a predicate.

Exercises

1. Recognition of simple predicate when it consists of one word
2. Recognition of simple predicate when it consists of more than one word
3. Recognition of simple predicate when it consists of a scattered group of words
4. Recognition of simple subject
5. Recognition of complete subject
6. Recognition of complete predicate
7. Recognition of simple and complete subject and predicate

II. Exercise 1. *How well can you recognize the word that makes the assertion in a sentence?*

EXPLANATION. Notice the italicized words in the following sentences:

1. The man *caught* the ball.
2. Those boys *went* to the city.
3. The students *wrote* their lessons well.
4. Several people *saw* her there.

In sentence 1, *caught* makes an assertion about the man, for it tells what he did. In sentence 2, *went* asserts something about the boys. In sentence 3, *wrote* tells what the students did; and *saw*, in sentence 4, makes an assertion about the people.

These words show how necessary to the sentence is the word that asserts. You cannot think of a sentence that does not contain at least one word that makes an assertion about some other word that is expressed or understood. This important word is called the simple predicate. Every sentence must have a predicate.

DIRECTIONS. *A.* Make a list containing the simple predicates of the following sentences. Number each.

1. I saw him yesterday.
2. The little girl sent her mother a basket of flowers.
3. Those strange men returned with two boats.
4. The thirsty boys drank the cold water.
5. My brother went away last night.
6. One circumstance made him very unhappy.
7. I read the sad story.
8. The woman did her work well.
9. The cook rang the bell.
10. Many American women worked in France during the war.
11. The choir sang a beautiful anthem.
12. She came to our school in February.
13. Many people go away in the summer.
14. I see her every day.

15. The teacher told the class an amusing story.
16. Some one took her bottle of ink.
17. We knew him years ago.
18. The boy fastened the rope to the window.
19. The little child lay there a long time.
20. He brought me some interesting books.

B. Write sentences in which the following words are simple predicates:

saw	broke	began
did	sat	rang
come	give	write
came	gave	drink
went	begin	wrote
run	sing	take
ran	ring	took
sit	drank	break
set		

II. Exercise 2.   *Are you able to find the simple predicate when it consists of more than one word?*

Explanation.   In *Exercise 1* we found that the simple predicate of each sentence consisted of only one word.   In what way do the predicates of the following sentences differ from those that we have studied?

1. The man *has taken* my book.
2. She *will go* to the city soon.
3. I *have seen* her every day.
4. The pupils *may read* now.
5. I *shall have finished* my dress by Friday.
6. The book *will have been returned* to the library before that time.

In each of these sentences we see that not one word but a group of words makes the assertion. In sentence 1, for example, an assertion is made about the man. We do not assert that the man *has,* nor that the man *taken,* but the assertion is " the man *has taken.*" Both of these words are necessary to tell what the man did. In sentence 5, the group of words *shall have finished* makes the assertion. In sentence 6, the assertion is stated by the four words *will have been returned.* A simple predicate may consist of as many as four words.

When a group of words is used to make an assertion, there is always a base word and one or more helpers or auxiliaries. If you wish to find the simple predicate, look for this main word and then see if there are any auxiliaries. The most common auxiliary words are: can, may, shall, will, must, am, was, are, have, had, has.

DIRECTIONS. *A.* Make a list containing the simple predicates of the following sentences. Number each.

1. I may take a trip to Alaska.
2. The teacher must see my papers.
3. The pupils will learn their lessons easily.
4. Some boys have brought me the evening paper.
5. Some one has laid my book away.
6. The child was seen in the store.
7. You may see her at any time.
8. The men have learned much at night school.
9. They should have taken their rubbers with them.
10. The poor boy has been gone a long time.
11. The little dog has stolen my slipper.
12. He should have come to our house today.
13. The children have broken the window.
14. I am studying music now.

15. These trees were struck by lightning.
16. The poor boy had been taken to the beach by a
    thoughtful man.
17. I will lie here for a while.
18. The kitten has drunk the milk.
19. The lad can win the race.
20. The work will have been done easily.

B. Write sentences in which the following words are
simple predicates:

have done	had taken
have seen	has rung
had come	have drunk
has broken	have sung
has gone	

II. Exercise 3. *Can you locate the simple predicate of
a sentence when it consists of a group of words that are
scattered?*

EXPLANATION. We have seen that the predicate of a
sentence may consist of one word or of a group of words.
Notice the italicized words in the following sentences:

1. *Have* you *seen* my book?
2. Where *will* he *meet* you?
3. I *do* not *read* those magazines.
4. I *had* fully *made* up my mind to go.

Unlike the simple predicates that we have studied thus
far, the words that make the assertion in each of these
sentences are not closely connected, but are scattered.
Although this is the case, they are the simple predicates
of the sentences, and are found by locating the base word

and then the auxiliaries. If a sentence asks a question, we can easily find the predicate by restating the sentence so that it will express a fact. For example, take the second sentence, " Where will he meet you? " Revising this, we have, " He will meet you where? " Stated this way, the two words of the simple predicate are connected, and there is no difficulty in recognizing it.

DIRECTIONS. *A.* Make a list of the simple predicates of the following sentences:

1. The child had never forgotten his father's face.
2. Jerry had been thoroughly trained for that kind of work.
3. He did not recognize his master's voice.
4. His master could even make him a prisoner.
5. The little dog could not be frightened into running away.
6. The pie had just been eaten by Johnny.
7. When will he return to America?
8. The old man had never seen such a sight before.
9. I will never bother you with my troubles.
10. Have you ever taken an ocean voyage?
11. I shall never hear another voice like hers.
12. Not as a miser had he collected all those interesting pieces of money.
13. They had long since gone into the darkness.
14. When shall you consider his plan?
15. The animal must have once seen a human being.
16. Where had he been living all these years?
17. The natives of that land had never feared any one.
18. Must you go soon?
19. Can you tell me the name of that building?
20. That doctor has never lost a patient.

B. In some book find fifteen examples of simple predicates that consist of groups of words that are scattered.
Copy the sentences and underline the simple predicates.

II. Exercise 4. *How well can you recognize the word
that names the person, the place, or the thing about which
an assertion is made?*

EXPLANATION. In the sentence, " The man caught the
ball," we know that *caught* is the predicate because it
makes an assertion about something. If we ask the question, " Who caught the ball? " the answer is *the man*.
The word *man* names the person about whom the assertion
is made. The word in a sentence that names the person,
the place, or the thing about which an assertion is made
is called the simple subject. Every sentence must have a
subject.

The subject of a sentence does not always precede the
predicate. Let us find the subject in the sentence, " Into
the room walked a strange old man." The predicate is
walked. When we ask the question, " Who walked? " the
answer is *man;* therefore *man* is the subject. If you will
always follow this method when trying to find the subject,
you will never have any difficulty in locating it.

Sometimes the subject of a sentence is not expressed.
Suppose we wish to find the subject of " Take your books
away." Following the usual method, we select the predicate; it is *take*. Asking the question, " Who takes? " we
find that the answer is *you take*. *You* is the subject, but
it is understood. In sentences that express a command or
an entreaty, the subject is generally *you* understood.

DIRECTIONS. *A*. Select the simple predicates and the
simple subjects from the following sentences. Write them

in two columns on the same paper so that the two parts of each sentence will be on the same line.

Note. If the subject is understood, place the word in parenthesis; as (you).

1. He found his way to the pantry.
2. The two men ate their dinner in silence.
3. The books have never been returned to the library.
4. You must come next Monday.
5. Every pupil can learn his lessons.
6. The seven children walked down the street together.
7. We saw strange things at the circus.
8. The poor man bought his sick child some fruit.
9. A wise person does not lose his temper.
10. Some birds sing beautifully.
11. Come to my room, please.
12. Into the room ran the child.
13. I shall go alone without you.
14. Take your books to your room.
15. When will the storm stop?
16. Do you like my new hat?
17. Whose pencils did she find?
18. I have read these articles.
19. Sing that song again.
20. Down the street with all his companions came Dick.

B. Take a composition you have recently written, and select from it ten sentences. Make a list of the simple predicates and simple subjects as you have in *A*.

II. Exercise 5. *Can you find the complete subject of a sentence as well as the simple subject?*

EXPLANATION. We have learned that the subject of a sentence is the word that names the person, the place, or the thing about which an assertion is made. In the sentence, " Several little boys play ball every evening," *boys* is the simple subject. There are, however, two words that give one a more definite idea about the subject *boys;* they are *several* and *little*. These words are said to modify the subject since they change its meaning. A group of words that consists of the simple subject with its modifiers is called the complete subject. *Boys* is the simple subject, and *several little boys* is the complete subject.

The simple subject need not necessarily have modifiers. In the sentence, " Mr. Smith is our neighbor," *Mr. Smith* is the simple subject and also the complete subject since it has no modifiers.

Directions. *A.* Select the simple predicates, the simple subjects, and the complete subjects from the following sentences. Write them in three columns on the same paper so that the parts of each sentence will be on the same lines.

1. Half a year after, a war vessel had poked her nose into the lagoon.
2. A few hours' labor of the men put that little matter right.
3. The tender tips of the fallen palms were eaten by the savages.
4. On deck Borckman kept a sharp eye out against danger.
5. Many eyes beheld the impending tragedy.
6. From the canoes on both sides uprose a glittering, glistening rain of tomahawks.
7. Jerry's heroic little heart of courage would have resented such treatment.
8. Eat your lunch now.

9. John could never win any affection from Jerry.
10. On rare occasions the wild savages had even eaten grass and leaves.
11. In that way he had slowly made a fortune.
12. In the meantime his interest in that line of work had not increased.
13. Never did the little dog receive a cross word from James.
14. Take those coats to my office.
15. Where has that child gone?

B. Select ten sentences from some paper that you have written either for English or some other subject. Make a list of the simple predicates, simple subjects, and complete subjects as you have in *A*.

II. Exercise 6. *Are you able to locate the complete predicate of a sentence as well as the simple predicate?*

EXPLANATION. In the sentence, " John returned his books to the library," *returned* is the simple predicate. There are other words in the sentence that tell something about the predicate. *His book* completes the simple predicate, and *to the library* tells where John returned the book. All of these words make the complete predicate. The complete predicate of a sentence consists of the simple predicate and all other words that complete its meaning or modify it.

We have learned that every sentence has two parts: a subject and a predicate. Every word in a sentence belongs either to the complete subject or to the complete predicate. A word cannot belong to both, however.

DIRECTIONS. *A.* Select the simple predicates, simple subjects, complete subjects, and complete predicates from the following sentences. Write them in four columns on the same paper so that the parts of each sentence will be on the same lines.

1. At the recognition of Skipper's voice, Jerry yelped eagerly.
2. In the loneliness of the dark the little dog whimpered like a lost child.
3. Then, with amazing abruptness, he was lifted out of the sea into the boat.
4. The poor little dog did not just calmly walk overboard.
5. About the fire the boys were grouped in a semi-circle.
6. Where shall we set the basket of fruit?
7. The flowers in the vase were brought to me yesterday.
8. Open all of the windows in this room.
9. How miserable the little boy looked!
10. Only for love of his child could the man have made the attempt.
11. Having lived in savagery all their lives, they knew naught else.
12. At that moment Anna, hearing the commotion upstairs, called for her father.

B. Add the complete predicates to the list made in *B* of *Exercise 5.*

II. Exercise 7. *How well can you recognize the parts of a sentence?*

EXPLANATION. Remember that every sentence has two parts: a subject and a predicate. Every word in a sentence belongs to one of these two parts. The simple predicate is the word or group of words that makes an assertion; the complete predicate consists of the simple predicate and the words that complete its meaning or modify it. The simple subject is the word that names the person, the place, or the thing about which the assertion is made; the complete subject is the simple subject and all the words that modify it.

You will have no difficulty in recognizing the parts of a sentence if you follow this method:

1. Select the word or words that make the assertion. This is the simple predicate.
2. Take the simple predicate and ask the question " Who? " or " What? " The answer will give you the simple subject.
3. Select all the words that modify the meaning of the simple subject. These words make the complete subject.
4. All the rest of the sentence is the complete predicate, — the simple predicate and all words that complete the simple predicate or modify it.

DIRECTIONS. Select the simple predicates, simple subjects, complete subjects, and complete predicates from the following sentences. Write them in four columns on the same paper so that the parts of each sentence will be on the same lines.

1. In the dark and dreary room sat my dear mother.
2. That interesting boy became the brightest student in his class at college.
3. You gave a very fine address today.
4. Never before have I seen such a beautiful sunset!
5. In the morning of the third day came a messenger from the king.
6. My mother brought us many beautiful things from Italy.

7. In this way he made a collection of rare paintings.
8. Do not fear the strange man.
9. For two years Henry studied foreign languages.
10. Down the stairs silently came two dear little children.
11. Not until two hours later did he awake.
12. The little boys on our street play ball every evening.

THE SENTENCE AS COMPARED WITH PHRASES AND CLAUSES

Purpose of Study

Some groups of words that seem to express complete thoughts are often mistaken for sentences. This is a serious mistake that no one should make. For that reason we must study such groups of words and be able to distinguish them from sentences.

Exercises

1. Recognition of phrases and completion into sentences
2. Recognition of clauses and completion of dependent clauses into sentences
3. Recognition of phrases and dependent clauses and completion into sentences

III. Exercise 1. *Are you able to recognize groups of words that seem to express complete thoughts but are not sentences?*

EXPLANATION. We have learned that a group of words must fulfill two requirements if it is a sentence: first, it must have a subject and a predicate; second, it must express a complete thought. Sometimes an expression that does not have a subject and a predicate contains words that are so closely related in thought that they are mistaken for a sentence. As an example, let us take the expression, " The poor old man, having walked many miles that day." Looking superficially at this group of words, one might think that it is a sentence since it seems to give the thought of the speaker. But what is the test of a sentence? A sentence must have a subject and a predicate. Does this group of words contain a subject and a predicate? Following our method for finding the subject and the predicate, we look first for a word that makes an assertion. We find there is none. We may assert " The man walked," or " the man had walked," but the expression, " the man having walked," makes no assertion. " Having walked that day " is merely a group of related words that tells something about " the man." Such a group of words is called a phrase. To make a sentence, we must insert a predicate; then we have, " The poor old man, having walked many miles that day, looked for a resting place."

Another kind of phrase is illustrated in " He cried often during the night." In this sentence, " during the night " is a group of closely related words that tells something about " cried." Since the group has no subject or predicate and does not express a complete thought, it is not a sentence.

It is clear to you now that there are groups of words that are as closely related as the words in a sentence, but they are not sentences because they do not contain a subject or a predicate, and do not express a complete thought. Such groups are called phrases. A phrase generally describes the subject or the predicate.

DIRECTIONS. *A.* Study the following groups of words. Complete the phrases, making them into sentences. Leave the sentences as they are.

1. During the earlier part of the afternoon.
2. With my mother acting as chaperon.
3. Seeing the rain fall.
4. A crew of six men working in the mines.
5. Called together for the purpose of selecting a new chairman.
6. The captain in command of the ship.
7. The winner of the race cheered by a crowd of admirers.
8. The boys having enjoyed the circus for half a day.
9. I love to see the rain falling.
10. While spending several weeks at the beach.
11. Discouraged by the latest reports.
12. Many pictures illustrating the benefits gained by the children.
13. Having greatly enjoyed seeing their daughters have such a good time.
14. With his little sister running behind him.
15. Surprised by the sudden appearance of a new face.
16. Mr. Smith arriving from New York.
17. Around the long tables of the council hall the leading statesmen of the world.
18. Having spent three years in a western university.

B. Write five phrases and use them in sentences.

III. Exercise 2. *Can you recognize groups of words that contain subjects and predicates, but are not sentences?*

Explanation. In the sentence, " I ran into the house when I saw him coming," you will notice that there are two assertions. One is " I ran into the house," and the other is " when I saw him coming." Each of these groups of words contains a subject and a predicate, and yet only one of the groups expresses a complete thought. " I ran into the house " gives a perfectly clear idea of the speaker's thought, but the other group, " when I saw him coming," is not complete in and of itself; it needs the first assertion to make it clear. A group of words that contains a subject and a predicate is called a clause. This sentence shows that there are two kinds of clauses: one that is independent, and one that is dependent. An independent clause states a complete idea; a dependent clause needs another clause to complete its meaning. A sentence may consist of one independent clause, but never of one dependent clause alone.

Notice the italicized clauses in the following sentences:

1. *If you were happy,* you would be well.
2. I know the man *whom you were watching.*
3. I will go *although I do not wish to.*

Each of these clauses is dependent because each depends upon another clause for its meaning. Notice that each of the dependent clauses is introduced by some word which makes it impossible for the clause to stand alone. In the first sentence, the word " if " introduces the dependent clause and also connects it to the independent clause. Look out for these introductory words in the sentences you write so that you will not make the serious mistake of writing a dependent clause for a sentence.

DIRECTIONS. *A.* Study the following groups of words. Make sentences of the dependent clauses by adding independent clauses. Do not change the groups that are sentences.

1. When I saw the old man hurrying along the street.
2. At the parties at which the dances were given, the parents were invited guests.

3. Her eyes which she rubbed again and again.
4. In his little room the birch-wood crackled in the stove.
5. As he lay in his comfortable bed, wrapped in his mother's blankets.
6. Because he was afraid of the noises he heard downstairs.
7. Should he flee from the affair?
8. The old chair which had belonged to the family for years.
9. When he wanted especially to succeed.
10. He left his work at once which, after all, was not a very wise action.
11. When a person knows where the Public Library is.
12. Because exits to fire escapes were locked.
13. If I had known the cause of the accident.
14. When I saw you bend your head to talk to her.
15. Inasmuch as it was warm in the waiting room.
16. Now that I have played for two years.
17. That I have never seen a circus.
18. When he was young and had not yet traveled far.

B. Write five dependent clauses and use them in sentences.

III. Exercise 3. *How well can you distinguish sentences from phrases and dependent clauses?*

EXPLANATION. We have learned that there are groups of closely related words that are not sentences, but are often mistaken for sentences. One of these groups is the phrase. A phrase never has a subject or a predicate, and, therefore, cannot possibly be a sentence. It generally tells something about the subject or the predicate.

The other group of closely related words that is often mistaken for a sentence is the dependent clause. Although a dependent clause contains a subject and a predicate, it does not give a complete thought, and for that reason cannot be a sentence. A sure test for the sentence is to see: (1) that it has a subject and a predicate, and (2) that it expresses a complete thought.

DIRECTIONS. *A.* Study the following groups of words and rewrite them so that each group will be a sentence. Do not change the wording; merely revise the grouping and end punctuation. Do not attempt to insert commas.

A farmer called on Earl Fitzwilliam. To tell him that his crop of wheat had been seriously injured in a field adjoining a certain wood. Where the earl and his friends had hunted during the winter. He said that the young wheat had been so cut up and destroyed. That in some places he could not hope for any produce. When the lord heard this. He said he should be glad to repay the injury. That his horses and hounds had made. Anticipating the earl's consideration and kindness. The farmer had a friend assist him in estimating the damage. Believing that the crop was entirely destroyed. They thought fifty pounds would cover the loss. As the harvest approached. The wheat grew, and in those parts of the field which were most trampled. The wheat was strongest and most luxuriant. The farmer went again to the earl and told him. That he had come to speak about the wheat in the field. Adjoining the wood. Earl Fitzwilliam immediately remembered the circumstance and asked if he had not given. Enough to cover all losses. The farmer then told the earl. That he had not had any losses. He explained that where the horses had most cut up the land. The crop was most promising. Having told all these facts. The farmer then returned the fifty pounds to the earl. The nobleman was greatly pleased to see such great honesty. He entered into a conversation with the farmer. Asking him several questions about his family, his children, and the age of each. His lordship then went into another room. On returning, he presented the farmer with a cheque for one hundred pounds. Being an independent man. The farmer did not wish to take the gift. The earl then told him to give it to his eldest son. When he had become of age. He also asked him to relate to the young man the event. Which had produced the money. This the farmer promised to do.

B. 1. What is the difference between a phrase and a sentence?

2. Write three sentences, each containing a phrase. Underline the phrases.

3. What is a clause?

4. What is the difference between a dependent and an independent clause?

5. Write three sentences, each containing an independent and a dependent clause. Underline the dependent clauses.

KINDS OF WORDS

Purpose of Study

If we are to express our thoughts correctly in sentences, we must have an understanding of the use of words, for every word in a sentence has some particular use in that sentence. Because of their special uses, words have been divided into kinds and are often called parts of speech. Before we can study the correct use of each kind of word, we must learn the names of the various parts of speech and gain the ability to recognize them in sentences. That is the purpose of this problem.

Exercises

1. Recognition of nouns
2. Recognition of common and proper nouns
3. Recognition of pronouns
4. Recognition of verbs
5. Recognition of adjectives
6. Recognition of adverbs
7. Recognition of conjunctions
8. Recognition of prepositions
9. Recognition of various parts of speech

IV. Exercise 1. *How well can you recognize words that are the names of persons, places, or things?*

EXPLANATION. Have you ever noticed how many words you use that are the names of things? In many statements you make, you use more words that name something than any other one kind of words. For example, in the sentence, " Mary goes to the store every day and buys groceries for her mother," there are five words that name something. These are: *Mary, store, day, groceries, mother*. A word that is the name of a person, a place, or a thing is called a noun.

DIRECTIONS. *A*. Make a list of the nouns in the following sentences:

1. While the man was cutting down some wood, he noticed a very thick branch of low brushwood.
2. No attention should be paid to those children.
3. Beauty comes from right living.
4. Every boy and girl should receive an education.
5. Night schools are held in all parts of the city.
6. Mr. Smith's address was received with great enthusiasm.
7. It is their plan to erect better and larger buildings.
8. The little boy asked for candy and cookies and many different toys.
9. Will that stove keep this room warm?
10. She is a poor little girl.
11. At Christmas when the tree is lighted, the master and mistress of the house join hands with the servants and sing old hymns around the blazing pine.
12. The bell rings early in the morning.
13. Rose flew to Uncle Alex for advice.
14. The minister was up in the old wooden pulpit gazing down upon his company.
15. The children were picking blackberries in the bushes beside the road when the soldiers passed.

B. Write five original sentences and underline all nouns.

IV. Exercise 2. *Are you able to distinguish between a noun that names some particular thing and a noun that names a class of things?*

EXPLANATION. In the sentence, " I hear that *Mary* visited the *White House* when she and the *girls* were in *Washington,*" each italicized word is a noun because it is the name of some person, place, or thing. Not all of these nouns, however, are of the same kind. " Mary," for example, names a particular person, while " girls " is the name of a class of people. You have doubtless noticed, too, that " Mary " is written with a capital and " girls " is not. These two words illustrate the two kinds of nouns. A noun that is the name of a class of persons, places, or things is called a common noun. A noun that is the name of a particular person, place, or thing is called a proper noun. A proper noun always begins with a capital letter.

A word may be a common noun in one sentence and a proper noun in another. Notice the use of " judge " in the first two sentences, and " hotel " and " street " in the last two.

1. Is Judge Smith coming tonight?
2. A judge has many responsibilities.
3. I shall go to my hotel on the next street.
4. The Clark Hotel is on Hill Street.

In sentence 1, " judge " is the name of a particular person and is a proper noun. In sentence 2, " judge " is the name of a class of people and is a common noun. The same difference is found in the words " hotel " and " street " in sentences 3 and 4. In the third sentence " hotel " and

" street " are common nouns because they name a class of objects; in the last sentence these same words are proper nouns because there they name particular objects.

DIRECTIONS. *A.* Rewrite the following sentences, capitalizing properly and placing the correct end punctuation marks:

1. the president spends much time at the white house
2. I am sorry helen could not attend the meeting of the ebell club
3. one of the largest cities in the eastern part of this country is chicago
4. john does not want mary to go to the party because she is so small
5. richard and robert are very good to their mother
6. when will jane return from new york
7. the higgens building is on second street
8. mildred came running up the stairs, laughing about howard's good fortune
9. I want to go to oregon on *the yale*
10. I have read many books by dickens and scott
11. did aunt stella send her pretty pictures from france and italy
12. oh, my father is coming home tonight
13. many times fathers and mothers are too absorbed in business and housekeeping to study their children
14. do you often read the atlantic monthly
15. I am sure that uncle fred will stay at a quiet hotel
16. he is attending east high school and enjoys his work very much
17. the president of the united states has more power than the king of england
18. they had not seen judge allen for many years

19. two days later the campbells went home, a larger
    party than when they came
20. there is one street in new york I can always find,
    and that is broadway

B. Write five sentences that contain common and
proper nouns. Underline the common nouns once and the
proper nouns twice.

IV. Exercise 3. *Can you recognize the words that are
used in place of nouns?*

EXPLANATION. Do you realize how often you use a word
that takes the place of your name? Suppose your name
is John, and you want to tell some one that you want your
book. You do not say, " John wants John's book "; instead you say, " I want my book." We very often use
such words in place of our own names, or the names of
some other person or thing. Such words are called pronouns, for a pronoun is a word that is used for a noun.
The most common pronouns are: *he, his, him, she, hers,
her, I, my, mine, me, you, yours, your, it, they, their, them,
who, whose, whom,* and *which*. The pronoun *I* is always
capitalized.

DIRECTIONS. *A*. Make a list of pronouns in the following sentences:

1. When will he bring your book to you?
2. I did not know who he was.
3. Those books were mine, but I gave them to her.
4. Is this pen yours, or is it hers?
5. They went into the room where mother was sitting,
   and gave her their flowers.

6. He gave them away most willingly because they belonged to his sister.

7. Boys like to have fun with their sisters.

8. Those are not my pictures.

9. How long will they be here?

10. I did not know to whom to tell my difficulty.

11. Why did she take it, do you suppose?

12. I am glad she had such a good conscience.

13. There are many people in this city who do not own their homes.

14. I think they are in a fair way to pay their debts.

15. You must not make fun of him, for he is a good fellow even if his clothes do not look like yours.

B. Write ten sentences that contain pronouns. Underline each pronoun.

IV. Exercise 4. *Are you able to find the words in a sentence that assert action or state of being?*

EXPLANATION. We have learned that every sentence contains a word that makes an assertion. In the sentence, " The boy ate his lunch," " ate " makes the assertion and expresses action. In " My bird is beautiful," " is " makes the assertion; but instead of expressing action it shows condition or state of being. Such words as " ate " and " is " are called verbs. A verb is a word that shows action or state of being. The predicate of a sentence is always a verb. Every sentence has at least one verb, for every sentence has a predicate.

We know that a verb may consist of as many as four words. The base word is the main verb, and the others are called auxiliary verbs. The most common auxiliary verbs are: *have, had, has, shall, will, should, would, can, may, might, do, did, does, must,* and *been*. Although the main verb and the auxiliary verb are often separated in a sentence, together they constitute the verb and simple predicate of the sentence.

DIRECTIONS. *A.* Make a list of the verbs in the following sentences. Do not separate the auxiliary verb from the main verb.

1. I had found the sea very calm, and I could easily go near the ship.
2. Did you say she was a quiet little girl and seldom cried?
3. I wished for the things I could not have, and then I enjoyed the things I already possessed.
4. We went to the pantry and filled our pockets with crackers.
5. They had lifted the huge stone and carried it many feet.
6. How long will you work before you eat your lunch?
7. I secured the necessary food and started out on my long walk.
8. We must have walked many miles before we came to any human beings.
9. I watched her as she studied her lessons.
10. Buck stood and looked at the other dogs.
11. She is a very fine student.
12. Nothing was too great for Buck when Thornton commanded.
13. Hans cast off the rope while the rest poled the boat out into the stream.
14. Had he sprung in, there would have been no accident.
15. Did he stagger to his feet and then fall down?
16. What a lonely old soul he is!

17. Those who were looking heard what was neither a bark nor a yelp.
18. Sometimes they went hungry, and sometimes they feasted riotously.
19. Why should he not do it?
20. It has been a hard trip, and the heavy work has worn them down.

B. Write ten original sentences and underline the verbs in each.

IV. Exercise 5. *Do you know the words that are used to describe or limit nouns?*

EXPLANATION. Read the following sentences and decide what makes the difference in their meaning:

1. I saw the man.
2. I saw the blind old man.

" Blind " and " old," you have doubtless noticed, are the words that make the difference, for they describe " man " and give a much more vivid picture than the one gained from reading the first sentence. We use many words of this kind when we describe the objects about which we talk. Such words are called adjectives. An adjective is a word that tells something about a noun or a pronoun.

In " She ate two apples," " two " tells how many " apples " were eaten. This shows that an adjective need not necessarily describe a noun; it may limit the meaning of a noun. Some of the adjectives that limit are: *several, few, much, many, three, five,* and other numbers.

The words, *the, a,* and *an,* which we use so often when speaking of some person or thing, are classified with the adjectives that limit, and are generally called articles.

Do not confuse a pronoun with an adjective. In the sentence, " Her hand is small," " her " is a pronoun that shows possession; it is not an adjective.

Adjectives derived from proper nouns should always be written with a capital. For example, " He knows his *English* lesson " and " The *French* language is very interesting."

DIRECTIONS. *A.* Make a list of all the nouns in the following sentences and another list of all adjectives. Write the adjectives after the nouns which they describe or limit. Do not omit the articles.

1. Those interesting books were purchased by the little Spanish girl.
2. Mr. Jones has a fine new home.
3. She had unexpected success in the hard task.
4. The small candle does not shed a very clear or steady light.
5. She manages her household affairs easily.
6. That man was in a miserable condition until he began to make greater effort.
7. We rode for hours on a calm sea.
8. Such workmanship is not often seen, for most English boys do not spend much time on their manual work.
9. I should like to read a long story about foreign travel.
10. A strange man came to our door and asked for a little money and some warm food.
11. She was a very happy old lady whenever her little grandchildren remembered to bring her some pink and white candy.
12. Jack was a very interesting little warrior, with a great black mustache over his rosy mouth.

B. Write the following words in sentences using them as adjectives:

1. slow
2. good
3. this
4. first
5. Latin

6. busy
7. patient
8. careful
9. smooth
10. English

IV. Exercise 6. *Are you able to find the words in a sentence that tell how, when, or where?*

EXPLANATION. Suppose you want to work after school or on Saturday, and the person whose name you give as a reference makes this statement about you, " He does his work." Your prospective employer would scarcely be satisfied with this reply, but would want to know how you do your work. It is often necessary to tell the manner in which an action is performed, for " He does his work well " gives a very different idea from " He does his work carelessly."

Study the italicized words in the following sentences and notice the explanation given in parentheses:

1. They will see her *soon.* (*Soon* tells when they will see her.)

2. He wants to go *there.* (*There* tells where he wants to go.)

3. She screamed *frightfully.* (*Frightfully* tells how she screamed.)

4. She is a *very* young woman. (*Very* tells how young she is.)

5. The man talked *very boastfully.* (*Boastfully* tells how he talked; *very* tells how boastfully he talked.)

Each of these sentences contains a word that tells how, when, or where something is done. Since they generally describe verbs, they are called adverbs. Not all adverbs describe verbs; " very " in sentence 4 tells something about the adjective " young," and " very " in sentence 5 describes the adverb " boastfully."

Do not confuse adjectives with adverbs. An adjective, you will remember, describes or limits a noun; an adverb usually describes the action asserted by a verb.

DIRECTIONS. *A.* Make a list of the adverbs in the following sentences and after each write in parentheses the word the adverb describes:

1. They entered the room slowly and silently.
2. How rapidly time flies!
3. Will she come soon?
4. Father looked at us quickly, and then asked us to show him our cards immediately.
5. I found the door first, and then I ran swiftly to a very safe place.
6. She ran away and was never seen again.
7. All I could do was to wait quietly.
8. There I lay until the water ebbed away.
9. When will you put your papers down?
10. I went early and met many interesting people there.
11. He always remembers to speak quietly.
12. I had scarcely taken my seat when I saw a very old man enter the room hurriedly.

B. Write the following words in sentences using them as adverbs:

1. well
2. fast
3. slowly
4. always
5. down
6. carefully
7. seldom
8. patiently

IV. Exercise 7. *Are you able to recognize connecting words?*

EXPLANATION. When we wish to talk about John and Mary, we use a word to connect these two names. We say, for example, " John *and* Mary will be here tomorrow." Suppose we wish to make two assertions that are closely connected in thought. Again we use a word to connect the two clauses, and we say, " I shall go now, *but* I shall return soon." Possibly we wish to make two assertions, one of which is dependent upon the other. To do this we use a word to connect the dependent and the independent clauses, and we say, " Mother will go *if* she can get away." These joining words are called conjunctions. A conjunction is a word that joins sentences or parts of sentences. There are many conjunctions in the English language; the most common are: *and, but, or, nor, if, as, as if, although, though, as though, unless, since, because, for,* and *till.*

In *Problem III* we learned that every dependent clause is introduced by a word that makes it impossible for the clause to stand alone. This word is generally a conjunction. The conjunction that introduces a dependent clause and connects it to an independent clause comes at the beginning of the sentence when the dependent clause stands first. For example, in " If she comes, I shall see her," the conjunction " if " connects the dependent and the independent clauses although it is the first word in the sentence. When the independent clause is stated first, it is easy to see that " if " is a conjunction; as, " I shall see her *if* she comes." Do not let the position of a conjunction confuse you into thinking it is not a connecting word.

DIRECTIONS. *A.* Make a list of the conjunctions in the following sentences:

1. Send those boys and girls to the library.
2. I cannot go unless I have some money.
3. Mary and Jane will go.
4. I should like to go, but I cannot.
5. I went out as he was entering the house.
6. He acted as if he were ill.
7. I cannot come to you, but I shall be glad to have you call on me.
8. Although he came, he was not very happy.
9. Neither James nor Henry will go.
10. He gave us his address, but I could not locate him.
11. Cornelius threw back his shoulders as the animal came nearer.
12. He has been here, because his hat and coat are here.
13. I have not seen him since I left Rochester.
14. Wait till mother comes.
15. They laughed, for the man was very funny.
16. By midday, on a smooth ocean floor, the clouds thinned and cleared, and sights of the ocean were obtained.
17. I asked her if she played golf.
18. He had not lain there long before he heard a dreadful noise.
19. If the natives become properly civilized, the trade of the traders will be gone.
20. As the noise died away, the woman led her children into the ruined house.

B. Write ten sentences containing conjunctions. Do not use the same conjunction twice. Underline each conjunction.

IV. Exercise 8. *Do you know how to recognize a phrase and the introductory word of a phrase?*

EXPLANATION. Sometimes we wish to describe an object or an action and not use separate adjectives or adverbs. For example, in the sentence, " She is going to the theater," " to the theater " tells where she is going and, therefore, is used like an adverb. Try to break up this group, and you will see that the words are so closely connected that they cannot be changed; they must be taken as they are or not at all. Such a group of words is called a phrase.

Let us look at the following sentences in which the italicized words are phrases:

1. He went *with his mother.*
2. They walked *over the slippery ice.*
3. I am going *to the mountains.*
4. The child ran *through the house.*
5. She fell *down the stairs.*

Each of these phrases begins with a word that is not a noun, a pronoun, a verb, an adjective, an adverb, or a conjunction. Yet in each case the word is of importance and cannot be omitted. For example, in the first sentence we cannot say, " He went his mother." The same is true of the phrases in the other sentences. Evidently, then, every phrase has a certain kind of word that introduces it. This word is called a preposition.

Now suppose some one said to you, " He went with." The thought would be incomplete, and you would immediately ask, " With whom? " The answer would be " with his mother." This illustration shows you that a preposition must have a word to complete it; this word is called the object of the preposition. A preposition and its object make a phrase.

Do not confuse prepositions with adverbs. The word " up " may be either a preposition or an adverb. When it is used by itself, it is an adverb; as, "Smoke goes *up*." If "up" is a preposition, it must have an object; as, "Smoke goes *up the chimney*." You can always test a preposition by seeing if it has an object to complete its meaning.

DIRECTIONS. *A.* In the following sentences select the phrases and underline the prepositions:

1. The next day he went out with his dog.
2. He walked down the dusty road and finally sat on a stone by the edge of the road.
3. The pictures on the wall are beautiful.
4. Several men came into the room and asked questions about the president.
5. The ship has come from Japan and has brought my cousin on it.
6. With a little dish of clay he made a useful lamp.
7. When we were at the beach, we saw holes in the rocks where the pigeons had made their homes.
8. At that time I was tired and could not write in my diary.
9. They came into our home and asked no questions of us.
10. Come to me and I will take your troubles from you.
11. The sweet clearness of her child's voice was pleasant to him, and he wondered why he had never noticed it in children's voices before.
12. He had been through a mutiny, where, in the prison yard with Gatling guns trained upon them, three hundred men had been disciplined with pick-handles wielded by brawny guards.

B. Write the following words in sentences using them first as adverbs and then as prepositions. Underline the adverbs in the first group and the phrases in the second. Remember that a preposition must have an object.

1. down   5. through
2. up   6. out
3. around   7. near
4. in   8. off

IV. Exercise 9.   *How well can you recognize the various parts of speech?*

EXPLANATION.   In the sentence, " Oh! I am so glad to be here," you know the name of every word except " oh." We often use such exclamations in our speech, and they are known as interjections.   An interjection is a word that expresses strong feeling.

It would be wise now for you to read over all the explanations given in the exercises of *Problem IV,* for it is very easy to confuse the different parts of speech.

Notice how flexible the English language is.   Take the word " watch."   When we use it in the sentence, " I have a new watch," it is a noun because it is the name of something; but in the sentence " I shall watch you," " watch " is a verb because it asserts action.   Take " each " as another example.   In " Each boy recited correctly," " each " is an adjective because it limits the noun " boy."   In " Each recited correctly," " each " is a pronoun because it is used in place of a noun.   The part of speech of a word is decided entirely by its use in a sentence.   Therefore, you should always study a sentence carefully to see how a word is used before deciding what part of speech the word is.   Ask yourself these questions: (1) " What does the word do in this sentence? " (2) " What part of speech is it? "

DIRECTIONS. *A*. There are eight parts of speech. Make a list of these and after each tell what you consider is the most important fact about each.

B. Write the following sentences and above each word state the part of speech. Use the following abbreviations:

noun.........n.	verb.........v.
pronoun......pro.	preposition....prep.
adjective.....adj.	conjunction...conj.
adverb.......adv.	interjection....int.

Notice that the abbreviations are followed by periods.

1. My poor grandmother has scarcely recovered from the fall she received in the winter.
2. This beautiful little girl is some man's child.
3. He thought about the long years of toil which had been spent in camps and in mines.
4. A woman in a soft, pretty gown came through the gate from the bungalow.
5. A tramp scrambled to his feet and stood watchfully and awkwardly.
6. He looked about him irresolutely, climbed the fence, crossed the bridge, and slouched along the road.
7. A few steps brought him into the main street of the village.

C. Write sentences containing the following words used in the ways as indicated in parentheses:

        every (pronoun, adjective)
        down (adverb, preposition)
        like (verb, preposition)
        out (adverb, preposition)
        sink (verb, noun)
        some (pronoun, adjective)
        thought (noun, verb)
        through (preposition, adverb)

ANALYSIS OF SIMPLE SENTENCES

Purpose of Study

Since we wish to write and speak sentences that are entirely correct, we must see to it that we understand thoroughly the sentences we use. In order to do this we shall first learn to separate sentences into their parts, and then study the relation of one part to another. This process is known as analysis.

We shall analyze sentences by means of diagrams. Just as an architect's plans are more easily understood than written directions, so the relation of various words in a sentence will be clearer if shown by diagraming than by written explanations.

Our first work will be with simple sentences, — that is, sentences that consist of only one independent clause.

Exercises

1. Analysis of sentences into subject and predicate
2. Analysis of sentences into subject, predicate, and object complement
3. Analysis of sentences into subject, predicate, and subjective complement
4. Analysis of sentences into subject, predicate, complement, and adjective modifiers

V. Exercise 1. *Can you analyze a sentence into simple subject and simple predicate?*

EXPLANATION. If you were an architect and wanted to show a person how to arrange the rooms in his house, would you write out the directions? Of course you would not; instead you would draw a plan or diagram that would indicate at a glance the relation of one room to another. We shall follow the same method in showing the relation of one word to another. Such a plan in our work is called a diagram.

The main parts of a sentence will always be placed on a straight line; as,

<u>main parts of a sentence</u>

Since there are two parts to every sentence, we shall show this in our diagram by drawing a line that will divide the sentence line into two parts; as,

Inasmuch as the subject generally precedes the predicate in a sentence, we shall place the subject before the predicate on the sentence line; as,

simple subject | simple predicate

We are now ready to begin to diagram a sentence. Let us take " The boys ate their lunch " as an example.

First we must find the simple predicate. Select the word that makes the assertion; this, we know, will be a verb. In this sentence it is "ate." Write it in the place for the simple predicate; as,

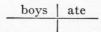

| ate

To find the simple subject, ask " Who ate? " The answer is " boys." Write it in the place for the simple subject; as,

boys | ate

Thus far we have analyzed the sentence into its simple subject and simple predicate.

DIRECTIONS. Analyze by means of diagrams the simple subjects and the simple predicates of the following sentences. Draw straight lines.

1. Children like candy.
2. Boys play ball.
3. The boys saw the circus.
4. The teacher assigned a lesson.
5. He ate the cherries.
6. Has that man taken a purse?
7. Those children drank the milk.
8. Several students made interesting speeches.
9. Go away.
10. I saw a big man.

V. Exercise 2. *Are you able to show by diagrams the simple subject, the simple predicate, and the word that completes the simple predicate?*

EXPLANATION. When we analyze the sentence, " The boys ate their lunch," we find that its simple subject and simple predicate are " boys ate." If we had only these two words, the sentence would be quite incomplete, and we should doubtless ask, " ate what? " Looking at the sentence again, we see that " lunch " tells what they ate, and completes the thought expressed by the verb. Since it completes the meaning of the verb, it is called the complement of the verb. You notice, too, that this word names the object that receives the action expressed by the verb; for this reason it is called the object complement. The object complement is generally a noun or a pronoun and always follows a verb of action.

The complement is a very important part of a predicate, but it must never be considered as the third part of a sentence, for we know that there can be only two main divisions to every sentence: the subject and the predicate. The relation of the object complement to the predicate is shown in this way:

$$\text{boys} \mid \text{ate} \mid \text{lunch}$$

The line that separates the complement from the predicate shows that the predicate has two parts: the verb and its complement.

To find the complement of a verb, take the simple subject and the simple predicate, and ask the question " What? " The noun or the pronoun that answers this question and completes the verb is the complement.

DIRECTIONS. Diagram the simple subject, the simple predicate, and the object complement of the following sentences. See that all lines are drawn carefully. Remember that there are only two main divisions to every sentence; consequently, only the line separating the subject from the predicate should cut the sentence line.

1. Children like candy.
2. Boys play ball.
3. The boys saw the circus.
4. The teacher assigned a lesson.
5. He ate the cherries.
6. Has that man taken a purse?
7. Those children drank the milk.
8. Several students made interesting speeches.
9. Go away.
10. I saw a big man.

V. Exercise 3. *How well can you find the simple subject, the simple predicate, and the complement of a verb that shows condition or state of being?*

EXPLANATION. In the preceding exercise we learned that the noun that completes a verb of action is called the object complement. Some verbs, however, do not show action; they merely assert condition or being. Notice the italicized verbs in the following sentences:

1. The girl *is* good.
2. Wilson *was* President.

In the first sentence the verb is incomplete and needs the adjective " good " to complete its meaning; therefore " good " is the complement of the verb. But it does not follow a verb of action, and cannot be an object complement. If you read the sentence carefully, you will see that " good " asserts a characteristic or attribute of the subject " girl." " President " in the second sentence names the subject. Such words are called subjective complements. The subjective complement is a word that completes a verb of being by describing or naming the subject.

The subjective complement is usually a noun, a pronoun, or an adjective. If it is a noun, it names the subject and is sometimes called a predicate noun; when it is an adjective, it describes the subject and is sometimes called a predicate adjective.

The relation of the subjective complement to the verb and the subject is shown in this way:

$$\underline{\qquad \text{girl} \mid \text{is} \diagdown \text{good} \qquad}$$
$$\mid$$

Notice that the line which separates the subjective complement from the verb slants toward the subject since the subjective complement describes or names the subject.

Always test the complement of a sentence in this way:

1. See if the verb has a complement. The word that completes the verb by answering the question " what " or " whom " is the complement. Not every verb has a complement.

2. Decide whether the complement is an object complement or a subjective complement.

   (1) If it is a subjective complement, it follows a verb that shows state of being and describes or names the subject.

   (2) If it is an object complement, it follows a verb of action and names the object that receives the action expressed by the verb.

The most common verbs that show state of being and take subjective complements are: *be, am, are, is, was, were, been, become, grow, feel, taste, smell, look, seem.*

DIRECTIONS. Diagram the simple subject, the simple predicate, and the subjective complement of the following sentences. See that all lines are drawn carefully. Opposite the subjective complement in each sentence tell whether it is a predicate noun or a predicate adjective.

1. Mr. Smith is the principal.
2. He is tired.
3. Is that man her uncle?
4. This house is her home.
5. The child grew better.
6. Job was a patient man.
7. The soldiers were weary.
8. The dog seems lame.
9. He became my friend.
10. That rose smells sweet.

V. Exercise 4. *Do you know how to find the subject, the predicate, the complement, and the adjectives that describe the subject and the complement of a sentence?*

EXPLANATION. When we were studying the parts of speech, we learned that certain words were used to tell something about other words. Such words are called modifiers, for a modifier is a word or a group of words that affects the meaning of another word. In the expression, " three old men," " men " is modified by the adjectives " three " and " old " since they affect the meaning of the noun.

The relation of adjectives to the noun they modify is shown in this way:

men
| old
| three

Both of these adjectives modify " men "; therefore the lines on which they are written must come to the line drawn from the noun.

In analyzing sentences find the simple predicate, the simple subject, and the complement; then locate the modifiers.

DIRECTIONS. *A.* Why does this diagram not show the real relation of the words " three old men"?

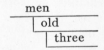

B. Diagram the following sentences. Draw all lines neatly and carefully.

1. The little children liked the good candy.
2. She is a good girl.
3. A poor old man became wealthy.
4. He has done good work.
5. Several little children recited poems.
6. Shakespeare was a great poet.
7. Many men help poor people.
8. We gained an easy victory.
9. Have those school children had a good time?
10. Take those pretty flowers.

V. Exercise 5. *Are you capable of analyzing sentences into subject, predicate, complement, and word modifiers?*

EXPLANATION. We know that adverbs as well as adjectives are modifiers since they affect the meaning of other words. An adverb may modify a verb, an adjective, or another adverb.

The relation of an adverb to the word it modifies is the same as the relation of an adjective to the noun or the pronoun it modifies. This is shown in diagrams thus: (*a*) The boys ate the candy quickly.

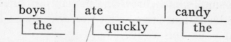

In this sentence the adverb " quickly " modifies the verb " ate."

(*b*) Some very good boys did the work.

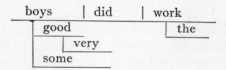

Notice that " very " does not describe " boys," but tells how " good " the boys are. Since it modifies an adjective, it is an adverb.

(*c*) I am not going.

$$I \mid am\ going$$
$$\mid \quad not$$

The word " not " makes the verb negative and is, therefore, an adverb.

We have learned that the only words that are modifiers are adjectives and adverbs. A pronoun which shows possession is diagramed like an adjective, but it remains a pronoun as far as its part of speech is concerned. The relation of a pronoun to the noun it modifies and to which it shows possession is indicated in this way:

```
she | has lost | doll
     |          | her
```

DIRECTIONS. Diagram the following sentences:

1. Those little boys are not reading their books carefully.
2. The small child threw the papers down.
3. Has he fallen down?
4. Send your dog away.
5. Has the postman brought any letters recently?
6. The woman was a very old person.
7. That ground is very hard.
8. Will you see her soon?

V. Exercise 6. *Do you know enough about the analysis of sentences to analyze simple sentences into subject, predicate, complement, word modifiers, and phrases that are used like adjectives?*

EXPLANATION. When we express our thoughts, we often use adjectives or adverbs to describe actions or objects. Not always, however, is it possible or best to use these modifiers. Sometimes we wish to use a group of words like an adjective, as in the sentence, " The men *of the church* gave their minister a beautiful gift." The italicized group of words modifies " men " just as a single adjective would. Since the group consists of closely related words introduced by a preposition which is completed by an object, it is a phrase. It is called an adjective phrase because it is used like an adjective.

The relation of the phrase to the word it modifies is shown thus:

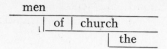

A preposition in and of itself is never a modifier. The phrase, which the preposition introduces, is the modifier. In the phrase the preposition " of " does not modify " men "; it merely introduces the phrase which as a whole modifies the noun. Never allow a preposition to stand in the position of a word modifier, for the word modifiers are adjectives, adverbs, and possessive nouns and pronouns.

Notice the relation of the various words in the following sentences:

(*a*) He wrote a story about a great man.

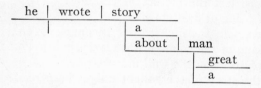

In this sentence the object complement " story " is modified by the article " a " and the adjective phrase, " about a great man."

(*b*) Write an article about Columbus in your note-book.

This sentence shows that a phrase does not always modify the word it stands next to in a sentence. You will see, too, that the object of a preposition does not necessarily have modifiers.

In analyzing sentences that contain word or phrase modifiers, there are four points to keep in mind:

1. Adjectives and adverbs (and possessive nouns and pronouns) are the only words that modify.
2. A preposition is never a modifier.
3. A phrase is a modifier when it is used like an adjective or an adverb.
4. A phrase is a group of words which has no subject or predicate but consists of a preposition and its object and modifiers.

DIRECTIONS. Diagram the following sentences:

1. A bottle of ink was broken.
2. She played a piece of music.
3. Has she lost the picture of the boy?
4. I had a dog of medium size.
5. The trees in the orchard are becoming green.
6. The king of the country was a very industrious man.
7. The pictures on the wall are pretty.
8. Has the story of the gallant knight been read?

V. Exercise 7. *How well can you analyze simple sentences into subject, predicate, complement, and modifiers?*

EXPLANATION. In the sentence, " He sent his child to the city," " to the city " is a phrase that is used like an adverb since it tells where. A phrase that is used like an adverb is called an adverbial phrase.

The relation of an adverbial phrase to the word it modifies is shown in this way:

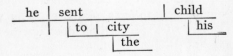

"To the city" is an adverbial phrase and modifies the verb "sent."

Always keep in mind these facts about phrases:

1. A phrase is a group of closely related words.
2. A phrase has no subject or predicate.
3. A phrase is introduced by a preposition that needs an object to complete its meaning.
4. A phrase is used like an adjective or an adverb.

DIRECTIONS.   Diagram the following sentences:

1. The boys sold the cans to the peddler.
2. I saw some papers in that box.
3. During the night I heard a very strange sound.
4. Does that boy sell papers on the corner?
5. Shall I buy this box of candy for you?
6. Into the room stumbled a poor old man.
7. The letters in that box are not old.
8. The story of Beautiful Joe is very interesting.

V. Exercise 8.   *Have you studied analysis of sentences enough to be able to analyze simple sentences?*

EXPLANATION.   We have learned in *Problem V* that there are two kinds of modifiers: word modifiers and phrase modifiers.   The words that modify are adjectives and adverbs; phrase modifiers are also adjective or adverbial since they are used like these parts of speech.

We know that a phrase consists of two parts: a preposition, which is never a modifier, and the object of the preposition.

Before concluding this problem, there are a few points that should be noticed.

(*a*) A phrase may modify the object of another phrase; as,

I know an interesting story about the picture of that man.

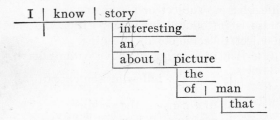

"Of that man" is a phrase that modifies the object of the phrase "about the picture."

(*b*) Two phrases may modify one word; as,

In the night he heard a strange sound in the kitchen.

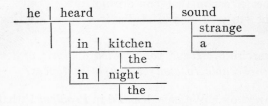

"In the kitchen" tells where he heard the sound, and "in the night" tells when; both phrases modify "heard."

If you will read again the explanations given in all the exercises of *Problem V*, you will be better able to take the test that finishes the Problem.

DIRECTIONS. Take each sentence you find below and follow this outline:

    1. Copy the sentence, and write the abbreviation
       for the part of speech above each word.

    2. Diagram the sentence.

1. The pictures in the front room were painted by a
    pupil of a great artist.

2. Does the kindergarten teacher tell the story of the
    three bears to her pupils?

3. For your English lesson write a composition about
    Columbus.

4. The president of the club was a woman of great
    ability.

5. In that room the king was sitting silently.

PROBLEM VI

ANALYSIS OF SIMPLE SENTENCES

Purpose of Study

Words are used in several special ways other than as subject, predicate, complement, or modifier. If we are to understand sentences thoroughly, we must know the use of every word in any sentence.

Exercises

1. Recognition of indirect object
2. Recognition of appositive
3. Recognition of a noun in direct address
4. Recognition of exclamatory nouns and other independent elements
5. Analysis of simple sentences

VI. Exercise 1. *Are you able to find the word in a sentence that names the receiver of the object complement?*

EXPLANATION. We have learned that the object complement names the direct receiver of the action asserted by the verb. Since this is so, it is sometimes called the direct object of the verb. In the sentence, " He gave his mother some flowers," the subject is " he "; the predicate is " gave "; and the object complement, or direct object, of the verb is " flowers," modified by the adjective " some." All words

60

in the sentence have been accounted for except "his mother." "His," we know, is a possessive pronoun that modifies "mother"; but how is "mother" used? If we change the sentence and place the object complement after the verb, we have "He gave some flowers," — where? — "to his mother." "Mother," then, tells to whom he gave the flowers; in other words, it names the person who receives the direct object, "flowers." Such a word is called the indirect object of the verb. The indirect object is never the complement of a verb; it is always a modifier of the verb. Its relation to the verb is shown in the diagram thus:

We see that the meaning of the sentence is, "He gave some flowers to his mother." The indirect object is not stated in phrase form, but virtually it is the same as a phrase with the preposition omitted. This is shown in the diagram by putting "x" in the place for the preposition.

It is very easy to confuse the object complement with the indirect object, for the indirect object always stands between the verb and the object complement. If you will remember that the object complement completes the verb by answering the question "what," you will have no difficulty in finding the direct and the indirect objects of a verb.

DIRECTIONS. *A.* Diagram the following sentences:

1. Those children in that house sent their sick sister ~~many~~ books.
2. He brought her three boxes of pens.

3. Give me those pencils.
4. Grant me my one request now.
5. The strange man suddenly told me his secret.
6. The frightened child would not tell the man her name.
7. Will you show me your new hat?
8. Write him a letter about the fire.

B. Write ten sentences each of which contains an indirect object.

VI. Exercise 2. *Can you analyze a group of words that explains a noun or a pronoun?*

EXPLANATION. If some one said to you, " Mr. Brown is here," you would probably wonder who " Mr. Brown " is. But if you were told, " Mr. Brown, the postman, is here," there would be no doubt in your mind as to who " Mr. Brown " is. We often use such explanatory groups of words when we are speaking of some person or thing. A group of words that is used to explain a noun or a pronoun is called an appositive. In every group of this kind there is a noun that is the base word of the appositive; it is called a noun in apposition. The other words in the group are the modifiers of this noun.

The relation of an appositive to the noun it explains is shown in the diagram thus:

(*a*) Mr. Brown, the postman is here.

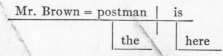

" Mr. Brown " is the subject, " the postman " is the appositive, and " postman " is the noun in apposition.

(*b*) I sent it to Kipling, the author of many books.

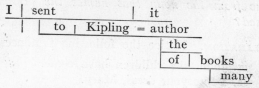

" Kipling " is the object of the preposition; " the author of many books " is the appositive, and " author " is the noun in apposition.

You have probably noticed that an appositive and the word it explains are virtually two names for the same person or thing. Any noun in a sentence — subject, complement, object of a preposition, or possessive noun — may have an appositive to explain it. Generally the appositive stands next to the noun it explains.

DIRECTIONS. *A.* Diagram the following sentences:

1. Mr. Brown, the postman, has not come to the house today.
2. *The Crisis,* a book by Churchill, is very interesting.
3. Mrs. Smith, the president of the club, gave several children tickets to the concert.
4. The Auditorium, a building in Chicago, has been bought by Mr. Jones, a very wealthy man.
5. A book was given to Mr. Smith, the winner of the prize.
6. They had always been hungry, those poor children!
7. Tomorrow will you send me the book, *The Jungle?*
8. My brother George became a noted educator.

B. Write ten sentences, each of which contains an appositive.

VI. Exercise 3. *Can you distinguish the subject of a sentence from the noun that names the person who is addressed?*

EXPLANATION. Notice the following sentences:

1. John, the children have come.
2. I like your dress, Mary.
3. Children, study your lessons.

In each of these sentences some particular person is addressed. In the first sentence it is " John," in the second it is " Mary," and in the third it is "children." Since these words name the person or persons addressed, they are known as nouns in direct address.

Let us analyze the first sentence carefully. The verb " have come " is the predicate. To find the subject we ask, " Who has come? " Is the answer " John " or " children "? " Children," of course, states who have come and is, therefore, the subject. Has the verb " have come " an object complement? Reading the sentence again, we see that " John " is the only word that has not been accounted for, but it cannot be the complement, for it does not complete the meaning of the verb. The verb has no complement. But what is the relation of " John " to the rest of the sentence since it is not the subject, the direct or indirect object, the object of a preposition, or a noun in apposition? It really is not needed, for one could make the statement, " The children have come," and be fully understood without using the term of address. Since this is so, it is said to be independent of the sentence, and its relation to the rest of the sentence is shown in this way:

```
        John
    ────────────────
      children │ have come
    ──────────────
         │ the      │
```

All nouns that name the person addressed are independent of the sentence.

Do not confuse the subject of a sentence with a noun in direct address. In the third sentence, what is the subject? Is it " children " ? Does " children " answer the question, " who studies? " No, the answer is " you study." " You," understood, is the subject, and " children " is a noun in direct address. Notice the diagram:

```
        children
     ───────────
      (you) | study | lessons
            |       | your
                    ─────────
```

A noun in direct address is never the subject of a sentence, and the subject is never a noun in direct address. A sentence always has a subject, but it does not necessarily contain a noun in direct address.

DIRECTIONS. *A*. What is the difference between the direct object and a noun in direct address?

B. Diagram the following sentences:

1. John, will you give me your pencil?
2. I will see you tomorrow, sir, in that office.
3. Boys, I have brought you some toys.
4. James, put that book on the desk.
5. Shall I see you next week, Mary?
6. Child, where are you going today?
7. Is this pudding very good, Mother?
8. Miss Jones, shall I bring you some flowers this afternoon?

C. Write five sentences, each of which contains a noun in direct address.

VI. Exercise 4. *Can you recognize exclamatory nouns and other words that are independent elements?*

EXPLANATION. In the preceding exercise we learned that a noun in direct address is an independent element since it is not necessary to the meaning of a sentence. We often use other words that are also independent of the sentence. For example, one may say, " Joy! my father is coming home." " Joy " is a noun that expresses an exclamation and is called an exclamatory noun. The thought of the sentence would be complete without this word, and consequently it is independent of the sentence. Its relation to the sentence is shown thus:

```
  Joy
  father    |  is coming
    | my    |      | home
```

All interjections are independent elements. Take, for example, the sentence, " Oh, I have lost my purse! "

```
     oh
   I | have lost | purse
     |           |  | my
```

The adverbs " yes " and " no " are always independent of the sentence, and in a diagram this fact is shown rather than their use as adverbs in expressing simple affirmation or negation. For example, take the sentence, " Yes, I shall go to the party." It is diagramed thus:

```
     yes
   I | shall go
     |   | to | party
     |          | the
```

If an independent element has a modifier, this is shown in the diagram like any other word that has a modifier. Notice the relation of " my " and " dear " to " girl," the noun in direct address, in the sentence, " My dear girl, are you very happy? "

In analyzing sentences, proceed as usual: find the simple predicate, the simple subject, the complement, the word and phrase modifiers. Then you can easily find any words that may be independent elements.

DIRECTIONS. *A.* Diagram the following sentences:

1. That little candle! how far it sends its rays!
2. My brother! send me your kindest thought.
3. Yes, Mr. Brown, the grocer, offered me a position yesterday.
4. How long have you known that, little rascal?
5. No, I cannot accept your offer, Mr. Smith.
6. Oh! when did he give me this beautiful gift?
7. Give me your best wishes, my dear friends.
8. Pshaw! when will he send me my receipt?

VI. Exercise 5. *How well can you analyze simple sentences?*

EXPLANATION. In *Problem VI* we have learned that words may be used independently of the sentence. Such words are nouns in direct address, exclamatory nouns, interjections, and the adverbs " yes " and " no."

We have also learned that a group of words may be used to explain a noun or a pronoun. Such a group is called an appositive. The base noun in the group is a noun in apposition.

Do not confuse a word that is used independently with a noun in apposition. An appositive explains a noun, and is another name for the noun; an independent element explains nothing and is not at all necessary to the meaning of the sentence.

It will now be profitable for you to read again the explanations given in all the exercises of *Problem VI*.

DIRECTIONS. *A*. What is the difference between a noun in apposition and an independent element?

B. Take each sentence that you find below and follow this outline:

1. Write the sentence and above each word tell the part of speech.
2. Diagram the sentence.
3. Tell how the underlined word is used.

1. Oh, he has not given *her* the right package.
2. *Mother,* may I send grandmother this book?
3. No, I cannot send this report to Mrs. Price, the *secretary.*
4. My dear *child,* you look very happy today.
5. *Goodness!* I have forgotten her new address.

ANALYSIS OF COMPOUND PARTS OF SIMPLE SENTENCES

Purpose of Study

We should always express our ideas in as clear a way as possible, but we should never repeat the same words again and again. In order to avoid this we must learn how to combine words so as to form compound subjects and predicates. Mistakes are often made in thinking that a compound subject is a sentence. For this reason we must be able to analyze our expressions and see if they are sentences that give complete thoughts, or if they are merely parts of a sentence.

Exercises

1. Analysis of compound subject
2. Analysis of compound predicate
3. Analysis of compound complements
4. Analysis of other compound elements
5. Analysis of simple sentences

VII. Exercise 1. *Are you able to find the compound subject of a sentence?*

EXPLANATION. If some one said to you, " Mary has eaten her lunch and Jane has eaten her lunch," you would think that the speaker had expressed his thought very

awkwardly, which would be quite true. Instead of repeat-
ing the predicate each time, he should have connected the
two subjects " Mary " and " Jane " with a conjunction and
expressed the predicate only once. Then he would have
said, " Mary and Jane have eaten their lunch." When the
subject consists of two or more words connected by conjunctions, it is said to be a compound subject.

Not all the conjunctions that we learned in *Problem IV*
can be used to connect the words of a compound subject.
We may say, " Mary *and* John," " *Neither* James *nor* John,"
" Mother *or* Father," because these conjunctions connect
words of the same kind. Such connecting words are called
coördinate conjunctions since they join words having equal
value; that is, a subject with a subject, a noun with a noun,
an adjective with an adjective.

Notice in the following illustrations how the diagrams
show: (1) the relation of one part of a compound subject
to another part, and (2) the relation of the entire compound subject to the rest of the sentence.

(*a*) Mary and John have eaten their lunch.

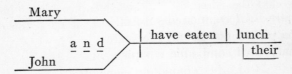

Notice the following points:

1. The conjunction is always written on a dotted line
   to show that it is not one of the subjects in the
   compound subject.
2. The two parts of the sentence, the subject and the
   predicate, are indicated by the line which divides
   the sentence line.

(*b*) The old lady and her daughter have bought a new house.

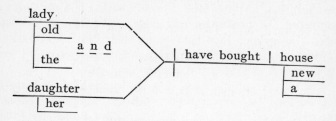

Notice that " the " and " old " modify " lady "; " her " modifies " daughter." To show this these words are placed under the nouns they modify.

(*c*) Those boys and girls are good.

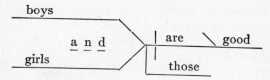

Note that the adjective " those " modifies both " boys " and " girls." This is shown by writing it on a line that leads to both subjects.

(*d*) Mary, John, and Jane are going.

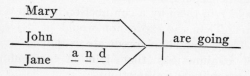

Some sentences have more than three subjects. Add necessary lines according to the number of subjects in the sentences.

DIRECTIONS. *A.* Diagram the following sentences:

1. Mary and John have given their mother a new machine.
2. Howard and Jack have bought a camp in the mountains.
3. The boys and the girls knew their lessons well.
4. Cats and dogs are domestic animals.
5. A poor old man and a little child went down the street.
6. John, those vases and pictures are very beautiful.
7. Many men, women, and children attended the concert.
8. The students and the teachers give the poor many gifts at Christmas.

B. Write five sentences containing compound subjects. Underline the compound subjects.

VII. Exercise 2. *Now that you can locate the compound subject of a sentence, can you find the compound predicate?*

EXPLANATION. We know that a person many times wishes to make one statement about several persons or things and uses a compound subject to do this. In the same way if one wishes to say, " John ran and John jumped," he should not repeat the subject monotonously, but should join them by a conjunction and use a compound predicate. Then the expression would be, " John ran and jumped." A compound predicate is joined by the same kind of conjunctions that join a compound subject; namely, co-ordinate conjunctions.

The following illustrations show: (1) the relation of one part of a compound predicate to another part, and (2) the relation of the entire compound predicate to the rest of the sentence.

(*a*) John ran and jumped.

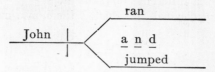

(*b*) John ate the sauce and washed the dish.

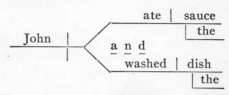

Note that the verbs in a compound predicate may be completed by different complements.

(*c*) Mary cleaned and dusted the house.

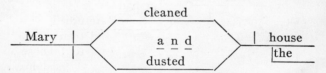

In this sentence note that both verbs have the same complement and must be diagramed so as to show this.

(*d*) They read their books, wrote their compositions, and studied their history.

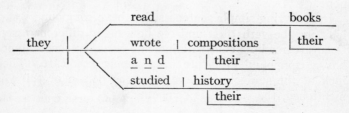

This sentence has three predicates, each of which is completed by a different complement.

(e) Mary cleaned and dusted the house carefully.

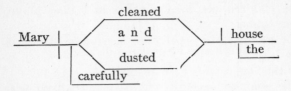

Note that the adverb "carefully" modifies both verbs and must be diagramed so as to show this.

(f) John paid the bill quickly and then returned to his house.

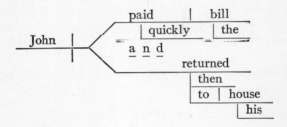

In this sentence the adverb "quickly" modifies "paid," and the phrase "to his house" modifies "returned." Notice that one verb has a complement and the other has none.

In analyzing simple sentences that have compound parts, look for the verbs first and see how many different assertions are made. This will indicate whether the sentence has a compound predicate or a simple predicate. Then look at the subject; if more than one person or thing is mentioned, the subject is compound.

DIRECTIONS. *A.* Diagram the following sentences:

1. The little child sang and whistled.
2. I sweep and dust my room every week.
3. Those children ate their lunches and then played their games.
4. In the evening Mary practices her music and reads her book.
5. Take this, or leave it here on the table.
6. I have seen her recently but have not talked with her.
7. They asked many questions and then went off without an answer.
8. The sun shines brightly and causes much happiness.

B. Write five sentences containing compound predicates. Underline the verbs that make the predicate in each sentence compound.

VII. Exercise 3. *Can you recognize the compound complement of a verb?*

EXPLANATION. Many times a compound complement completes a verb. This may be an object complement or a subjective complement. The following diagrams illustrate the relation of the compound complement to the rest of the sentence.

(*a*) The man was poor but happy.

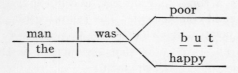

(*b*) I bought cheese, bread, and apples.

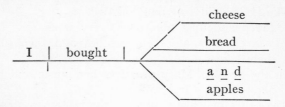

DIRECTIONS. *A.* Diagram the following sentences:

1. She was old and wrinkled.
2. I ate bread, butter, and cheese.
3. In August I shall buy a house and a machine.
4. We packed our hats and coats away carefully.
5. The little children were noisy but very happy.
6. The speaker's words were clear and distinct.
7. I shall soon be happy and contented.
8. Where did he leave his books and pencils?

B. Write four sentences containing compound object complements, and four sentences containing compound subjective complements. Indicate which are the object complements, and which are the subjective complements.

VII. Exercise 4. *Do you understand the compound elements of a sentence well enough to recognize the compound object of a preposition and compound modifiers?*

EXPLANATION. A sentence may have other compound elements besides a compound subject, a compound predicate, or a compound complement. The following diagrams illustrate other compound elements:

(*a*) She bought many presents for her mother and father.

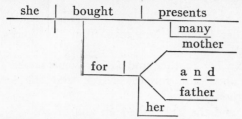

"Mother" and "father" are the compound object of the preposition "for."

(*b*) She ran around and around.

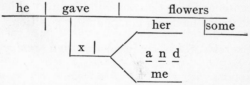

"Around" and "around" are compound modifiers.

(*c*) He gave her and me some flowers.

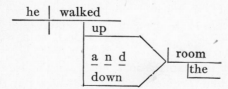

"Her" and "me" are the indirect object of the verb "gave."

(*d*) He walked up and down the room.

" Up " and " down " make a compound preposition.

DIRECTIONS.   *A.*   Diagram the following sentences:

1. His mother brought him toys from the stores and shops.
2. They gave her mother and father some books.
3. They blamed him for the wreck and the loss of their money.
4. The boy and the girl rushed up and down.
5. Shall I send you and your father these flowers?
6. They sent things from the book store, the grocery store, and the jewelry shop.
7. Give that to him or me.
8. He ran up and down the stairs.

B.   Write the following sentences:

1. A sentence having a compound object of a preposition.
2. A sentence having compound modifiers.
3. A sentence having a compound indirect object.
4. A sentence having a compound preposition.

VII. Exercise 5.   *How well can you analyze simple sentences that have compound elements?*

EXPLANATION.   Any part of a sentence may be compound.   The subject, for example, may consist of two or more nouns or pronouns connected by coördinate conjunctions.   In the same way a sentence may have a compound predicate, a verb may have a compound complement, a preposition may have a compound object, or a word may have compound modifiers.

Read again the explanations given in the exercises of *Problem VI* and *Problem VII,* and study the diagrams so that you will have absolute mastery of the analysis of simple sentences.

Always read a sentence before attempting to analyze it. If you do not follow this advice, you will find that you will spend much time in making corrections and rewriting papers.

DIRECTIONS. Diagram the following sentences:

1. Into the room she went and set her basket of eggs upon the table.
2. The child walked behind his father with a slow and deliberate gait.
3. The little children gave their friends pictures and books.
4. The paintings and the furniture were sent to various stores in New York and Chicago.
5. On the steep and narrow trail stood a big mountain lion.
6. Jerry, give Mary and me your box of pens and pencils.
7. Last night mother and I saw John and Henry on the street.
8. Those roses and violets were beautiful.

PUNCTUATION OF SIMPLE SENTENCES

Purpose of Study

In order to write sentences correctly and express our thoughts intelligently, we must not only be able to analyze sentences and know the relation of one part to another, but we must punctuate the sentences we write so that those who read them will be able to understand our thought. There are some very simple rules for punctuation which one must know if he is to write correctly.

The purpose of punctuation is to make the thought clear to the reader.

Exercises

1. Punctuation of ends of sentences
2. Punctuation of abbreviations
3. Punctuation of words in direct address
4. Punctuation of appositives
5. Punctuation of series of words, phrases, and clauses
6. Punctuation of exclamatory nouns and other independent elements
7. Punctuation of simple sentences

VIII. Exercise 1. *Can you punctuate the ends of sentences correctly?*

EXPLANATION. We are studying these problems and exercises for one purpose; namely, to express our thoughts in correctly spoken and written sentences. We know that the sentence is the unit of thought. When we write sentences, there are a few facts that we must always keep in mind These are:

1. A sentence is a group of words expressing a complete thought.
2. A sentence always has a subject and a predicate. The subject may be understood, but it exists, nevertheless.
3. A sentence begins with a capital.
4. A sentence ends with a mark of punctuation which is decided by the thought expressed.

It is very necessary that we use the end punctuation correctly so that our readers can understand our thought readily. Sentences that ask questions are followed by the question mark. Sentences that express strong feeling or sudden thought are followed by the exclamation mark. All other sentences are followed by the period.

Sentences have been given certain names because of their use. We need not know these names in order to write and punctuate sentences correctly, but it is a help to know them when we wish to speak about the various kinds of sentences. For that reason we shall learn the names of the kinds of sentences when classified according to their use or meaning.

1. A sentence that states a fact is called a declarative sentence.
2. A sentence that asks a question is called an interrogative sentence.

3. A sentence that expresses sudden thought or strong feeling is called an exclamatory sentence.

4. A sentence that makes a request or a command is called an imperative sentence.

DIRECTIONS. *A.* What are the four kinds of sentences when classified according to their use? Write two illustrations of each with the correct punctuation.

B. Insert the correct end punctuation and capitalize the first word of every sentence in the following group of words:

have you ever read the biography of Guglielmo Marconi the inventor of the wireless it is as fascinating as any story of adventure that was ever written let me tell you a few interesting things that the author tells about this remarkable man Marconi was born into a home of wealth in Italy he never lacked money for an education which could fit him for his wonderful work in addition he was always able to buy any apparatus that was needed for his experiments what do you suppose he invented first when he was five years old he made an indelible ink from wild berries with this he marked his clothes then for eleven years he made no more discoveries are you wondering why he stopped so suddenly like all children he wanted the appreciation of his mother and when she did not seem to appreciate this first attempt at invention the little child was too discouraged to try anything else at the age of sixteen he began to experiment with a crude apparatus which he had made himself when he was twenty-one Marconi took out his first wireless patent how he was ridiculed at first but did he stop his work because of this no he went on as though nothing had been said by the time he was twenty-four years of age he had shown the world that messages could be transmitted without wires he soon became world famous his fame seemed to make as little impression upon him as did the ridicule that he had received earlier in his life he continued to be simple in his tastes and unassuming in his actions do you want to know more about this man read his biography

VIII. Exercise 2. *Do you know how to punctuate abbreviations?*

EXPLANATION. Instead of writing out such words as doctor, mister, ante meridian (before noon), post meridian (after noon), and mistress, we use abbreviations that have become so common that every one understands them. An abbreviation is always followed by a period. If it comes at the end of a sentence, one period serves both purposes; as, " The boys left at 2 P.M."

Abbreviations are not in good taste in letters or any other kind of writing. Only a few abbreviations are used in good literature; these are:

i. e.	that is	Mr.	mister (with name)
e. g.	for example	Mrs.	mistress (with name)
q. v.	which see	Dr.	doctor (with name)
A.M.	before noon	A.D.	in the year of our Lord
P.M.	after noon	B.C.	before Christ
viz.	namely	Messrs.	sirs (plural of mister)

DIRECTIONS. *A.* Punctuate the following sentences:

1. Dr Marks called at 3 PM
2. Mrs Price has gone to see her sister Miss Hunt
3. If I do not order the groceries by 9 AM, I shall not get them until afternoon

4. Messrs Jones and Allen are thinking of buying that hotel
5. Columbus discovered America in 1492 AD

B. Write ten sentences containing abbreviations that are considered good form.

VIII. Exercise 3. *Are you able to punctuate words in direct address?*

EXPLANATION. Notice the punctuation of the following sentences:

1. Mother, may I go to the store?
2. You may go, John, but hurry back.
3. I wish I had been with you, Jane.

Each of these sentences contains a noun in direct address. In the first sentence it is " Mother," in the second it is " John," and in the third it is " Jane." If you have looked at the punctuation carefully, you have noticed that each of these nouns is set off from the rest of the sentence by the comma. In the first sentence only one comma is used to set off " Mother " from the rest of the sentence because it is the introductory word of the sentence. In the second sentence two commas are used, for " John " appears within the sentence. The third sentence ends with the term of direct address, and only one comma is used. These three illustrations show that words in direct address are set off from the rest of the sentence by commas. If the word comes at the beginning or at the end of a sentence, it is set off by one comma; if it appears within the sentence, it is preceded and followed by a comma.

DIRECTIONS. *A.* Punctuate the following sentences:

1. John I wish you would bring me that book
2. Which house did you visit Mary
3. I saw you sir as you came into the house
4. Boys here is my brother
5. Doctor will you come in
6. It seems to me my friend that your advice is very timely
7. I like your boat Captain
8. How do you like my hat Mary and my new cape
9. Nancy you should behave differently
10. Mr Grant there must be a package here for me
11. You funny girl don't you know who I am
12. Surely John you can come and help me a little
13. Poor little boy have you lost your mother
14. Never mind sonny she will be here soon
15. Look here Buddy you must go with me

B. Write ten sentences containing nouns in direct address. Punctuate each carefully.

VIII. Exercise 4. *Do you understand how to punctuate an appositive?*

EXPLANATION. In the sentence, " Mr. Harding, the President of the United States, lived in Ohio," the group of words, " the President of the United States," is an appositive since it explains the noun, " Mr. Harding." Look at the punctuation of the appositive, and you will see that it is set off from the rest of the sentence by commas. Notice that a comma precedes and follows the explanatory expression. If the appositive comes at the end of a sentence, only one comma is necessary to set it off from the rest of the sentence; as, " I once saw Mr. Roosevelt, the President of the United States."

Remember that an appositive is a noun in apposition and all of its modifiers.

DIRECTIONS. *A.* Punctuate the following sentences:

1. They talked about operations a topic of interest to many people

2. In this attitude of thankfulness I went home to my castle a little tent on the shore of the lake

3. I once knew a man a peculiar old fellow who would not wear a collar

4. My friends Mary and Jane came to see me every day until I was well

5. Abraham Lincoln the famous president of the United States was once a country boy

6. He is the son of Mr Snyder the Mayor

7. I tried to lift the gun a heavy antique thing

8. Howard Smith a resident of San Francisco was a passenger on the boat

9. We arrived in Albany the capital of New York

10. Joe the grocery boy has a remarkable memory

11. My hearth an open place filled with square tiles was the center of my new home

12. Mr. Smith's daughters Eunice and Eurina will go to Canada next summer

13. Before I could publish the document, Colonel House President Wilson's associate arrived in London

14. Mr Steele a leading newspaper man returned to Chicago early in the winter

15. Tolstoy a great Russian writer desired universal peace

B. Write ten sentences containing appositives. Punctuate each correctly.

VIII. Exercise 5. *Are you able to punctuate a group of words, phrases, or clauses that have the same use in the sentence?*

EXPLANATION. Notice the wording and punctuation of the following sentences:

1. Mother, Father, Mary, and John went to the beach.
2. We walked slowly, thoughtfully, and carefully.
3. They went to the beach, to the city, and to the country to find her friend.
4. I came, I saw, I conquered.

A careful reading of these sentences shows you that each contains a group of words that are the same kind and are used in the same way. For example, sentence 1 has a group of nouns that make the compound subject. Sentence 2 has a group of adverbs that modify the verb. Sentence 3 has a group of adverbial phrases, and sentence 4 has a group of independent clauses. Such groups are known as series of words, phrases, or clauses.

Look at the punctuation again, and you will see that the comma is used to separate the terms of each series. Notice that the comma is not omitted before the conjunction that connects the last term of the series with the others. This comma is sometimes omitted, but it is always better to use it. Suppose you have the sentence, " Mary, John, and James are coming." What change does the omission of the comma before the conjunction make? The sentence would then be, " Mary, John and James are coming." When the sentence is written this way, the subject is " John and James," and " Mary " is a noun in direct address. You can see how the omission of this comma causes a decided change in the meaning of the sentence. Because of the confusion that may arise from omitting the comma before the conjunction in a series, it is always best to use it.

If conjunctions are used to connect the terms of a series, commas are not used; as, " Mother and father and Uncle Joe went to the mountains."

DIRECTIONS. *A.* Punctuate the following sentences:

1. He traveled through Washington Oregon and California
2. I had lost my boat my gun and my dog
3. He rang the bell waited a moment looked through the window and finally opened the door
4. My dog and my cat and my parrot were now my only friends
5. Day after day week after week month after month he worked without a thought for himself
6. He sold butter and cheese and milk
7. I went up the hill to see how the shore lay how the current set and how the boat could leave the channel
8. He carried in his belt a saw a hatchet and two powder pouches
9. At my back I carried my basket on my shoulder I had my gun and over my head I raised a great clumsy ugly goat's-skin umbrella
10. I listened I looked around me I could hear nothing and I could see nothing
11. I lay down and slept soundly and awoke much refreshed
12. I should like to visit Norway Holland and Italy
13. I took with me six candles a tinder-box a gun and some biscuits

14. I had two little goats several parrots and many tame
    sea-fowls
15. He visited us in January in March and in August

B. Write ten sentences, each containing a series of
words, phrases, or clauses. Punctuate correctly. Remember that the words in a series are always used in the same
way.

VIII. Exercise 6. *Do you know how to punctuate exclamatory nouns and other independent elements?*

EXPLANATION. Notice the punctuation of these sentences:

1. Yes, you may have my book.
2. Mercy! how can he be so cruel.
3. Oh, come with me.
4. Alas! I shall never see her again.

In each of these sentences there is an independent element which is set off from the rest of the sentence by some
mark of punctuation. In the first sentence the independent element is the adverb " yes." " Yes " and " no " are
always set off from a sentence by a comma.

In the second sentence, the independent element is an
exclamatory noun. It is set off from the sentence by an
exclamation mark.

The third and fourth sentences contain interjections.
" Oh " in the third sentence is followed by a comma because it expresses a mild exclamation. " Alas " in the
fourth sentence is followed by an exclamation point because it expresses strong feeling. An interjection may be
followed by a comma or an exclamation point.

These illustrations and rules will guide you in punctuating all independent elements that we have studied.

DIRECTIONS. *A.* Punctuate the following sentences:

1. Yes I can do this for you
2. My but she plays beautifully
3. Goodness how she does cry
4. No he cannot go
5. Alas I have lost my English paper
6. Well I will do what I can for you
7. Heavens she is alone on that raft
8. Home how I wish I were there
9. Oh my child is not here
10. Hey can't you hear me

B. Write ten sentences that illustrate the facts you have learned in *Exercise 6.*

VIII. Exercise 7. *How well can you punctuate simple sentences?*

EXPLANATION. You should now be able to punctuate correctly almost any simple sentence that you may wish to write. Let us summarize the points we have learned in *Problem VIII.*

1. Every sentence is followed by some mark of punctuation. The thought expressed in the sentence decides what the mark must be.
2. An abbreviation is followed by a period.
3. Words in direct address are set off from the rest of the sentence by commas.
4. An appositive is set off from the rest of the sentence by commas.
5. Commas are used to separate the terms of a series.

6. Independent elements are set off from the sentence by commas or, in the case of exclamatory words, by exclamation marks.

DIRECTIONS. Punctuate the following sentences. Number each punctuation mark. Below the sentence write the reason for the marks of punctuation, numbering each according to the number in the sentence; for example,

   1   2   3   4

Mr. Jones, the doctor, came.

1. Abbreviation
2. Appositive
3. Appositive
4. Declarative sentence

1. Send your bill Mr Nash to my daughter the treasurer of the association
2. Eat less candy drink more milk and sleep more at night
3. Hark I hear some one at the door John
4. Yes I will send your name to Mr. Jones the real estate agent
5. I like cheese and crackers and sardines
6. A boomerang the weapon used by natives of Australia was sent to me by my nephew
7. I did not know that Dr. Smith John's friend had been here
8. Jane Mrs Smith your cousin visited us last night
9. Open the desk take out the paper and write me a letter
10. Aha I caught you this time you little rascal

ANALYSIS AND PUNCTUATION OF COMPOUND SENTENCES

Purpose of Study

We often wish to make two or more complete assertions that are closely connected in thought. We can do this by using simple sentences, but such a method results in expressions that are very childish and tiresome. A better way is to join the simple sentences together and have a compound sentence. In order to do this correctly, we must study the construction of such sentences. Furthermore, we must know how to punctuate them so that our readers will be able to understand our thought easily.

Exercises

1. Analysis of compound sentences
2. Analysis of compound sentences
3. Analysis of compound sentences
4. Punctuation of compound sentences
5. Punctuation of compound sentences
6. Punctuation of compound sentences
7. Analysis and punctuation of compound sentences

IX. Exercise 1. *Now that you know how to analyze simple sentences, can you analyze compound sentences?*

EXPLANATION. We have learned that a clause is a group of words containing a subject and a predicate. When a clause expresses a complete thought, it is an independent clause. If a sentence contains only one independent clause, it is a simple sentence. " Mary did her work " is a simple sentence because it is an independent clause.

Suppose one wishes to make two statements; as, " John took his little sister to the circus. Mary went with them." These two simple sentences are connected in thought, and would sound much better if they were joined. Then the sentence would be," John took his little sister to the circus and Mary went with them." When expressed this way the sentence is compound, for a compound sentence is one that contains two or more independent clauses. The clauses of a compound sentence are usually connected by a coördinate conjunction.

Notice the relation of the clauses of a compound sentence as shown in the diagram.

(*a*) John went but Mary stayed.

The clauses in this sentence are of equal value, both being independent, and therefore are placed on the same line. A coördinate conjunction connects the two clauses.

(*b*) John took his little sister to the circus, Mary went to the theatre, but Jane could not leave the house.

```
 Mary | went                    Jane | could leave | house
        |      | to | theatre _but_      |    | not       | the
               | the
```

Notice that there are three clauses in this sentence.

The conjunction is omitted between the first and second clauses, and a cross (x) is put on the dotted line for the conjunction.

When analyzing compound sentences, read carefully and select the different clauses first; then diagram.

DIRECTIONS.   Diagram the following sentences:

1. Paderewski, the noted pianist, is a native of Poland, but he has spent much time in America.
2. He gave me some cherries, and I shall give him some candy.
3. We enjoyed the music and the reading, but we did not like the location of our seats.
4. John, will you bring me your books, or must I send William for them?
5. Edmund Henry, the only son of George Henry, went to college for a short time, and then he was sent to the Orient on an important mission.
6. Captain Hervey received severe wounds in a battle at sea, but he soon recovered.
7. Last week I saw a pretty hat in the store, but today it was gone.
8. That man amassed a great fortune, and then he gave it away to his son and daughter.

IX. Exercise 2.   *Are you able to analyze compound sentences?*

EXPLANATION. We have learned that a compound sentence consists of two or more independent clauses which are closely connected in thought. Not all independent clauses can be united and made into compound sentences. For example, one should not make a statement like this: " I must study, and mother has coffee for her breakfast." Such a sentence is foolish, for the two statements are in no way connected in thought. Be sure that the independent clauses of any compound sentence that you write express thoughts that can be connected.

In analyzing compound sentences, find the independent clauses and then proceed as if they were simple sentences.

DIRECTIONS. Diagram the following sentences:

1. I enjoy many kinds of books, but I do not read books about war.

2. He ate his pie greedily, but he left the bread and butter on his plate.

3. Those little children seem happy, but their mother is very sad.

4. I shall go to my work early and the manager of the store will be glad.

5. One sees many interesting advertisements in newspapers and magazines.

6. One evening in December Mrs. Smith attended a concert, Mr. Smith went to his club, and the children stayed at home with the nurse.

7. Mother bought a new suit for John, Howard brought mother a beautiful vase, and father sent Auntie, his sister, a lovely book.

8. John, can you telephone the message, or must some one deliver it personally to Mr. Jones?

IX. Exercise 3. *How well can you analyze compound sentences?*

EXPLANATION. Sometimes a simple sentence contains a compound predicate, the parts of which are so long that a person becomes confused and considers them the clauses of a compound sentence. For example, take the sentence, " He has gone to the store but will return soon." This is a simple sentence with a compound predicate. " He " is the subject of " has gone " and " will return." Notice how the relation of the two predicates is shown in the diagram:

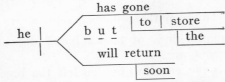

Do not say that the subject of *will return* is *he* understood. The only sentences in which the subject is regularly understood are imperative sentences.

The one main point to be kept in mind when writing compound sentences is this: a compound sentence consists of two or more independent clauses closely connected in thought.

DIRECTIONS. Diagram the following sentences:

1. I rode on the street car for a few miles but later went in an automobile.
2. The buildings in New York are very tall, but they are perfectly safe.
3. Give me your bundle, mother, and I will carry it for you.
4. What beautiful eyes that child has, and how little she is!

5. This street car travels very slowly, but I shall be patient and read my book.

6. I shall see you at the theater and introduce my father and brother to you.

7. These are very beautiful plants, but I shall not buy any of them.

8. The rich men of the city have done much for little children and will do more.

IX. Exercise 4. *Are you able to punctuate compound sentences?*

EXPLANATION. Notice the punctuation of the following sentences:

1. John took his books to the library, but James sent his by his brother.

2. Margaret ate her breakfast quickly, but her sister refused to eat anything.

Each of these sentences is compound because each contains two independent clauses connected by a coördinate conjunction. Look at the punctuation again, and you will see that a comma precedes the conjunction in each sentence. In a compound sentence a comma is placed before the coördinate conjunction that connects the independent clauses. This rule should always be observed unless the clauses are very short.

In punctuating compound sentences, do not forget how to punctuate an appositive, a noun in direct address, and the other points you learned in *Problem VIII*.

DIRECTIONS. *A.* Punctuate the following sentences:

1. Who is that strange man and where is he going

2. I do not know his name or where he is going but I am willing to ask him

3. The little girls were tired and sleepy but they insisted on staying up until their mother returned

4. There were several men and women in the library but I could not find Mr Smith among them

5. I must go now but sometime I'll come back again

6. I could spend much more money than I have but I am really very happy with what I now possess

7. Our childhood days are our happiest ones but one seldom knows it at the time

8. At four o'clock a special edition of the paper is sold and every one buys it most eagerly

9. I once went through the southern part of Iowa with a two-horse covered sleigh and the trip lasted two whole months

10. We invaded Denver and our traveler Charley Cranston took an order from a Denver bookseller for several hundred volumes of standard poems

11. Dr Hornaday was one of the world's foremost naturalists and his last book came with authority from a man of ability

12. I was a boy just out of college and Mr Allison appeared to me to be a person of great age and dignity

13. The football team won every game but the baseball team was not so successful

14. He may have put limitations upon himself but he never shrank from doing his duty

15. Mr Allison did not stand in the class with Lincoln but he did belong to that class of statesmen who made possible the success of representative government

16. I came here intending to open a shoe store but it was impossible to find a vacant room

17. Buildings were going up by the hundred and the noise of the hammer was ceaseless

18. Mr Robertson also started a shoe business and we supplied shoes to all the inhabitants of our little village

19. The discomforts of life on the frontier were innumerable but many men and women endured them

20. After breakfast we talked business and the old man gave me a larger order

B. Write five compound sentences in which the independent clauses are connected by coördinate conjunctions.

IX. Exercise 5. *Do you understand compound sentences well enough to punctuate them correctly?*

EXPLANATION. In the sentence, "The poor child had no friends or relatives; he had only a miserable old dog to love him," there are two independent clauses; consequently it is a compound sentence. The two independent clauses, however, are not joined by a conjunction, nor is a comma used; instead a semicolon separates the clauses. When the independent clauses of a compound sentence are not connected by a coördinate conjunction, a semicolon is used. Two or more independent clauses should not be grouped together in this way unless they are very closely connected in thought.

DIRECTIONS. *A.* Punctuate the following sentences:

1. I will study and finish my work I won't be a failure

2. It is hard to leave off old customs it is harder to go against one's own will

3. America is the melting pot of God it is the great melting pot where all races are fusing and re-forming

4. An honest man is a great man he is beautiful great and strong

5. The largest and noblest and most valuable qualities of manhood are not showy the largest and noblest of men are alike unshowy

6. Every day is a new life every sunrise is but a new birth

7. We have committed the golden rule to memory now let us commit it to life

8. There is only one real failure possible that is not to be true to the best one knows

9. Pessimism leads to weakness optimism leads to power

10. Hypocrisy desires to seem good rather than to be so honesty desires to be good rather than to seem so

11. Nothing great is achieved without the severest dis-cipline of heart and mind nothing is well done that is done easily

12. We measure a man's intellect by his achievements we measure his achievements by his difficulties

13. The Government should help the farmers to get a start it should not tax them to begin

14. A camel can easily carry a weight of one thousand pounds on its back this is four times as much as a horse can carry

15. The camel begins work at the age of four years and is useful for half a century the horse is generally played out at fifteen years of age

16. This is the best day in the year every day is the best of all days

17. Wealth has no power to produce happiness it takes away the spur of necessity which is a man's great developer

18. None knew what the sign meant no one dared to ask

19. There is no table talk like laughter at meals it is the great enemy of dyspepsia

20. Her heart lived always in the summer the winter of age could touch only her body

B. Write five original compound sentences, each of which is punctuated by a semicolon.

IX. Exercise 6. *Are you able to punctuate any compound sentence that you write?*

EXPLANATION. Many compound sentences contain independent clauses that are connected by such words as *hence, therefore, thus, so, however, then, still, moreover,* and *nevertheless.* These words are called conjunctive adverbs since they are adverbs that serve the purpose of conjunctions. When two independent clauses are connected by a conjunctive adverb, a semicolon precedes it; as, " He received a letter from his lawyer; therefore he made an early visit to the city."

If a coördinate conjunction is also used with the conjunctive adverb, a comma precedes the coördinate conjunction and the semicolon is omitted; as, " He received a letter from his lawyer, and therefore he made an early visit to the city."

The relation of the conjunctive adverb to the rest of the sentence is shown in this way:

he	received		letter
	from	lawyer	a	x
		his	

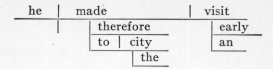

Notice the following sentence:

Father sent Mary, James, and me many interesting souvenirs of France, Italy, and Greece; but everything was lost in the fire, and we shall never be able to duplicate them.

In this sentence there are two independent clauses connected by a coördinate conjunction. One would naturally think that a comma should separate the two clauses, but instead a semicolon is used. The reason is this: when two clauses of a compound sentence are long and commas are used within one or both, a semicolon precedes the coördinate conjunction that connects the clauses.

DIRECTIONS. Punctuate the following sentences:

1. Do not become discouraged always keep your enthusiasm
2. Our little daughter has work she does every morning then she plays as she wishes the rest of the day
3. He felt that he was becoming very useless therefore he decided to spend more time in study
4. The world is full of opportunities all gates are open to him who can use them
5. I have my health and my friends what more do I want
6. All our worries were needless and not a single thing occurred to mar the happiness of all
7. I will send him all that I can moreover I will not let him repay it

8. He has read the story and he has seen the author still he insists that he has no remembrance of either

9. There are twenty ways of going to a point but there is always one that is the shortest

10. I know he was in the city last week here is the letter in which he says so

11. Look up and not down look forward and not back

12. I slept very late in fact it was noon before I awoke

13. The chairman made the statement that every man and woman in the audience was selfish then there began a veritable combat of words

14. He made no pretense of liking the house he showed clearly that he thought it was no place for him and his family

15. At eight o'clock we retired to our berths thus we failed to see their departure

16. First you mix your eggs and milk and then you let them boil for five minutes

17. The boys are far more systematic about their football practice they make more of a business of it

18. I expressed a wish to see the institution therefore John sent me an invitation to visit them for a week

19. We hurriedly ate lunch put our hats on rushed out the door and then remembered that we had forgotten the cat

20. Any place is home where chlidren dwell and are loved and no place is a home if no children are ever there

IX. Exercise 7. *How well can you analyze and punctuate compound sentences?*

EXPLANATION. There are four important points to remember when writing compound sentences:

1. A compound sentence contains two or more independent clauses.
2. In compound sentences a comma is placed before the coördinate conjunction that connects the independent clauses.
3. When the independent clauses of a compound sentence are not connected by a coördinate conjunction, a semicolon is used.
4. If the two clauses of a compound sentence are long and commas are used within one or both, a semicolon precedes the coördinate conjunction that connects the clauses.

Read again the explanations and illustrations given in *Problem IX* before trying to work this exercise.

DIRECTIONS. *A.* Write three sentences to illustrate each point in 2, 3, and 4 in the explanation above.

B. Take each sentence that you find below and follow this outline:

1. Write the correct punctuation. Number each mark and give the reason below.
2. Diagram.

1. She brought me a lovely fan from Italy from India she sent Mary some jade beads
2. He had promised her a gown from Paris therefore he sent it
3. My son was happy in his work and did much for others
4. A man should think first of his character and then he can consider his condition
5. Many times he asked for flowers but the days were cold and dreary and we could find none in the fields and pastures

ANALYSIS OF COMPLEX SENTENCES

Purpose of Study

In order to vary the expression of our written and spoken ideas, we often wish to give more importance to one thought than to another. This is done by making one statement depend upon another statement, or, to use grammatical terms, by making one clause depend upon another clause. Sentences that contain such a combination of clauses are known as complex sentences. If we are to construct complex sentences correctly, we must understand the relation of one part to another part. For this reason we must learn how to analyze complex sentences.

Exercises

1. Recognition of dependent clauses
2. Analysis of complex sentences containing adjective clauses
3. Analysis of complex sentences containing adverbial clauses
4. Analysis of complex sentences containing noun clauses
5. Analysis of complex sentences containing parenthetical clauses
6. Analysis of complex sentences

X. Exercise 1. *Are you able to recognize dependent clauses?*

EXPLANATION. In *Problem III* we learned that a group of words that expresses a complete thought and contains a subject and a predicate is called a clause. We have found, too, that some clauses are independent, and others are dependent. When analyzing sentences, we saw that a simple sentence always contains one independent clause and a compound sentence always consists of two or more independent clauses.

There is a kind of sentence that contains a dependent clause as well as an independent clause. For example, take the sentence, " I saw the house where Shakespeare was born." This sentence contains two clauses: one is " I saw the house," a clause that expresses a complete thought and is independent; the other is " where Shakespeare was born," a clause that depends for its meaning upon the independent clause. A sentence that contains one independent clause and one or more dependent clauses is called a complex sentence.

Notice the following sentences:

1. Mr. Jones is the man *who will be elected.*
2. I do not know *where he lives.*
3. I shall be glad to see you *if I am at home.*
4. He went *although I told him not to.*
5. The man *who was here* is her uncle.

Each of the italicized groups is a clause, which has a subject and a predicate. But none of the clauses makes sense without the rest of the sentence; each is, therefore, a dependent clause.

Notice that the dependent clause in each sentence is introduced by some word that connects it to the rest of the sentence. In sentence 1 and 5 the connecting word is a pronoun, in 3 and 4 it is a conjunction, and in 2 it is a word that seems to be a conjunction and an adverb. Every dependent clause has an introductory word which indicates that it is a dependent clause.

In selecting the dependent clause of a complex sentence, first find a verb and its subject and complement; this with the modifiers will constitute one clause. The rest of the sentence will be the other clause. When the different clauses have been found, you will have no difficulty in telling which is dependent and which is independent.

DIRECTIONS. *A*. Select the dependent clauses in the following complex sentences and underline the connectives:

1. He looked as if he were hungry.
2. I gave him the picture that I liked best.
3. Unless I see you tomorrow, I cannot do your work for you.
4. The little lady, whose purse you found, is here now.
5. I will read the article if you ask me to.
6. Where is the house that he bought?
7. They sent the child to a school where he knew the teacher.
8. I ate some candy that James gave me.
9. I wish I had a machine that would run without gasoline.
10. When you came, I was fast asleep.
11. The knight, who won the prize, went away suddenly.
12. Who is the author of the book that you mentioned?
13. We finally found our way though we had been lost for three days.
14. The house that Mr. Ryan owned was sold for ten thousand dollars.
15. I shall go where I can get the best offer.

B. Write five sentences each of which contains a dependent and an independent clause. Underline the introductory word of each dependent clause.

X. Exercise 2. *Can you analyze complex sentences that contain adjective clauses?*

EXPLANATION. In *Exercise 1* we learned that a dependent clause is one that does not make a complete thought. Dependent clauses are used in various ways. In the sentence, " I know the man who owns this house," " who owns this house " is a dependent clause that tells something about the word " man "; it is, in fact, a modifier of " man." Since it modifies a noun, it is an adjective clause.

The introductory word of the clause, " who owns this house," is the pronoun " who." It refers to the word " man " in the independent clause. Because it is used to relate to a preceding noun, it is called a relative pronoun. The relative pronouns that introduce adjective clauses are: *who, which,* and *that.* Who has two other forms: *whose,* and *whom.*

The relation of a dependent clause to an independent clause is shown in the diagram in this way:

```
I | know | man
  |            the
        who | owns | house
               |      this
```

You see that a clause is a modifier just as a phrase is. Notice that the dependent clause is placed below the independent clause since it does not have the same value.

Study the analysis of the sentence, " The man who sold the house is my uncle."

```
  man  |  is  \  uncle
  _____
    the    |      | my
  _____
    who    | sold | house
  _____
           |      | the
```

In this sentence the dependent clause, " who sold the house," does not come at the end of the sentence, but appears within the sentence. One must watch carefully in order to recognize dependent clauses.

An interesting point about adjective clauses is seen in the diagram of the sentence, " Those boys whom you saw know their lessons."

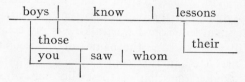

Notice that the subject of a dependent clause does not necessarily come first. One must select the clause carefully; then he must take the verb and ask the question *who* or *what* to find the subject. For example, " saw " is the verb. Ask the question, " Who saw? " The answer " you " is the subject. To find the complement, take the subject and the predicate and ask the question " you saw what? " " Whom," the pronoun used in place of the noun " boys," is the answer and tells what the complement of the verb is.

Another important point about adjective clauses is seen when we analyze the sentence, " I do not know the man for whom you are looking." (Some people express this thought in this way: " I do not know the man whom you are looking for." It is better to place the preposition before the end of the sentence.)

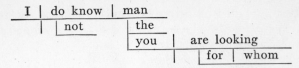

In this sentence the relative pronoun that connects the independent and dependent clauses is the object of a preposition.

DIRECTIONS. *A.* Diagram the following sentences. Before diagraming, select the independent and the dependent clauses. Diagram the independent clause first.

1. The man, who arrived late, had very little dinner.
2. Do you know the boy whom the teacher wants?
3. The man to whom I was talking is my cousin.
4. Will you send me the names of the people who are interested in this course?
5. I asked a question of the policeman who stood on the corner.
6. People who are industrious generally succeed.
7. The person who gives happiness to others finds happiness for himself.
8. I will send you some books that you will like.

B. Write five sentences containing adjective clauses. Underline the dependent clause in each sentence.

X. Exercise 3. *Do you know how to analyze complex sentences that contain adverbial clauses?*

EXPLANATION. In *Exercise 2* we saw that many complex sentences contain adjective clauses. In the sentence, " He studies when he can," the dependent clause, " when he can," is used like an adverb because it modifies the verb by telling when he studies. A clause that is used like an adverb is called an adverbial clause. Notice the relation of the adverbial clause to the rest of the sentence as shown in the following diagrams:

(*a*) I shall go if my mother comes.

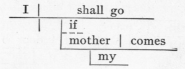

(*b*) He studies when he can.

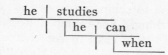

In each of these sentences the dependent clause is introduced by a connecting word. In sentence *a*, the dependent clause is introduced and connected to the independent clause by " if." Because it connects clauses of unequal value, it is called a subordinate conjunction. The most common subordinate conjunctions are: *if, lest, since, that, till, unless, then, as, because.*

In sentence *b*, the dependent clause is introduced and connected to the independent clause by a word that is also used like an adverb since it gives the idea of when. Because of this double use, such a word is called a conjunctive adverb. Some common conjunctive adverbs that connect dependent and independent clauses are: *when, where, while, why, how, whenever.* These conjunctive adverbs are not used like those that connect the independent clauses of compound sentences, nor is the punctuation the same. It would be wise to read *Problem IX* again in order to know the difference between them.

Another point about adverbial clauses is illustrated in

the sentence, "As he shut the door, the phone rang." Although the dependent clause is stated first, its dependence upon the other clause must be indicated by placing it below the independent clause. Notice the diagram:

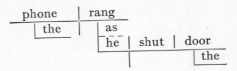

One other kind of adverbial clause must be mentioned. Many times we wish to compare one person or thing with another person or thing. For example, we say, "John is older than Mary." It is easy to see that one clause is "John is older," but the words "than Mary" do not make sense until we add the verb "is." Then the expression becomes "John is older than Mary is." This group of words, we see, is a complex sentence containing an adverbial clause. It is analyzed in this way:

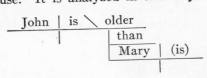

The verb "is" is placed in parentheses because it is not expressed. In adverbial clauses that show comparison, the verb is generally omitted.

DIRECTIONS. *A.* Diagram the following sentences:

1. She knows her lesson better than he.
2. The boys in that class are more industrious than I.
3. When he heard his mother's voice, he ran rapidly into the house.

4. John is younger than I.
5. Those boys are hungrier than Mary and I.
6. She works more earnestly than he.

B. Write ten sentences containing adverbial clauses. Underline the connective in each sentence.

X. Exercise 4. *Do you understand complex sentences well enough to analyze sentences which contain clauses that are used like nouns?*

EXPLANATION. We have seen that dependent clauses may be used as adjectives or as adverbs. There is another way in which a dependent clause may be used. In the sentence, "He ate what he wanted," the dependent clause, "what he wanted," completes the verb and is used like a noun because it names what he ate. Any clause that is used like a noun is a noun clause.

A noun clause may be used in any way that a noun is used; for example,

(*a*) A noun clause may be the object complement of a verb.

He ate what he wanted.

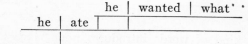

(*b*) A noun clause may be the subject.

Whatever is good is worthy of the price.

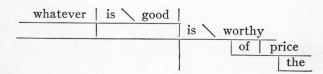

(*c*) A noun clause may be the subjective complement. That is what he thought.

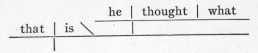

(*d*) A noun clause may be the object of a preposition. They listened to what the poor man said.

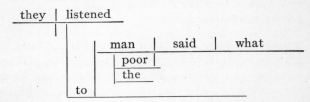

(*e*) A noun clause may be in apposition with a noun or a pronoun.

The rumor, that he has inherited great wealth, has no truth in it.

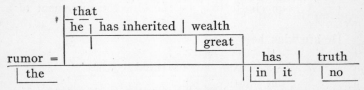

No one kind of words introduces noun clauses. Some of those most commonly used are: *whatever, whoever, whichever, who, which,* and *what.*

DIRECTIONS. *A.* Diagram the following sentences:

1. I know whom you want.
2. Tell me who your friends are.
3. Do you know who will be elected?

4. I do not know for whom he is looking.

5. Have you forgotten whom he invited?

B. Write five sentences that contain noun clauses and underline the introductory word in each.

X. Exercise 5. *Are you capable of analyzing complex sentences that have clauses which have been inserted but are not necessary to the meaning of the sentences?*

EXPLANATION. Sentences often have clauses in them which sometimes cause considerable trouble in correct speech. In this sentence, " He is the man who they say will be elected," we see that the main thought is " He is the man who will be elected." In addition there is the clause, " they say," which has been inserted and is not dependent upon the independent clause. In other words, it is neither an independent clause nor a dependent clause. It has been thrown into the sentence and is called a parenthetical clause.

The relation of the parenthetical clause to the rest of the sentence is shown in this way:

You will see that the complex sentence is complete without these words, but since they are expressed, we must be able to analyze them. Inasmuch as they do not belong to either clause, they are placed at one side.

DIRECTIONS. *A.* Diagram the following sentences:

1. Margaret is the candidate who most people think will be president next year.

2. Who do most people think will be president next year?

3. Will you give some flowers to the students who the judges think are the best speakers?

4. The voters of the community elected a man who the politicians thought could do the work.

5. The girl whom I think the student body would select can not be an officer.

6. I heard the boy who the judges said was a very remarkable speaker.

B. Write five sentences that contain parenthetical clauses and underline each.

X. Exercise 6. *How well can you analyze complex sentences?*

EXPLANATION. Let us summarize what we have learned in this problem:

1. A complex sentence consists of an independent clause and one or more dependent clauses.

2. An independent clause may be a sentence in and of itself, but a dependent clause can never stand alone.

3. Dependent clauses are used as adjectives, adverbs, or nouns, depending upon the thought they contain and their relation to other words in the sentence.

4. Every dependent clause is introduced by some word that connects it to an independent clause, and indicates that it is a dependent clause.

In analyzing sentences, select the different clauses. If there is one dependent clause in the sentence, it is a complex sentence.

Test every sentence to see that it expresses a complete thought and does not consist of a dependent clause alone.

DIRECTIONS. *A.* Diagram the following sentences:

1. John, did you see the man who brought me the box of flowers?
2. I do not know with whom I shall spend my vacation.
3. He is older than she.
4. Several boys whom I saw on the field were talking about the game.
5. She sent flowers to the boy who they considered deserved them.
6. He is the man who some people think will be elected.
7. Where are the boys to whom I should give these books?
8. Do you know any of the women whom the little children have invited to their party?

B. Write three sentences illustrating the three kinds of dependent clauses. After each tell the kind. Underline the introductory word of each dependent clause.

PUNCTUATION OF COMPLEX SENTENCES

Purpose of Study

Now that we have learned how to analyze and construct complex sentences, we must learn how to punctuate them so that a reader can understand our thought easily.

Exercises

1. Punctuation of complex sentences when the dependent clause stands first
2. Recognition and punctuation of restrictive and non-restrictive clauses
3. Punctuation of complex sentences

XI. Exercise 1. *Are you able to punctuate complex sentences when the dependent clause stands first?*

EXPLANATION. In the sentence, " While we were eating and drinking several men entered the room," we see that a comma is needed after " drinking " as an aid to rapid reading. With the comma inserted, the sentence becomes clear at a glance, — " While we were eating and drinking, several men entered the room." Since confusion often arises in this kind of a sentence, a comma is used to set off the dependent clause when it stands first in a sentence.

When punctuating a complex sentence, locate the dependent clause. If it stands first, set it off from the rest of the sentence by a comma.

The end punctuation of a complex sentence depends upon the thought of the main clause.   For example, the sentence, " Did you know the man who made the report? " is interrogative because the independent clause, " Did you know the man," asks a direct question.

DIRECTIONS.   *A.*   Punctuate the following sentences:

1. If he comes before I return tell him to wait for me
2. While he was sitting there in walked his sister Jane
3. When he heard his mother's voice he ran into the next room
4. While he sat there reading his book the train left the station
5. If you want me to do this work for you say so
6. While he was in Australia he purchased many interesting souvenirs
7. As soon as she came into the house she made every one happy
8. After he had been gone about a month we heard that he was doing very well in his business
9. While he was studying his brother entered the room and took his hat
10. When I go into a bookstore I always want to buy something
11. As soon as I saw him he asked if mother was home
12. When he saw us he was very much surprised
13. If you want to succeed in life start at once to do your work to the best of your ability
14. As soon as he went down the elevator fell
15. While the teacher was working at her desk several visitors entered
16. Although he was no financier he was able to gain considerable wealth

17. When he asked me for my opinion I was very loth to give it
18. After he had counted the votes he posted the results
19. When the telephone rang I was talking with the laundry man
20. Whenever she comes to my house I am tempted to tell her the secret

B. Write five original complex sentences in which the dependent clauses stand first.

XI. Exercise 2. *Can you punctuate complex sentences which contain clauses that describe and clauses that limit?*

EXPLANATION. Notice the dependent clauses in the following sentences:

1. All men that make strenuous effort should win.
2. James, who made a greater effort than all others, should win.

In sentence 1 the dependent clause, " that make strenuous effort," is absolutely necessary to the meaning of the sentence. If we were to omit it and say, " All men should be rewarded," we should lose the thought of the sentence as it now stands. Clauses that are so necessary to the meaning of a sentence are called restrictive clauses since they limit closely the word they modify. A restrictive clause is never separated from the rest of the sentence by commas.

In sentence 2 the dependent clause, " who made a greater effort than all others," is not so vital to the meaning of the sentence and could be omitted. Such clauses are called non-restrictive clauses since they merely add a new thought to the sentence and do not limit the word they modify. A non-restrictive clause is always set off from the word it modifies by a comma. If the clause comes in the middle of a sentence, two commas are needed to set it off from the rest of the sentence.

Clauses that are introduced by " who " and " which " are generally non-restrictive because they give additional thoughts; such clauses are set off by commas. Clauses that are introduced by " that " are usually restrictive because they limit the word they modify. For this reason a clause beginning with " that " is not generally set off by commas.

Test every sentence you write to see if the dependent clause is restrictive or non-restrictive. Follow this method:

1. Select the dependent and independent clauses.
2. See if the independent clause has the same meaning with the dependent clause omitted as it does when it is expressed. If it does, the dependent clause is non-restrictive and commas should be used to set it off from the rest of the sentence.
3. If the omission of the dependent clause changes the thought expressed in the independent clause, the clause is restrictive and it should not be set off by commas. For example, " James should win " has the same meaning as sentence 2 above. But " All men should win " does not have the same meaning as sentence 1.

DIRECTIONS. *A.* Punctuate the following sentences:

1. Mildred Smith whose mother is a musician cannot read a note of music
2. All things that man has made will some day pass away
3. The music that Handel composed is better than mine

4. I saw the poor little child whom the truck had struck
5. The clothes which I put on the line last night are not dry yet
6. The boys that left the building early must remain later tonight
7. The book which I bought for mother has been stolen
8. The trip which I chose for my vacation costs too much for one of my means
9. I made a great fire upon the hearth which I had paved with some square tiles
10. Mr Spense who cannot speak one word of French is trying to carry on a conversation with a Frenchman
11. I had my long sail boat with which I could escape from my place of captivity
12. The man that invented the telephone is my greatest benefactor
13. All amusements that are really harmful should be prohibited
14. I refuse to ride on any street car that is operated by one man
15. Any man that is a gentleman will treat a lady with respect
16. I know a place where there is a hidden treasure
17. The children that were present every day were given special recognition
18. Here is Oscar who has won the prize for three years
19. I will give a dollar to anyone that can answer this question
20. James who was ready to go told the others to hurry

B. Write five sentences that contain non-restrictive clauses and five sentences that contain restrictive clauses.

XI. Exercise 3. *How well can you punctuate complex sentences?*

EXPLANATION.   There are three points that we must keep in mind when we write complex sentences.   These are:

1. A comma is used to set off a dependent clause when it stands first in a sentence.
2. A non-restrictive clause is always set off from the word it modifies by a comma.   If the clause comes in the middle of a sentence, two commas are needed.
3. A restrictive clause is never separated from the word it modifies.

DIRECTIONS.   *A.*   Punctuate the following sentences. Number each mark of punctuation, and below the sentence give the reason for the mark.   If a sentence contains a restrictive clause, mention that fact.

1. While he was studying into the room walked his father and mother
2. I have found my pearl necklace which my brother sent me from Japan
3. Just as I had set my mast and sail I saw some alteration of the current was near
4. Shall the person that found your purse be rewarded
5. They that know what it is to be rescued from thieves may guess what my joy was
6. The inlet which was as narrow as a brook was a beautiful place for a boating trip
7. Robinson Crusoe was able to make a suit of clothes wholly of skins although he was not a tailor by trade

8. When I had no need of my umbrella I could close it and carry it under my arm

9. After he had resided on the island many years he returned to his native country

10. When Mr. White retired from business he took a long trip around the world

B. Write ten sentences that illustrate the various kinds of complex sentences. Punctuate each carefully.

ANALYSIS AND PUNCTUATION OF SENTENCES

Purpose of Study

Now that we have finished the problems on analysis and punctuation of simple, compound, and complex sentences, it will be profitable for us to assemble the information we have gained and test our ability in analyzing and punctuating all kinds of sentences. Such is the purpose of this problem.

Exercises

1. Analysis and punctuation of sentences
2. Analysis and punctuation of sentences
3. Analysis and punctuation of sentences
4. Writing and punctuating original sentences

XII. Exercise 1. *Are you able to analyze and punctuate simple, compound, and complex sentences?*

EXPLANATION. Since this problem is for the purpose of summarizing the preceding problems, it is not necessary to give any explanation. It will be profitable for you to read again all the explanations given in the problems you have completed.

When analyzing each sentence, find the clauses first; then show the relationship of the words and the clauses.

DIRECTION. *A.* Take the sentences that are given below and follow this outline:

(*a*) Write with the correct punctuation marks. Number each mark and below the sentence give the reason, using the same number as in the sentence.

(*b*) Above each word write the part of speech.

(*c*) Diagram.

(*d*) Tell the kind of sentence: simple, compound, or complex.

(*e*) Give the use of the italicized words.

(*f*) Give the reason for capitalization.

1. *bob* john has sent mildred and *me* a picture of his new home it is very beautiful

2. is your son *who* lives in chicago older than *I*

3. we have just read a book by kipling the english *poet but* we have not returned it to the library

4. *when* he comes here I shall give *him* this magazine

5. is he the interesting *man who* you said will be at the hotel tonight

B. Write two illustrations of each of the following:

1. Indirect object

2. Non-restrictive clause

3. Dependent clause standing first

XII. Exercise 2. *Can you analyze and punctuate sentences?*

EXPLANATION. If you made any mistakes in *Exercise 1,* look up those particular matters and make sure that you overcome the difficulties now. There is no reason why you should not have absolute mastery of this subject.

DIRECTION. *A.* Take the sentences that are given below and follow this outline:

(*a*) Write with the correct punctuation marks. Number each mark and below the sentence give the reason, using the same number as in the sentence.

(*b*) Above each word write the part of speech.

(*c*) Diagram.

(*d*) Tell the kind of sentence: simple, compound, or complex.

(*e*) Give the use of the italicized words.

(*f*) Give the reason for capitalization.

1. mr wallace the *instructor* in music gave his *friends* a rare treat he played and sang many of his pieces

2. are you going sooner *than we*

3. do you know for *whom* that man is looking *mary*

4. *as* he was reading his children ran into the room hurriedly *but* he paid no attention to them

5. the man *whom* you saw here gave mother and *me* tickets to the lecture but we cannot use them

B. Write two illustrations of each of the following:

1. Series without commas

2. Appositive

3. Compound sentence with semicolon

XII. Exercise 3. *How well can you analyze and punctuate sentences?*

Explanation. You should now know all the fundamental points about analyzing and punctuating. If there is any point that you have not yet mastered, conquer it before finishing this exercise. Study once more the explanations given in the preceding problems.

Direction. *A.* Take each sentence that is given below and follow this outline:

(*a*) Write with correct punctuation and capitalization. Number each punctuation mark and below the sentence give the reason, using the same number as in the sentence.

(*b*) Above each word write the part of speech.

(*c*) Diagram.

(*d*) Tell the kind of sentence: whether simple, compound, or complex.

(*e*) Give the use of the italicized words.

1. the boys *whom* the teacher recommended were rewarded by mr smith and *me*

2. *goodness* I thought *you* had gone *but* here you are again

3. this pretty cloth *which* she will make into dresses was a *gift* from mildred and *me*

4. he often asked *her* and me strange questions but *we* never answered them

5. *mother* I will do this work *for* you must rest now

B. Write two illustrations of each of the following:

1. Restrictive clause
2. Non-restrictive clause
3. Series without commas
4. Series with commas

XII. Exercise 4. *How well can you write your own illustrations of all the points studied in the preceding problems?*

EXPLANATION. If you have worked carefully all the exercises of this problem, you will be able to write sentences that will illustrate these points. In writing the assignments of all your lessons and in writing letters, you will often need to know how to use this information.

Directions. Write in sentences an illustration of each of the following points:

1. A noun in direct address
2. An independent element
3. An appositive
4. A parenthetical clause
5. An adjective phrase
6. An adverbial clause
7. A compound sentence that demands a comma for its mark of punctuation
8. An indirect object
9. A predicate noun
10. A non-restrictive clause
11. "*For*" as a conjunction
12. A complex sentence with a dependent clause standing first
13. An abbreviation
14. A restrictive clause
15. A predicate adjective
16. An adverbial phrase
17. An adjective clause
18. A series with commas
19. A compound sentence that demands a semicolon for its mark of punctuation
20. A restrictive clause

A STUDY OF THE FORMS OF PRONOUNS AND NOUNS

Purpose of Study

Our aim in this course is to eliminate all errors in our written and spoken English so that the sentences in which we express our thoughts will be absolutely correct. There are two kinds of errors that people make: one is the kind that deals with the construction and punctuation of sentences; the other consists of words that are used incorrectly.

We have studied the construction of simple, compound, and complex sentences, and should be able to write and speak correctly constructed sentences. We have also learned how to punctuate these sentences, and we should do this so perfectly that our readers will be able to understand our thought easily.

There remains one other kind of error which we must try to eliminate entirely. That is the error of using the incorrect forms of various words. In order to free our sentences from such errors, we shall make a study of correct forms and learn when to use them.

Pronouns cause considerable difficulty at times. For that reason we shall study everything about pronouns that will help us to use them correctly.

Exercises

1. Recognition of the number of pronouns and nouns
2. Recognition of the gender and person of pronouns and nouns
3. Recognition of pronouns in the nominative case
4. Recognition of pronouns in the objective case
5. Recognition of pronouns and nouns in the possessive case
6. Recognition of the forms of various pronouns
7. Recognition of the case of pronouns
8. Recognition of the number, gender, person, use, and case of pronouns
9. A study of all the properties of pronouns

XIII. Exercise 1. *Are you able to tell how many persons or things are referred to by a pronoun or a noun?*

EXPLANATION. What is the difference between these two sentences?

> The boy broke the chair.
> The boys broke the chair.

The difference in the written form is so slight that one might easily overlook it, but the difference in the meaning is considerable. In the first sentence " boy " denotes one person; in the second " boys " means more than one person. Nouns and pronouns may denote only one object, as " boy "; or they may be changed to denote more than one object, as " boys." This change in the form of a noun or a pronoun by which one or more objects is indicated is called number. When a noun or a pronoun denotes one object, the word is in the singular number; when it denotes more than one object, it is in the plural number.

Notice the italicized words in the following sentences:

1. Our *navy* is small.
2. The *committee* on finances made its report.
3. The *army* moved slowly.
4. A *flock* of birds passed over our house.

Each of these words names a collection of individuals or objects which are considered as one body. Such nouns are called collective nouns, and when the group is thought of as one, the noun is in the singular number.

The plurals of nouns are formed in various ways, but regularly by adding " s " or " es " to the singular. The spelling of the plurals of nouns should be studied carefully as a part of one's work in composition and will be omitted here.

Pronouns form their plurals quite differently from nouns. For example, in the sentence, " I enjoyed the concert," " I " is singular since it denotes only one person. Change it to the plural and it becomes," We enjoyed the concert." We shall study the formation of the plurals of pronouns more in detail later; for the present get the meaning that is expressed. If only one is meant, the pronoun is singular; if more than one is meant, the pronoun is plural.

The following pronouns are always singular: *every one, every, each, anybody, everybody, either, no one, nobody.*

DIRECTIONS. *A.* Give the number of the italicized words in the following sentences:

1. *Each* of the *boys* has a new cap.
2. An *army* generally moves slowly.
3. A *flock* of *birds* is flying southward.

4. *They* have taken *their* books.
5. The *committee* has decided to meet again.
6. *Everybody* knows something *he* likes to do.
7. *We* shall take *our* car with us.
8. *Nobody* likes to work all the time.
9. Almost *every one* has a pet hobby.
10. *Either* of those *hats* is becoming to you.
11. Is that *yours?*
12. The *United States* is a young nation.
13. *Some one* has put *his* books on my desk.
14. The *army* is smaller than *it* was during the war.
15. The *committee* have signed *their* names to the report.
16. Were *you* here last night?
17. *They* were going home.
18. Every *pupil* in this class should do his work to the best of *his* ability.

B. Write the following sentences:

Three sentences containing singular pronouns
Three sentences containing plural pronouns
Five sentences containing collective nouns
(try to use some not given in this exercise)

XIII. Exercise 2. *Can you recognize other characteristics about pronouns and nouns besides number?*

Explanation. All nouns and pronouns have certain characteristics which are known as properties. We learned in the last exercise that nouns and pronouns have the property of number. In this exercise we shall study two other properties of nouns and pronouns.

In the sentence, " The woman came," " woman " is a noun that names an individual that is female. In " Several men were missing," " men " names individuals that are male. "Box" in the sentence, "The box is large," denotes an object that is neither male nor female. In the sentence, "The child is lost," "child" names an individual that is either masculine or feminine.

The property of a noun that names the sex of an object is called gender. There are four genders, each of which indicates certain kinds of objects.

1. Masculine gender indicates that the individual is of the male sex.
2. Feminine gender indicates that the individual is of the female sex.
3. Neuter gender indicates that the object is of neither sex.
4. Common gender indicates that the object is of either male or female sex.

In the sentence, "The man left his book here," the masculine form "his" is used because it refers to the noun "man," which is masculine. The word to which a pronoun refers is called its antecedent.

Notice the sentence, "Some one has left his book here." Probably you are saying, "How do we know that the 'some one who left the book' is masculine?" We do not; but when the antecedent of a pronoun is of the common gender, the pronoun is always of the masculine gender.

Let us look at another property of pronouns and nouns for a moment. Some pronouns have different forms which indicate whether a person is speaking, is spoken to, or is spoken of. This property is called person.

The pronouns *I, we, us, our,* and *me* denote the person speaking and are of the first person.

The pronouns *you* and *your* denote the person spoken to and are of the second person.

The pronouns *he, she, it,* and *they* denote the person spoken of and are of the third person.

Nouns also have the property of person, but they do not change their form to show it. They are generally of the third person. A noun in direct address is of the second person since it is the person spoken to.

DIRECTIONS. *A.* Tell the number, gender, and person of the italicized words:

1. *Each* of the *boys* has brought *his sister*.
2. *She* will be here soon with *her* mother.
3. *No one* that is unwilling to work should apply for that position.
4. *Any one* of the students has ability to do that.
5. *I* have not read the *book*.
6. The *teacher* did not come today.
7. An *army* is composed of many *individuals*.
8. I have lost *my* cat; have you seen *it?*
9. *We* will not lose *your* sister.
10. *Anybody* should have enjoyed that concert.
11. *Neither* of the girls has seen her father or mother.
12. *Some* like to go to the beach, but *I* prefer to go to the mountains.

B. Write eight sentences that contain nouns and pronouns. Tell the number, gender, and person of each of these nouns and pronouns.

XIII. Exercise 3. *Do you understand the relation of pronouns and nouns to other words in a sentence?*

EXPLANATION. Notice how the noun *girl* is used in the following sentences:

1. The *girl* has a new dress.   (subject)
2. I saw the *girl*.   (object complement or direct object)
3. She is a little *girl*.   (subjective complement)
4. He gave the *girl* a flower.   (indirect object)
5. Give that flower to the *girl*.   (object of preposition)
6. Little *girl*, what makes you cry?   (noun in direct address)
7. Mary, the largest *girl* in the class, is absent today. (noun in apposition)

These illustrations show that a noun may be used in various ways. It may be the subject of a sentence, the object complement or direct object of a verb, the subjective complement, the indirect object of a verb, the object of a preposition, a noun in direct address, or a noun in apposition.

The property of a noun that shows its use in a sentence and its relation to other words is called case.

A noun is in the nominative case when it is:

1. The subject of a verb
2. The subjective complement
3. A word in direct address
4. In apposition with a noun in the nominative case

Pronouns also have the property of case. Just as they change their form to indicate their person and number, so many of them change their form to show their case. This changing from one form to another is one cause of many errors in speech.

A pronoun is in the nominative case under the same circumstances as a noun.

The italicized words illustrate the ways in which a pronoun or a noun may be in the nominative case:

1. *He* has my purse. (subject)
2. It is *she*. (subjective complement)
3. *Mary,* take your hat away. (noun in direct address)
4. Mr. Smith, the *printer,* has not come. (noun in apposition with a noun in the nominative case)

Directions. *A.* Tell the use and the case of each of the italicized words in the following sentences. Be very explicit; for example, if a word is the subject of a verb, state the verb.

Note: Decide what the relation of the noun or the pronoun is to the rest of the sentence. If there is any doubt in your mind, think how the sentence would be diagramed; then you will easily see what the use of the word is in the sentence.

1. *He* has left the room.
2. Are the boys more advanced than *we?*
3. I do not know *who she* is.
4. Is it *she* whom you want?
5. May *we* go to the circus, mother?
6. That is *he.*
7. She is not so clever as *he.*
8. It is *I.*
9. I have seen the girl *who* they think will be our next president.
10. That was *I who* spoke to you last night.
11. It is not *we who* lost the books.
12. *We* boys voted for the proposition.

B. Write ten sentences, each of which contains a pronoun in the nominative case. Underline the pronouns that are in the nominative case.

XIII. Exercise 4. *Do you know when a pronoun or a noun is in any case other than the nominative? Do you know the name of the cases?*

EXPLANATION. We have learned that a noun or a pronoun may be used in a number of different ways, and that the use of a word in a sentence determines its case. It is in the nominative case when it is the subject, the subjective complement, a word in direct address, or in apposition with another noun that is in the nominative case.

These, however, are not the only relations that nouns and pronouns have with words in a sentence. They are often used in other ways and then are said to be in the objective case. A noun is in the objective case when it is:

1. The object complement (direct object)
2. The indirect object
3. The object of a preposition
4. In apposition with a word in the objective case.

The italicized words illustrate the ways in which a pronoun or a noun may be in the objective case:

1. He saw *me*. (object complement or direct object)
2. He gave *me* a flower. (indirect object)
3. Take this to *her*. (object of a preposition)
4. I saw Mr. Smith, the *postman*. (in apposition with a word in the objective case)

DIRECTIONS. *A.* Tell the use and case of the italicized words in the following sentences. Be very explicit; for example, if a word is the object of a preposition, state the preposition.

1. He gave *me* a piece of cake.
2. *Whom* do you want?

3. All is over between you and *me.*
4. Will you do that for Mary and *me?*
5. Do you know *whom* you saw?
6. Send *me* your new address now.
7. The angry man drove *her* and her children from the house.
8. There has been a little misunderstanding between *him* and *her.*
9. I shall do all I can for the little child who is so dear to you and *me.*
10. They sent *him* and *me* some complimentary tickets.
11. The man *who* they thought had caused the trouble could not be located.
12. *Whom* do you expect?

B. Write ten sentences each containing a pronoun in the objective case. Underline all pronouns that are in the objective case.

XIII. Exercise 5. *Can you recognize a noun or a pronoun that shows possession?*

Explanation. We know that nouns often show possession or ownership as " boy's " does in the sentence, " The boy's cap is lost." Such nouns are in the possessive case.

Nouns have certain forms that show possession. As an illustration notice the italicized words in the following sentences:

1. The *boy* is here. (" Boy " is singular.)
2. The *boy's* hat is here. (" Boy's " is singular possessive.)
3. The *boys* are here. (" Boys " is plural.)
4. The *boys'* hats are here. (" Boys' " is plural possessive.)

It is readily seen that the singular possessive of a noun is formed by adding an apostrophe and " s " to the singular form. The plural possessive is formed by adding an apostrophe to the plural form provided it ends in " s." If the plural does not end in " s," an apostrophe and " s " are added to the plural form. For example:

Singular	Singular possessive	Plural	Plural possessive
man	man's	men	men's

The formation of the possessive of nouns is a very important point in spelling correctly and should be mastered in connection with writing compositions. We shall not consider it more in detail here. One rule may be of value: when you wish to write the plural possessive of a noun, make it plural first and then add the sign that indicates possession.

The words *hers, yours, his, its,* and *theirs* are the possessive forms of the pronoun and are never written with the apostrophe. Do not confuse " its " with " it's." " Its " is the possessive of the pronoun; " it's " is a contraction of " it is."

Pronouns generally change their form to indicate the possessive case. The italicized words in the following sentences illustrate various possessive pronouns:

1. That is *his* cap.
2. I am *her* sister.
3. *My* hat is new.
4. *Your* paper is well written.
5. *Its* wing is broken.
6. Have you seen *their* new home?

DIRECTIONS. *A.* Tell the number and the case of the italicized words in the following sentences:

1. The *boy's* game was interrupted.
2. The *boys'* game was interrupted.
3. The *lady's* gloves were lost.
4. I am going to the *grocer's* to buy something for *our* lunch.
5. I shall soon have four *weeks'* vacation.
6. The *men's* hats had been misplaced.
7. Did you see the *children's* theater?
8. The *child's* toys have been broken.
9. Is that *yours?*
10. The *ladies'* umbrellas cannot be mended.
11. That poor bird has had *its* wings broken.
12. Do you know if that is *hers?*
13. The *women's* clubs met today.

B.   1. Write five sentences, each containing nouns in the possessive case.

2. Write the following possessive pronouns in sentences:

theirs   its
hers   yours

XIII. Exercise 6. *Can you recognize the various forms of pronouns?*

EXPLANATION.   Pronouns change their form to indicate person, number, and case.   The changing from one form to another often causes errors unless one understands all the forms thoroughly.   It is our purpose to study these in this exercise.

Pronouns of one group indicate by their form whether the person is speaking, is spoken to, or is spoken of.   Such pronouns are called personal pronouns.   The following arrangement shows the case forms for the three persons in the singular and plural numbers.

| | FIRST PERSON | | SECOND PERSON | |
	Singular	Plural	Singular	Plural
Nom.	I	we	you	you
Poss.	my, mine	our, ours	your, yours	your, yours
Obj.	me	us	you	you

| | THIRD PERSON | | | Plural |
| | Singular | | | |
	MASCULINE	FEMININE	NEUTER	
Nom.	he	she	it	they
Poss.	his	her, hers	its	their, theirs
Obj.	him	her	it	them.

We should know these forms, but merely memorizing them will not help us to use them correctly. We must know when to use the objective form " me " and when to use the nominative " I."

Can you tell why the italicized forms are correct?

1. It is *she*. (nominative case)
2. Give her and *me* some candy. (objective case)
3. She is as tall as *he*. (nominative case)
4. *We* boys went to the beach. (nominative case)
5. Between *you* and *me* there can never be any trouble. (objective case)

Read again the explanations given in *Exercises 3* and *4* so that you will know when and why certain forms are used.

In the sentence, " I saw the man who won the prize," we know that " who " is a pronoun used to introduce the dependent clause that modifies " man." Since it refers or relates to " man," it is called a relative pronoun. There are four relative pronouns: *who, which, what,* and *that. That* and *what* always remain the same. The forms for *who* and *which* are as follows:

Nom.	who	which
Poss.	whose	(whose)
Obj.	whom	which

Each of the relative pronouns is used to refer to a certain kind of word. The word to which a pronoun refers is called its antecedent.

1. *Who* is used when the antecedent is the name of a person. " I know the *man who* did the work."
2. *Which* is used when the antecedent is the name of some thing. " I saw the *house which* he built."
3. *That* is used when the antecedent is the name of a person or a thing. " The *man that* sang is my friend." " The *house that* was burned belonged to me."
4. *What* has no antecedent. It is never used when speaking of persons or things. Generally it refers to an idea or a thought; as, " I know what he wants."

Relative pronouns are sometimes written with the word " ever " or " soever," as *whoever* and *whosoever.* These words are known as compound relative pronouns. Their case forms are the same as those of the relative pronouns. If you can always use the relative pronouns correctly, you will never make any mistake with the compound relative pronouns.

Before attempting the assignment, be sure that you read once more the explanations given in *Exercises 3* and *4* so that you will know when a pronoun is in the nominative case and when it is in the objective case.

DIRECTIONS. *A.* In the following sentences tell the use and the case of each italicized word:

1. *Whom* did *you* see?
2. Is it *she whom* you want?
3. The girl *whom they* selected was very beautiful.
4. At *whom* were you looking?
5. *Who* is your dentist?
6. *Its* foot is badly hurt.
7. Father gave those books to mother and *me*.
8. Do you know *whom* the judges selected?
9. Please save these for Marion and *me*.
10. Though her brother remonstrated, the girl, who was older than *he,* won.
11. Are you as well qualified as *he?*
12. To *whom* were you talking?
13. It is *he who* the boys say will win the scholarship.
14. I shall give my books to those *who* I think deserve them.
15. *Who* can it be?

B. Write the following words in sentences:

1. " Whom " as object complement
2. " She " as subjective complement
3. " Who " as subject
4. " Him " as indirect object
5. " I " as subjective complement
6. " Whom " as object of a preposition
7. " He " as subjective complement

XIII. Exercise 7. *Are you able to tell the case of any pronoun and why it is in that case?*

EXPLANATION. Every pronoun that we use has a certain case form which is decided by its use in the sentence. It is in the nominative case if it is:

1. The subject
2. The subjective complement

It is in the objective case if it is:

1. The object complement
2. The indirect object
3. The object of a preposition

It is in the possessive case if it shows possession.

Before you decide the reason for the case of any pronoun, consider what its use in the sentence is; that will be the reason for its particular case form.

DIRECTIONS. *A.* Tell the use and the case of the italicized words in the following sentences:

1. Please do this for Jane and *me.*
2. To *whom* did you write?
3. I could not believe it was *he.*
4. The blame of the affair rested on George and *me.*
5. John Hitchcock is the man *who* we think should be made chairman.
6. Is it *he whom* you think you know?
7. It is not *we whom* you asked.
8. Please do not refer to *us* boys when you mention the matter.
9. *Whom* do you think I saw at the store?
10. Do you know *who* that woman is?

B. Write sentences containing pronouns used as:

1. Subject
2. Subjective complement

3. Object complement
4. Object of a preposition
5. Indirect object

Note: Underline the pronoun in each sentence.

XIII. Exercise 8. *Are you able to tell the number, gender, person, use, and case of any pronoun?*

EXPLANATION. We have learned that every pronoun has these properties:

1. Number (singular or plural)
2. Gender (feminine, masculine, neuter, or common)
3. Person (first, second, or third)
4. Use (as subject, subjective complement, object complement, object of preposition, or indirect object)
5. Case (nominative, possessive, or objective)

If we understand these properties and then use our knowledge in all written and oral expression, we shall never be guilty of using incorrect English.

Let us look at the properties of " she " in the sentence, " It is she." " She " is singular number, feminine gender, third person, is the subjective complement of " is," and therefore is in the nominative case.

Notice *who* in the following sentences:

1. Do you know the man *who* was here?
2. Do you know the women *who* were here?

How can we tell the number, gender, and person of " who " in sentence 1 and in sentence 2, for the word itself gives us no definite idea? The only way to know is to look at the antecedent of the pronoun. In sentence 1 it is " man," and in sentence 2 it is " women." Since the antecedent is different in each sentence, the properties of the relative pronouns are different though they happen to be the same word. Let us compare them:

Who (sentence 1)	Who (sentence 2)
Singular number	*Plural* number
Masculine gender	*Feminine* gender
Third person	Third person
Subject of " *was* "	Subject of " *were* "
Nominative case	Nominative case

These sentences show that a pronoun agrees with its antecedent in number, gender, and person.

A pronoun does not agree with its antecedent in case. For example, in " I saw the man who was here," " man," the antecedent of " who," is in the objective case because it is the object complement of " saw "; the relative pronoun is in the nominative case because it is the subject of " was."

DIRECTIONS. *A.* Tell the number, gender, person, use, and case of the italicized words in the following sentences. If the antecedent is expressed, give it.

1. *He* and *I* went to the city.
2. When will you send *us* your picture?
3. Was that *she who* phoned?
4. It is *I*.
5. I do not know *who* he is.
6. I shall select a person *who* you know will be satisfactory.
7. Is that *she who* gave the address?
8. Can you tell me *whom* they chose for secretary?
9. *Who* do you think is coming?
10. Father sent mother and *me* some laces from Italy.

B. 1. Write five sentences containing pronouns in the objective case. Underline each pronoun and explain its use.

2. Write five sentences containing pronouns in the nominative case. Underline each pronoun and explain its use.

XIII. Exercise 9. *How well can you tell why certain forms of pronouns and nouns are used rather than other forms?*

EXPLANATION. Try to make all the facts given in these exercises yours, just as your personal possessions are yours. Always think before you speak and try to choose the correct form. In time you will acquire the habit of correct speech, which is one of the finest possessions you can possibly have.

Read again the explanations given in *Exercises 3* and *4* on the use of the nominative and objective cases.

Remember that these words are always singular: *each, every, either, neither, one, some one, any one, everyone, anybody, everybody, nobody, one, a person.* If any one of them is the antecedent of a pronoun, that pronoun must be singular also. Recall that when the gender of the antecedent is common, the pronoun that refers to it is always masculine.

DIRECTIONS. *A.* Why are the italicized words in the following sentences used? State every reason that you know.

1. When a pupil finishes the exercises of a problem, *he* should be able to pass the test.

2. Mary, will you go the *milliner's* and get my hat?

3. The boy *that* saved the child's life was soon forgotten.

4. Some one sent my brother and *me* a lovely plant.

5. Do you know *whom* they want?

6. Every one in the audience wanted to do *his* part to help.

7. That book is *hers*.

8. Everybody likes to feel that *he* is doing something worth while.

9. We heard that John is one *whom* they were discussing.

10. *One's* idea of a city often changes after *he* has lived in it for some time.

11. The *lady's* gloves were found on the car.

12. It is *she* for *whom* we are looking.

13. That man is a friend of my *father's*.

14. Mother bought some dress goods for *her* and *me*.

15. I have talked with the man *who* they think will be the superintendent.

B. Write the following pronouns in sentences as subjects. In each of these sentences use a personal pronoun to refer to the subject.

1. each
2. one
3. neither
4. anybody
5. some one
6. every one

C. If your teacher wishes you to do so, give all the properties of the nouns and pronouns in the sentences in this exercise. (The process of giving all properties of a word is called parsing.)

THE CORRECT USE OF PRONOUNS

Purpose of Study

It is our aim to write and speak correctly and thus eliminate from our sentences every error in pronouns. In order to do this we must know what the correct forms are. These we learned in the preceding problem. Now we must have much practice with these forms so that we shall acquire the habit of using pronouns correctly. Such is the purpose of this problem.

Exercises

1. Correct usage of personal pronouns
2. Correct usage of compound personal pronouns
3. Correct usage of personal and compound personal pronouns
4. Correct usage of relative pronouns
5. Correct usage of pronouns and antecedents
6. Correct usage of the possessive case with verbal nouns
7. Correct usage of pronouns

XIV. Exercise 1. *Are you able to use the correct forms of personal pronouns?*

EXPLANATION. Because personal pronouns change their form to show case and number and person, they often cause considerable difficulty. We can eliminate practically every incorrect form of pronouns from our written and spoken expressions if we will keep in mind four short rules that we learned in *Exercises 3* and *4* of *Problem XIII.*

1. The subject of a verb is in the nominative case.
2. The subjective complement of a verb is in the nominative case.
3. The object complement of a verb is in the objective case.
4. The object of a preposition is in the objective case.

Try to make each of these rules help you to speak correctly. Keep them in mind constantly until you use the correct forms of pronouns from force of habit.

DIRECTIONS. *A.* Write the following sentences, filling each blank with one of the words found in parentheses at the end of the sentence. State briefly the reason for your choice by giving the use and the case of the word.

If there is any doubt in your mind as to the use of a word, diagram the sentence and its place in the sentence will become clear at a glance.

1. —— and —— went to the city. (her, she; me, I)
2. Please give your books to Grace and ——. (I, me)
3. Mother brought Mildred and —— some interesting books. (me, I)
4. When will you send —— your plans? (we, us)
5. Did you see John and —— last night? (me, I)
6. It is ——. (me, I)

7. Was that —— who called yesterday?   (she, her)
8. —— boys want to go to the circus.   (we, us)
9. My mother always prepares a good dinner for my sister and ——.   (I, me)
10. It is a question between —— and ——.   (he, him; I, me)
11. Is it —— who are to blame?   (we, us)
12. —— Americans love the name of Lincoln.   (us, we)
13. I have seen —— and his daughter in the theater many times.   (he, him)
14. My father is sending my brother and —— some books about Alaska.   (me, I)
15. Will you please prepare the dinner for my mother and ——?   (me, I)
16. —— boys will go swimming after school.   (us, we)
17. He is not so tall as ——.   (she, her)
18. Everything is over between —— and ——.   (him, he; I, me)
19. The teacher did not refer to Henry and ——.   (I, me)
20. Some of —— boys did not see the play.   (us, we)
21. Was it —— ?   (them, they)
22. They sent us, Harry and ——, to the warehouse.   (me, I)
23. You ought to consider —— and his friends.   (he, him)
24. Did she send that to you and ——?   (I, me)
25. Mother gave —— and —— some money.   (him, he; I, me)

B.   Watch your speech and that of your classmates, and make a list of any incorrect forms of pronouns that you hear. Write the sentences as they were given originally, and after each make the correction. Do not do this in a spirit of criticism but rather as a means of eradicating errors in English.

XIV. Exercise 2. *Do you know how to use the personal pronouns to which " self " or " selves " has been added?*

EXPLANATION. One occasionally hears such words as *himself, themselves,* and *herself.* Since these words are formed by adding *self* or the plural *selves* to a personal pronoun, they are called compound personal pronouns. We need to know how to use these pronouns correctly, for they often cause trouble.

There are only two ways in which a compound personal pronoun may be used. In the sentence, " I hurt myself," " myself " is the object complement of " hurt " because it names the object that receives the action expressed by the verb. At the same time it refers to the subject; it is, in fact, the same person as the subject. When a compound personal pronoun is used as the object complement and refers or reflects back to the subject, it is known as a reflexive pronoun. This is a correct use of the compound personal pronoun. The object of a preposition may sometimes be a compound personal pronoun; as, " He is always thinking of himself."

Another way in which a compound personal pronoun may be used is shown in the sentence, " I myself will do that work." The speaker evidently wished to emphasize the fact that it is " I " who will do the work; consequently he intensified the meaning by adding the pronoun " myself." He might have expressed the same thought by saying, " I will do that work myself." When a compound personal pronoun is used in this way, it is known as an

intensive pronoun. It is correct to use a compound personal pronoun this way.

In the following sentences the compound personal pronouns are used correctly:

1. They hurt *themselves*. (reflexive)
2. He did the work *himself*. (intensive)
3. The little child can dress *herself*. (reflexive)
4. She *herself* told me. (intensive)
5. She always talked about *herself*. (reflexive)

There are some things we must never do.

1. We must not coin new compound personal pronouns, as " hisself." This is not an English word. The only forms that are correct are these:

myself	yourself	herself	themselves
ourselves	yourselves	himself	
		itself	

2. We must never let a compound personal pronoun stand alone as the subject of a verb. For example, " My friend and myself will go " is incorrect. The sentence should be, " My friend and I will go."

3. We must never use a compound personal pronoun unless we are absolutely certain it is used correctly; that is, it must be either a reflexive pronoun or an intensive pronoun.

DIRECTIONS. *A*. Write the following sentences, filling the blank spaces with the correct form of a personal or a compound personal pronoun:

1. I hope —— and your guests will be able to call on my mother and ——.

2. Did he hurt —— badly?
3. She threw —— on the bed.
4. The President —— was present at the convention.
5. The children can wash ——.
6. The author —— revised the manuscript.
7. My brother and —— visited our sister in Chicago.
8. We shall expect to see —— and your mother next Tuesday.
9. This box of candy is for your brother and ——.
10. He said the princess —— had given —— the ring.
11. My friend and —— shall go abroad next summer.
12. My cousin and —— were invited to go to the theater.

B. Write each of the following words in sentences to illustrate the two correct ways of using compound personal pronouns:

himself	myself	herself
themselves	ourselves	yourself

XIV. Exercise 3. *How well can you use personal and compound personal pronouns?*

EXPLANATION. When a person speaks of himself and others, it is good form to mention one's self last; as, " John and James and I bought a boat." When one does this he not only shows that he understands what correct English is, but he also shows that he is well bred.

Another important fact that one must remember is that the pronoun " them " is never used for the adjective " those." It is correct to say, " She likes those pictures "; but it shows great ignorance of good English to say, " She likes them pictures." " Them " is a pronoun in the objective case; therefore it cannot be used with a noun as a modifier.

It is permissible to say " we boys " in the nominative case and " us boys " in the objective case. Long usage has made these expressions acceptable, but they are the only instances where any pronoun may stand with a noun unless the pronoun is a possessive modifier. For that reason " them boys " is not allowed.

One other point should always be borne in mind; that is, never to express the subject more than once unless it is the intensive pronoun. For example, " My brother he went away," is a very awkward expression because there are two subjects. A compound subject is quite different from this kind of repetition.

In the first three exercises of *Problem XIV*, you have learned the facts that will help you to use personal and compound personal pronouns correctly. Read again the explanations given in *Exercises 1, 2,* and *3*.

DIRECTIONS. *A.* Write the following sentences, filling each blank with one of the words found in parentheses at the end of the sentence. State the reasons for your choice.

1. I have asked —— children to be quiet. (them, those)
2. The man gave —— and —— some oranges. (she, her; I, me)
3. My father and —— will be there at noon. (myself, I)
4. —— and —— went to the city last night. (me, I; him, he)
5. Was that —— who brought this lovely fruit to my mother and ——? (she, her; myself, me, I)

6. His mother and —— were expected to arrive last night. (he, himself)

7. —— and their guests were badly frightened by the fire. (themselves, theirselves, they)

8. The little boy hurt —— while he was playing in the tree. (himself, hisself)

9. —— and her brother have often inquired about the price of the house. (her, she, herself)

10. Harry took —— and —— for a ride. (she, her; I, me)

11. Where did you put —— cakes? (those, them)

12. Did your father send —— books to your mother and ——? (them, those; you, yourself)

13. —— girls enjoyed our picnic at the beach. (we, us)

14. Please send —— and —— to the store. (she, her; me, I)

15. The minister —— swept the little church. (he, himself)

16. Give —— and —— some of your fruit. (him, he; I, me)

17. A lovely lady told an interesting story to —— children. (us, we)

18. My mother —— likes to have my friends come to our house. (she, her)

19. Mother, please read Mary and —— a story about Indians. (me, I)

20. —— and John and James are going away. (I, me)

B. Write the following words correctly in sentences:

1. himself
2. him
3. me
4. myself
5. them
6. us
7. her
8. themselves
9. yourself
10. I (as subjective complement)

C. Make a list of expressions which you hear that contain the incorrect use of pronouns. Notice how many you can hear, but do not let one of your classmates hear you expressing your thoughts incorrectly.

XIV. Exercise 4. *Are you able to use the correct forms of the relative and interrogative pronoun "who"? Do you know which relative pronoun to use in any sentence?*

EXPLANATION. In *Problem XIII* you learned that the forms of the relative and interrogative pronoun *who* are:

> Nominative..... who
> Possessive...... whose
> Objective....... whom

Their case depends upon their use in a sentence. A relative pronoun is in the nominative case when it is:

1. The subject
2. The subjective complement

It is in the objective case when it is:

1. The object complement (direct object)
2. The indirect object
3. The object of a preposition

Do not think that *who* can do the work of the other relative pronouns *which, that,* and *what.* Each of these pronouns is used for special purposes. Notice what these are:

1. Who..... refers to persons and has the name of a
   (whose) person for its antecedent; as, "He is the
   (whom) *man who* bought the piano."

2. Which... refers to things and has the name of an object or an animal for its antecedent; as, "The *paper, which* you sent me, contains several interesting articles."

3. That.....refers to persons or things and may have the name of either for its antecedent. It generally introduces a restrictive clause; as, "Any *man that* is really unselfish will not think of himself when others are suffering."

4. What.... usually refers to a thought or an idea and rarely has an antecedent expressed; as, "I do not know *what* he said."

Read again these notes and the illustrations of the use of the relative pronoun. Study them until you are certain that you understand and possess the information.

Interrogative pronouns and compound relative pronouns, such as *whosoever* and *whomsoever,* will cause no trouble when you understand relative pronouns. If you are in doubt as to what form of *who* to use, diagram the sentence and you will see immediately what its work in the sentence is.

DIRECTIONS. *A.* Write the following sentences, filling each blank with one of the words found in parentheses at the end of the sentences. State the reason for your choice.

1. I know the man —— you are looking for. (who, whom)

(*Note.* It is not the best policy to end a sentence with a preposition. However, many people do it and possibly you do occasionally. If you do, are you sure that you select the correct pronoun? That, after all, is the important point.)

2. That was —— —— you saw on the street. (I, me; who, whom)

3. Was that —— —— called to you last night? (she, her; who, whom)

4. Do you know —— that man is? (who, whom)

5. —— do you want to talk to? (who, whom)

6. Is it —— —— they want? (I, me; who, whom)

7. This check was sent to me by my brother —— you know is a very generous person. (who, whom)

8. —— do you think that man is? (who, whom)

9. They sent tickets to those —— they thought would enjoy the concert. (who, whom)

10. They were very kind to my sister and —— —— you know are alone in this city. (myself, me; who, whom)

11. —— did they send? (who, whom)

12. The man —— gave his last dollar to buy bread for the starving children was unselfish. (who, whom, what, that, which)

13. We are not so ambitious for fame as ——. (them, they)

14. She was kind to —— men. (we, us)

15. Is it —— boys —— are to blame for what —— girls did? (us, we; who, whom; them, those)

16. A large amount of money was left to —— and her mother. (herself, she, her)

17. I was glad when I heard —— Mr. Smith had chosen for his new secretary. (who, whom)

18. Have you invited those —— you know will be able to come? (who, whom)

19. I hope that nothing will ever come between —— and ——. (she, her; I, me)

20. All the responsibility of the work rests upon you and ——. (I, me)

B. Write ten sentences illustrating the correct use of all relative pronouns. Underline each relative pronoun.

XIV. Exercise 5. *Do you understand the properties of pronouns well enough to make a pronoun agree with its antecedent?*

EXPLANATION. In the sentence, "Each of the girls has sent her money," "her" refers to the subject "each" and not to "girls," the object of the preposition. Because "each," the antecedent of "her," is singular, the personal pronoun is singular also. This is an important rule in the correct use of pronouns. It is very easy to think that "girls" is the antecedent and to use a plural personal pronoun to refer to it. The sentence could stand without the phrase; it would then be "Each has sent her money." If you have difficulty in locating the antecedent of a pronoun in sentences like this one, recast the sentence without any of the phrases, and you will then know what the antecedent of the personal pronoun is.

Remember that *somebody, anybody, nobody, every one, some one, any one, no one, each, every, either,* and *neither* are singular and must agree with the singular personal pronouns.

Another point to be remembered is that the gender of the personal pronoun is masculine when its antecedent is of the common gender; as, "Every one tried to do *his* best."

DIRECTIONS. A. Write the following sentences, filling each blank with one of the words found at the end of the sentence. In parentheses state the reason for your choice.

1. Each of the pupils did —— work well. (his, their)
2. If any one does not like this, let —— say so now. (them, him)
3. Every pupil should show —— loyalty by good scholarship. (his, their)
4. Each of the boys sent —— mother some flowers. (their, his)
5. Every one who was present received —— reward. (their, his)
6. Five trains went by, each with —— load of brave men. (their, its)
7. Each of them has —— trials. (their, his)
8. No one would want to lose —— way in this forest. (their, his)
9. They were told that each of the students would have to wait —— turn. (their, his, her)
10. If anybody calls, tell —— I shall be back soon. (them, her, him)
11. Has each of them fully decided to remain here during —— vacation? (their, his)
12. On Sunday everybody puts on —— best clothes. (their, his)
13. The students entered, each with —— diploma. (their, his)
14. Will either of the boys bring —— sister? (their, his)
15. No one has any idea what —— mark will be. (their, his)

B. Use each of the following words as the subject of a sentence and in each sentence use a personal pronoun to refer to the subject:

1. one	8. a person
2. any one	9. either
3. some one	10. neither
4. any body	11. somebody
5. nobody	12. everyone
6. some one	13. no one
7. each	14. either

15. neither

XIV. Exercise 6. *Can you recognize verbal nouns and always use the possessive case with them?*

EXPLANATION. Notice the italicized words in the following sentences:

1. *Skating* is good exercise.
2. I never heard of *his failing*.
3. They enjoy *John's singing*.
4. We saw him without *his knowing* it.

In each of these sentences there is a verb ending in " ing " that is used like a noun. In sentence 1 " skating " is the subject; in 2 " failing " is the object of a preposition; " singing " in sentence 3 is the object complement, and in 4 " knowing " is the object of the preposition " without." Such words are called verbal nouns since they are verbs used like nouns.

If you should say, " He never spoke of his mother," you would naturally use the possessive pronoun " his " with the noun " mother." A verbal noun ending in " ing " is the same as any other noun in this regard. A noun or a pronoun that modifies a verbal noun must be in the possessive case. See if the verb is used like a noun; if it is, it requires a possessive noun or pronoun as its modifier.

DIRECTIONS. *A.* Write the following sentences, filling each blank with one of the words found at the end of the sentence. State the reason for your choice.

1. I had not heard of —— being promoted. (John, John's)
2. No one would have thought of —— coming now. (you, your)
3. There is no use of —— going to the office. (him, his)
4. She left without —— knowing it. (me, my)
5. There was no enjoyment in hearing —— singing. (him, his)
6. I do not like to think of —— being so far away. (mother, mother's)
7. There is no danger of —— seeing us. (him, his)
8. The possibility of —— going never occurred to us. (him, his)
9. Who ever heard of —— paying a fine? (them, their)
10. The idea of —— trying to buy the machine seemed impossible. (father, father's)

B. Write ten sentences containing verbal nouns ending in " ing," each modified by a possessive noun or pronoun.

XIV. Exercise 7. *How well can you use pronouns, and how well do you know the reasons for their use?*

EXPLANATION. You should now have mastery of the correct use of all pronouns. If you know that you make mistakes in pronouns, you must watch yourself closely and put this information to use. Do not allow yourself to be judged as ignorant and uneducated because you are careless in your speech or written work.

Read again all the explanations given in the exercises of *Problems XIII* and *XIV*. Watch your speech and make a determined effort to master this matter of the correct use of pronouns.

DIRECTIONS. *A.* Write the following sentences, filling each blank with one of the words found at the end of the sentence. In parentheses state the reasons for your choice.

1. No one may enter the gymnasium without —— card. (their, his)
2. Who ever heard of —— being a musician? (him, his)
3. —— did he say the president of the organization is? (who, whom)
4. Is that —— —— you are looking for? (she, her; who, whom)
5. You have had as much experience as ——. (I, me)
6. The man —— I believe is the best fitted for the position is manager. (who, whom)
7. Send your address to the secretary or to ——. (I, me)
8. She is taller than ——. (he, him)
9. I know the man with —— you were talking. (who, whom)
10. The boy —— we paid was the one —— brought the letter. (who, whom)
11. —— and my sister are going away. (myself, I, me)
12. When can you take —— and my friend to the country? (me, I)
13. Harry and John —— have not been here for a long time. (they)

14. A person likes to be free to express —— ideas on a subject. (their, his)
15. He hurt —— when he was getting Marian and —— a drink. (himself, hisself; I, me)
16. —— playing is always enjoyed. (Mary, Mary's)
17. Neither of the women will allow —— children to play on the street. (their, her)
18. You may tell —— you meet. (whoever, whomever)
19. No one regretted —— knowing about the matter more than ——. (him, his; me, I)
20. —— do you think is the best architect in this city? (who, whom)

B. Write sentences containing the following:

1. "What" as a relative pronoun
2. "That" as a relative pronoun
3. "I" as a subjective complement
4. "Whom" as an object complement
5. "Himself" as a reflective pronoun

A STUDY OF THE FORMS OF VERBS

Purpose of Study

More errors are made in the use of verbs than in any other part of speech. Since it is our aim to speak and write sentences that are entirely free from all mistakes, we must study the properties of verbs in order to know what the correct forms are. This is the purpose of *Problem XV*.

Exercises

1. Transitive and intransitive verbs
2. Active and passive voice
3. Principal parts
4. Tense
5. Tense
6. Person and number
7. Mood
8. Infinitives
9. Participles
10. A study of all the properties of verbs

XV. Exercise 1. *Can you recognize the two kinds of verbs?*

EXPLANATION. Notice the verbs in the following sentences:

1. John *hit* the ball.
2. The ball *was hit* by John.
3. The train *went* rapidly.

In sentence 1 the object complement, "ball," names the object that receives the action expressed by the verb; in 2 the subject, "ball," names the receiver of the action; in sentence 3 "went" expresses action, but nothing receives the action. These sentences illustrate the two kinds of verbs: (1) those that have a receiver of the action, and (2) those that have no receiver of the action.

A verb that asserts action that is received by some person or thing is called a transitive verb. The verbs in these sentences are transitive:

1. The boy *ate* the candy. ("Candy" receives the action.)
2. The dress *was ironed* by the woman. ("Dress" receives the action.)

A verb that asserts being or action not received by any person or thing is called an intransitive verb. The verbs in the following sentences are intransitive.

1. The man *is* tall. ("Is" asserts being, not action.)
2. The girl *went* away. (Nothing receives the action asserted by the verb.)

Every verb is transitive or intransitive. Some verbs are always transitive, and others are always intransitive. There are very many verbs that may be transitive or intransitive; that is, they may or may not have a receiver of the action.

If you wish to know whether a verb is transitive or intransitive, see if it has a receiver of the action. If it does, it is transitive; if not, it is intransitive.

DIRECTIONS. *A*. Select the verbs in the following sentences and tell whether they are transitive or intransitive. If they are transitive, name the receiver of the action.

1. In this way the battle went on for some time.
2. They established missions in various parts of the country.
3. California was discovered many years ago.
4. The line soon broke.
5. Captain Preston waved his sword and uttered a command which could not be heard distinctly.
6. Lincoln's family came to America from England.
7. He set the lamp on the desk.
8. They have sat there for some time.
9. Please raise the window.
10. He rose as the women entered.
11. The little boy awoke at six and immediately waked his mother.
12. The child has lain there for hours.
13. Please set your books on the table.
14. Do you sit here every day?
15. He laid the blankets in the closet.
16. If your mother has awaked, lay the sheets in the drawer of the dresser.
17. Wake your father now.
18. Those children have sat in that room too long.
19. I will lie down for an hour.
20. A beautiful little lake lies up in the mountains.

B. Write five sentences containing transitive verbs and five containing intransitive verbs. Indicate which verbs are transitive, and which are intransitive.

XV. Exercise 2. *Are you able to recognize a property that all transitive verbs possess?*

EXPLANATION. In the sentence, "The child ate his dinner," the subject "child" names the doer of the action. If the sentence is changed to "The dinner was eaten by the child," the subject "dinner" names the receiver of the action. We see that the verbs in both of these sentences are transitive since each has a receiver of the action. There is, however, a difference between them. In one the subject names the doer of the action; in the other the subject names the receiver of the action. The property of a verb that shows whether the subject names the doer or the receiver of the action is known as voice. There are two voices: active voice and passive voice.

A verb is in the active voice when the subject names the doer of the action and the object complement names the receiver of the action.

A verb is in the passive voice when the subject names the receiver of the action.

Since verbs in either the active or the passive voice must have a receiver of the action, it is evident that only transitive verbs have voice.

DIRECTIONS. *A*. Select the verbs from the following sentences and tell whether they are transitive or intransitive, and give the voice of the transitive verbs.

In order to determine whether a verb is active or passive, make this test:

1. See if the verb is transitive; that is, if it has a receiver of the action.

2. Look at the subject and see whether it names the doer or the receiver of the action. If the subject names the doer, the verb is active. If the subject names the receiver, the verb is passive.

3. If the verb is intransitive, do not give the voice.

1. The captain gave orders for unmooring the ship.
2. We arrived in Chicago on the first of April.
3. We hired horses and rode to the beach.
4. The whales were seen at a distance as we lay in the harbor.
5. Everything wore the appearance of a holiday.
6. When our duties had been discharged, we were allowed a few hours for amusement.
7. After the arrangements had been made, we sent for Cousin George.
8. Notes should not be used in debates.
9. It was a very interesting story.
10. He nodded his head and smiled faintly.
11. The president will be at the theater tonight.
12. I was greatly influenced by that book.
13. No principle was involved in the last issue.
14. When the noise was heard, the children ran out of the room.
15. A very important question was discussed by the members of the club.

B.   Change each of the active verbs in these sentences to passive voice and each of the passive verbs to active voice.   Notice how this is done:

Active Voice........... The boy hit the ball.
Passive Voice.......... The ball was hit by the boy.

The complement of the active verb becomes the subject of the passive verb, and the subject of the active verb becomes the object of a preposition.   The passive verb always has some form of the verb " be."

C.   Write five sentences in which the verbs are in the active voice, and five in which they are in the passive voice.

XV. Exercise 3. *Do you know the three parts of every verb?*

EXPLANATION. In the following sentences notice the various forms of the verb " go ":

1. I *go* to school every day.
2. She *went* there yesterday.
3. My friend *has gone* to Alaska.

If we should use this verb in all the ways we possibly could, we should find that there would be three different forms: *go, went, gone.* These forms are called the principal parts of the verb and are known as the present, the past, and the past participle.

Practically every verb has these three forms. The past and past participle of many verbs are formed by adding *d* or *ed* to the present. Such verbs are said to be regular. The verb " walk " illustrates this kind.

Present	walk
Past	walked
Past Participle	walked

There are other verbs that form their past and past participle by making some change in the word itself, generally in the vowel. These verbs are called irregular verbs. " See " is one of this kind.

Present	see
Past	saw
Past Participle	seen

People often confuse the past with the past participle and make very serious mistakes. As it is our aim to free our speech and written expression from all errors, we must know the principal parts of the verbs we use.

There are many irregular verbs. The principal parts are given in the dictionary, which you should consult again and again until you are certain that you know the correct forms. The following list contains the principal parts of the verbs that are often misused:

Present	Past	Past Participle
see	saw	seen
do	did	done
come	came	come
go	went	gone
run	ran	run
sit	sat	sat
lie	lay	lain
lay	laid	laid
give	gave	given
begin	began	begun
ring	rang	rung
sing	sang	sung
write	wrote	written
take	took	taken
break	broke	broken
drink	drank	drunk
forget	forgot	forgotten
draw	drew	drawn
blow	blew	blown

DIRECTIONS. *A.* Write the following sentences, filling each blank with the form suggested in the parentheses:

1. I —— him yesterday. (Past of " see ")
2. He has —— his glasses. (Past participle of " break ")
3. He has —— there two hours. (Past participle of " lie ")

4. Have you —— about the party? (Past participle of " forget ")
5. He —— to work last week. (Past of " begin ")
6. How many glasses of water have you ——? (Past participle of " drink ")
7. The boy was not ——. (Past participle of " drown ")
8. After he had —— down, his mother entered the room. (Past participle of " lie ")
9. I —— to school early this morning. (Past of " come ")
10. They —— their lessons well. (Past of " do ")
11. My brother —— too fast when he was little. (Past of " grow ")
12. Have you —— him recently? (Past participle of " see ")
13. It was so cold that the milk was ——. (Past participle of " freeze ")
14. I —— to school this morning. (Past of " run ")
15. She —— a beautiful picture. (Past of " draw ")
16. Mother —— my books away. (Past of " lay ")
17. She —— on the bed as she read. (Past of " lie ")
18. Are those bottles ——? (Past participle of " break ")
19. He —— the ball a long distance. (Past of " throw ")
20. The man —— the horn. (Past of " blow ")

B. What are the principal parts of the following verbs? Consult a dictionary.

awake	lose
bring	steal
choose	wake
flee	dive

fly	swim
flow	prove
get	burst
lead	know

be

C. Write ten sentences, each containing either the past or the past participle of some verb listed in this exercise.

XV. Exercise 4. *Can you recognize the time asserted by a verb?*

EXPLANATION. Notice that the verb in each of the following sentences asserts an action performed at some time:

1. I broke the dish. (" Broke " denotes past time.)
2. I break the dish. (" Break " denotes present time.)
3. I shall break the dish. (" Shall break " denotes future time.)

All verbs denote time. This property is called tense. The illustrations show that verbs denote three different times or tenses: present tense, past tense, and future tense.

The present tense denotes that the action is taking place in the present time. It usually consists of one word; as, " I *forget* the man's name."

The past tense denotes that the action took place in the past time. It usually consists of one word; as, " I *forgot* the man's name."

The future tense denotes that the action will take place at some time in the future. " Shall " or " will " is always a part of the verb in the future tense; as, " I *shall forget* the man's name."

In the following sentences notice that the verbs denote an action as being completed or perfected at some time.

1. I *have broken* the dish. (" Have broken " asserts an action completed at the present time.)
2. I *had broken* the dish. (" Had broken " asserts an action completed at some time in the past.)
3. I *shall have broken* the dish. (" Shall have broken " denotes an action that will be completed at some time in the future.)

Since these tenses indicate an action completed or perfected, they are known as the perfect tenses, and are the present perfect, the past perfect, and the future perfect.

The present perfect tense denotes an act completed in or continued to the present time; as, " I *have made* my new dress." The verb consists of " have " or " has " and the past participle.

The past perfect tense denotes a past act completed before some other action of the past occurred; as, " I *had made* my new dress before I saw her." The verb consists of " had " and the past participle.

The future perfect tense denotes an action that will be completed before some other event will occur; as, " I *shall have made* my dress when I see you again." The past participle of the verb is added to " shall have " or " will have " to form the future perfect tense.

Every verb has the property of tense and denotes one of the six tenses. The present and the past tenses generally consist of one word, while the future is formed by adding " shall " or " will " to the present. The perfect tenses always consist of some form of the auxiliary verb " have " and the past participle.

The important point in the formation of the tenses is not to confuse the past tense with the past participle. It shows great ignorance of correct English to say, " I seen " for " I saw." " Seen " is the past participle and must be used with the auxiliary " have "; then the expression becomes " I have seen " or " I had seen."

Watch everything you say and write in order to correct any bad habits you may have acquired in the use of verbs. Possibly this plan will assist you:

Formation of Tenses

Present tense
    one word   I *see* you.
Past tense
    one word   I *saw* you.
Future tense
    shall or will + present   I *shall see* you.
Present perfect tense
    have (has) + past participle   I *have seen* you.
Past perfect tense
    had + past participle   I *had seen* you.
Future perfect tense
    shall have or will have   I *shall have* seen you.
    + past participle

DIRECTIONS. *A.* Write the following sentences, filling the blank in each with the tense of the verb indicated in parentheses:

1. The man —— his daughter away. (Future tense of " take ")
2. I —— my work now. (Present perfect tense of " do ")
3. They —— us at the theater. (past tense of " see ")
4. The children —— the dish before I came. (Past perfect tense of " break ")

5. When he comes, I —— to the city. (Future perfect of " go ")
6. The boys —— three bottles of milk before I could stop them. (Past perfect of " drink ")
7. The man —— there all night. (Present perfect of " lie ")
8. Those flowers —— too rapidly. (Past of " grow ")
9. I —— here until he comes. (Future of " sit ")
10. The girls —— those dresses since Christmas. (Present perfect of " wear ")
11. Before father came in, mother —— to prepare supper. (Past perfect of " begin ")
12. I —— those boys as they were hunting for the treasure. (Past tense of " see ")
13. The dog —— the child. (Present perfect of " bite ")
14. That skirt —— in the washing. (Past of " shrink ")
15. The sun —— all day. (Present perfect of " shine ")
16. She —— before you can get there. (Future of " freeze," passive voice)
17. The girls —— the table while father and mother rested. (Past of " set ")
18. Some boys —— the little child. (Present perfect of " wake ")
19. That boy —— a fine ball. (Present perfect of " throw ")
20. The teacher —— down to rest. (Past of " lie ")

B. Write sentences containing the following:

1. Past tense of " lie "
2. Present perfect tense of " run "
3. Past perfect tense of " choose "
4. Past tense of " lead "
5. Present perfect tense of " drink "

6. Past tense of " do "
7. Present perfect tense of " go "
8. Past tense of " see "

XV. Exercise 5.   *Are you able to write a verb in any of the six tenses?*

EXPLANATION.   In *Exercise 3* we learned that every verb has the property of tense.   There are three ways of forming the various tenses.   The most common way was shown in the preceding exercise.   Another way is to use the auxiliary " do " in the present tense and " did " in the past tense.   This is known as the emphatic form, and is used to give emphasis to an assertion.

> *Present*   I *do take* my work seriously.
> *Past*   I *did take* my work seriously.

We often wish to represent an act as continuing or progressing at a certain time.   This form is known as the progressive form, and it consists of the verb " be " and the form of the verb that ends in " ing," known as the present participle.

Present	I *am making* a dress.
Past	I *was making* a dress.
Future	I *shall be making* a dress.
Present perfect	I *have been making* a dress.
Past perfect	I *had been making* a dress when you entered.
Future perfect	I *shall have been making* a dress when you come again.

These two methods just illustrated rarely cause any trouble, for the past participle is not used.   They are given so that you may know ways of varying your expressions.

The past participle is the cause of most of the trouble with verbs. However, if one will learn the principal parts of troublesome verbs and then use the knowledge he has gained, he need never be guilty of this error. It is not a difficult thing to form tenses correctly, if one makes a determined effort to do it right each time.

A summary of the information that has been given in *Exercises 3* and *4* may be of help in forming the various tenses.

Tense

1. Tense is a property of all verbs.
2. There are six tenses.

   a. *Primary tenses*   *Formation* (common method)
   - (1) Present   (1) Present form of verb
   - (2) Past   (2) Past form of verb
   - (3) Future   (3) " Shall " or " will " and present form of verb

   b. *Secondary tenses*   *Formation*
   - (1) Present perfect   (1) " Have " (has) and past participle
   - (2) Past perfect   (2) " Had " and past participle
   - (3) Future perfect   (3) " Shall have " or " will have " and past participle

3. The emphatic form of a verb is used to give emphasis. It consists of " do " or " did " with the present tense of the verb. The emphatic form has only the present and past tenses in the active voice.
4. The progressive form of a verb is used to show the continuance of an action. It consists of some form of the verb " be " and the present participle. The progressive form has all tenses, but only the active voice.

DIRECTIONS. *A.* Write the following sentences, filling the blank in each with the tense of the verb indicated in parentheses.

1. He ——— into the room just as I was leaving. (Past tense of " come ")

2. Some one ——— my new glass vase. (Present perfect tense of " break ")

3. How much milk ——— you ——— before I came? (Past perfect tense of " drink ")

4. How many times do you think that bell ———? (Present perfect tense of " ring ")

5. She ——— to take music lessons when she was very young. (Past tense of " begin ")

6. They ——— when I arrived. (Past perfect tense of " go ")

7. The teacher ——— the boy close his book. (Past tense of " see ")

8. The choir ——— a beautiful anthem at the beginning of the service. (Past tense of " sing ")

9. ——— she ——— there long? (Present perfect tense of " lie ")

10. I ——— my work as well as I could. (Past tense of " do ")

11. The boys ——— down the hall shouting and laughing. (Past tense of " run ")

12. That little dog ——— up and down the street trying to find his master. (Present perfect of " run ")

13. The frightened child ——— before we could talk with him. (Past perfect tense of " go ")

14. I ——— you, but you were too busy to see me. (Past tense of " see ")

15. You might ——— when the others ———. (Present perfect tense of " drink," past tense of " drink ")

B. Write sentences containing the following:

1. Past tense of " see "
2. Past perfect tense of " come "
3. Past tense of " do "
4. Present perfect tense of " go "
5. Past tense of " run "
6. Past tense of " begin "
7. Present perfect tense of " drink "
8. Past tense of " come "

XV. Exercise 6. *Can you tell the person and the number of a verb?*

EXPLANATION. We know that nouns and pronouns have the properties of person and number. The same is true of verbs. The person and the number of a verb are the same as the person and the number of its subject. For example, in the sentence, " She has eaten her lunch," the subject is in the singular number and the third person, and the verb is the same.

Notice the change in the form of the present tense to show person and number.

Singular

First person	I make my dresses.
Second person	You make your dresses.
Third person	She *makes* her dresses.

Plural

First person	We make our dresses.
Second person	You make your dresses.
Third person	They make their dresses.

The only change in the form of the present tense is found in the third person singular which ends in " s." The same is true of the present perfect tense.

	Singular	*Plural*
First person	I have seen her.	We have seen her.
Second person	You have seen her.	You have seen her.
Third person	He *has* seen her.	They have seen her.

These two changes to show number and person are the only changes that occur regularly. They are very important, however, and should be observed carefully.

The verb " be " is very irregular and shows differences in person and number by various forms in different tenses. Many changes appear in the present and past tenses. These forms are as follows:

Present Tense

	Singular	*Plural*
First person	I *am* well.	We *are* well.
Second person	You *are* well.	You *are* well.
Third person	He *is* well.	They *are* well.

Past Tense

First person	I *was* well.	We *were* well.
Second person	You *were* well.	You *were* well.
Third person	He *was* well.	They *were* well.

Notice especially that the form for the second person singular and plural in the past tense is " You were." This is often spoken and written incorrectly. Be sure that you always use it correctly.

When you are writing or speaking, see that the verbs in your sentences agree with their subjects in person and number. You will have no difficulty in observing this rule if you will remember these points:

1. A singular subject takes a singular verb.
2. A plural subject takes a plural verb.

3. *Each, every, anyone,* and other words of this kind are singular and take a singular verb.
4. A collective noun is singular when the group is considered as one, and takes a singular verb.
5. A compound subject generally has a plural verb.
6. If the tense is present or present perfect, the form for the third person singular ends in " s."

DIRECTIONS. *A.* Write the following sentences, filling the blank in each with the correct form for the tense, person, and number of the verb indicated in parentheses. Select the subject first and see if it is singular or plural; then write the verb.

1. Each of the men —— to do his work. (Present perfect of " come ")
2. —— you here yesterday? (Past of " was ")
3. He —— not present today. (Present of " be ")
4. Every pupil in this room —— his work alone. (Present perfect of " do ")
5. The mob on the streets —— its leader. (Present perfect of " lose ")
6. The boys and the girls —— that play. (Present perfect of " see ")
7. —— I not a help to you? (Present of " be ")
8. This automobile with all its equipment —— for one thousand dollars. (Present of " sell ")
9. Either John or James —— the book. (Present of " have ")
10. Every one of those pupils —— to succeed. (Present of " want ")
11. There —— many boys and girls in this room. (Present of " be ")
12. Every one of the girls —— to go to camp. (Present of " like ")

13. Into the room —— each of the boys with a flag and
a banner. (Present of " come ")

14. Neither of us —— anxious to go again. (Present
of " be ")

15. There —— several men waiting in the office. (Past
of " be ")

16. One of the inspectors —— to see us today. (Present
progressive of " come ")

17. Do you know if any of the men or women —— my
books? (Present perfect of " see ")

18. There —— several questions that should be answered.
(Present of " be ")

19. Everybody in that room —— the answers. (Present perfect of " write ")

20. We —— here on time. (Past of " be ")

B. 1. Write sentences containing the following:

(1) Second person singular, past tense of " be "
(2) Third person singular, present tense of " go "
(3) Third person singular, present perfect tense of
" see "

2. If you do not yet understand tense, select a paragraph from some book and tell the tense of each verb.

XV. Exercise 7. *How well can you recognize the manner in which an assertion is made?*

EXPLANATION. Verbs make assertions in various ways.
They are used to make a statement of a fact, to ask a
question, to give a command, to state a condition, or to
make a wish. The property of a verb that denotes the
manner in which the assertion is made is called mood.
There are three moods: indicative, imperative, and subjunctive.

A verb is in the indicative mood when it is used in the statement of a fact, or when it asks a question.

A verb is in the imperative mood when it is used in expressing a command or an entreaty.

A verb is in the subjunctive mood when it is used in expressing a wish, a condition contrary to fact, or something that is uncertain.

The only mood that we need to study carefully is the subjunctive, since verbs in that mood have a different form from those in the indicative or the imperative. In the sentence, " If she were here, I could do my work," the dependent clause expresses a condition that is contrary to fact; therefore the verb is in the subjunctive mood. Notice the form of the verb. Ordinarily the third person singular of the past tense of " be " is " was." We say " She was here." In the condition contrary to fact, however, the verb has a different form. The same is true of the first person. When we state a fact, we say, " I was there." Change this to a condition contrary to fact, and it becomes " If I were there, I should be glad." The subjunctive forms of the verb " be " in the present and past tenses are as follows:

Present Tense (Notice that each form has " be ")

	Singular	*Plural*
First person	If I be there	If we be there
Second person	If you be there	If you be there
Third person	If he be there	If they be there

Past Tense (Notice that each form has " were ")

First person	If I were there	If we were there
Second person	If you were there	If you were there
Third person	If he were there	If they were there

The subjunctive forms of the verb " be " are so different from the regular forms that many mistakes are made in them. In order to be certain that you use them correctly, first remember that the subjunctive mood is used only to express wishes, statements that are uncertain, and conditions that are contrary to fact. Then be sure that you know the correct forms, and make a conscious effort to use them.

DIRECTIONS. *A.* Tell the mood of the italicized verbs in the following sentences and give the reason:

1. I wish she *were* here now.
2. If he *were coming,* he would have telegraphed us.
3. If he *is* here when I return, let me know at once.
4. I do not know if he *is coming.*
5. If he *were coming,* he would be here now.
6. If that *is* the right thing to do, we will do it at once.
7. If that *were* my book, I should not use it so carelessly.
8. I wish I *were going* to the mountains.
9. If those two boys *were invited,* there would be too much excitement.
10. If I *were* you, I should smile.
11. If he *were* here, he would amuse us with anecdotes of his life in Alaska.
12. If you *were* I, should you go there?
13. The little child wished he *were* a grown man.
14. He acted as if he *were* a child.
15. The boys were wishing they *were* away in the mountains.

B. Write ten sentences, each containing the verb " be " in the subjunctive mood.

XV. Exercise 8. *Can you recognize verbs that are used as nouns?*

EXPLANATION. Notice the italicized words in the following sentences:

1. I wanted *to go* to the city.
2. *To read* good books is a liberal education.
3. The child would like *to have seen* the play.

In each of these sentences there is, in addition to the predicate, a verb which is preceded by the word "to." Such words are called infinitives. Read the sentences again, and you will see that each infinitive is used like a noun. In sentence 1 "to go" is the object complement of "wanted"; in sentence 2 "to read" is the subject of "is"; "to have seen," in sentence 3, is the object complement of the verb "would like."

The relation of an infinitive to the rest of the sentence in shown in the diagram.

(*a*) To go to school is the duty of all.

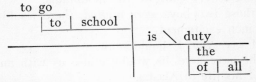

The infinitive is the subject of the sentence. Notice that it is modified by an adverbial phrase.

(*b*) She wanted me to go to school.

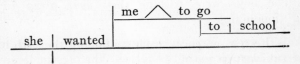

The infinitive is the object complement of " wanted."
The pronoun " me " is the subject of the infinitive and is
in the objective case.   The subject of an infinitive is always
in the objective case.

(*c*) Whom do you want the leader to be?

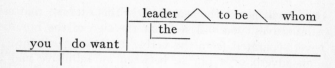

Notice that the interrogative pronoun " whom " is the
complement of the infinitive " to be."   In preceding problems where a subjective complement followed the verb
" be," the subjective complement was in the same case as
the subject; namely, the nominative case.   Inasmuch as
the subject of an infinitive is in the objective case, the complement of the infinitive " to be " is in the objective case
instead of the nominative case.

(*d*) Let me go to the city.

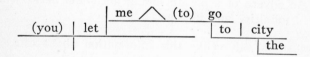

In this sentence " to," the sign of the infinitive, is
omitted.   The sign of the infinitive is generally omitted
after these verbs: *let, hear, make, feel, see,* and *bid.*

These illustrations show that an infinitive may have a
subject and a complement and modifiers.   The entire group
is called an infinitive phrase.

Like all verbs, infinitives have the property of tense.
There are, however, only two tenses: the present tense and

the perfect tense. An infinitive should be in the present tense unless it represents an action taking place before that of the predicate; for example,

Present........   I hope *to see* her soon.
Perfect........   He ought *to have paid* his bills.

If you will notice the sentences in this exercise that contain infinitives, you will see that the sign of the infinitive is never separated from the verb. It is very bad form to put an adverb or a phrase between an infinitive and its sign.

There are a few facts that must be remembered in connection with infinitives:

1. A verb that is preceded by " to " expressed or understood is an infinitive.
2. An infinitive is a verbal noun.
3. Infinitives have two tenses: the present and the perfect.
4. The subject and the complement of an infinitive are in the objective case.
5. An adverb or a phrase should not stand between an infinitive and its sign.

Directions. *A.* Give this information about each of the following sentences:

1. The infinitive phrase and its use   (Underline the infinitive.)
2. The tense of the infinitive
3. The case and the use of the underlined words
   1. He wanted *me* to show *him* the flowers.
   2. They invited Mary and *me* to go with them.
   3. Let him and *her* go with us.
   4. *Whom* did you hope to see when you went there?

5. We expected the winner to be *him*.
6. *He* would like to have eaten the pie.

B. Write ten sentences containing present and perfect infinitives. Underline each infinitive.

XV. Exercise 9. *Can you recognize verbs that are used like adjectives?*

EXPLANATION. Notice the italicized words in the following sentences and determine what the use of each is.

1. *Rising* from the chair, he made a low bow.
2. The *rising* tide threatened the campers.
3. The heirloom, *made* hundreds of years ago, is treasured by the old lady.

Each of these words is a verb and each modifies a noun. In other words, each is a verb used like an adjective. Such words are called participles.

Participles, like infinitives, have tense. There are three tenses: the present, the past, and the perfect. The present participle expresses action as still in progress; as, " The boys run about the house *laughing* and *shouting*." The past participle expresses action completed in past time; as, " He wore an old coat *patched* with many pieces of cloth." The perfect participle expresses action completed in the past before some particular time; as, " *Having heard* that her son was near, the woman could not rest until she saw him."

Though a participle never has a subject, it may be completed by a complement with modifiers. The entire group is called a participial phrase. A diagram shows the relation of a participial phrase to the word it modifies. For example, take the sentence, " Having arrived at the camping place, we started to get our dinner."

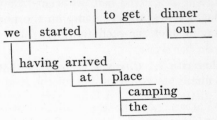

In this sentence " having arrived at the camping place " is the participial phrase. " Having arrived " is a perfect participle, modified by the prepositional phrase, " at the camping place." " Camping " is a present participle that modifies the noun " place." Notice, too, that the object complement of " started " is the infinitive phrase " to get our dinner."

Do not confuse the past participle that is a part of the predicate in the perfect tenses with the past participle that is used like an adjective. When a participle is used to form a perfect tense, it becomes the predicate of a clause and is not a participle in the sense of its being a modifier. The same is true of the present participle when it is used to form a progressive verb.

A participle is always a modifier. If there is no word in the sentence that it modifies, then it is not used correctly, and the sentence must be revised. This is often a very serious matter in compositions. Watch your sentences and see that the participles are used like adjectives.

DIRECTIONS. *A.* Diagram the following sentences:

1. Seeing his father in the distance, little Harry began to shout.

2. She ran about the yard, gathering flowers for her mother.
3. Having heard the bell, we went to our lunch.
4. She saw her father sitting on the porch.
5. Having laid the clothes away, the woman began to do her work.
6. This article, written originally for a newspaper, was finally accepted by one of the leading newspapers.
7. A little brooklet, flowing thru the fields, was our only comfort in those days.

B. Write ten sentences, each containing a participle or a participial phrase. Underline each participle.

XV. Exercise 10. *How well can you give the properties of verbs? How well can you recognize infinitives and participles?*

EXPLANATION. Our study of verbs in this problem has shown us that a verb may be used in three different ways: as the predicate, as an infinitive, or as a participle.

The predicate makes the assertion and is absolutely necessary to the meaning of a clause. A predicate has these properties:

1. Class (or kind)
   (1) Transitive   (has a receiver of the action)
   (2) Intransitive (has no receiver of the action)
2. Voice (if transitive)
   (1) Active (the subject is the doer of the action)
   (2) Passive (the subject is the receiver of the action)
3. Tense
   (1) Present

(2) Past

(3) Future (" shall " or " will " + present)

(4) Present perfect (" have " or " has " + the past participle)

(5) Past perfect (" had " + the past participle)

(6) Future perfect (" shall have " or " will have " + the past participle)

4. Person (the same as that of the subject)

5. Number (the same as that of the subject)

6. Mood

(1) Subjunctive (used to express a condition contrary to fact, a wish, a statement that denotes uncertainty)

(2) Indicative (used to state a fact or ask a question)

(3) Imperative (used to express a command)

7. Principal parts

(1) Present

(2) Past

(3) Past participle (used to form perfect tenses)

There is some special fact about each of these properties that you must master. Read again the explanations given in the preceding exercises.

An infinitive is a verbal noun. There are two kinds of infinitives:

1. The infinitive in " ing "

2. The infinitive with " to "

The infinitive in " ing " we studied in *Problem XIII* and learned that it is modified by a possessive noun or pronoun; as, " John's whistling becomes rather tiresome." Since " whistling " is a verbal noun, it is an infinitive.

The infinitive with " to " is easily recognized. The most important fact to remember about it is that an adverb or a phrase must never separate the infinitive from its sign.

A participle is a verbal adjective. The most necessary thing to remember about participles is that they must always be modifiers. There will be no loose or dangling participles in correctly written sentences.

Every verb is used in one of these three ways. When you wish to tell the properties of a verb, decide first whether it is a predicate, an infinitive, or a participle. After you have decided this, you are ready to tell its properties.

Directions. *A.* Classify all the verbs in the following sentences as:

1. Predicates
2. Infinitives
3. Participles

1. She would like to see you and your mother in the library.
2. Not having read the letter, I had not heard of his going.
3. Whom do you expect him to see when he *goes* into the office?
4. I do not want him to hear her singing.
5. The train *was wrecked* because some careless person had forgotten to signal the man stationed at the junction.
6. We *have* not *seen* her for months.
7. If I *were* you, I should study more each evening.

B. Give the properties of the italicized words.

C. Tell how each infinitive and participle is used.

CORRECT USE OF VERBS

Purpose of Study

More than half of all the mistakes that are made in the use of words are made with verbs. Since this is so, we must have much drill in the use of the correct forms of verbs, for it is our aim to make our speech and written expressions absolutely correct.

Exercises

1. Agreement of subject and predicate
2. Use of the past tense and past participle
3. Use of transitive and intransitive verbs
4. Use of "shall" and "will"
5. Use of the subjunctive mood
6. Correct use of infinitives
7. Correct use of participles
8. Harmony of tense and voice
9. Correct use of verbs
10. A study of the correct use of all verb forms

XVI. Exercise 1. *Are you able to make the subject and the predicate of a sentence agree?*

EXPLANATION. The subject of a sentence must always agree in number with the predicate. If the subject is singular, the predicate must be singular; if the subject is plural, the predicate must be plural.

A few definite rules and illustrations may help you to master this subject.

1. " You " always takes a plural verb; as, " *Were* you there last week? " It is never correct to say, " We was " or " You was." This is a mistake that is inexcusable, for it shows very great ignorance and carelessness.

2. A compound subject takes a plural verb; as, " Mother and I *are* going to the country," and " *Were* Henry and James here last night? "

3. Where *either, neither, each, someone, any one,* and other words of this kind are used as the subject, they are singular and take a singular predicate; as, " Neither of the boys *is* intending to go to the picnic." Notice that the subject is " neither " modified by the phrase " of the boys." Do not let the plural object of the preposition confuse you; it is not the subject and can not govern the number of the verb.

4. In such a sentence as " Either Mr. Smith or Mr. Jones *is* coming," the verb must be singular. The meaning is this: " Either (one) of the two men (Mr. Smith or Mr. Jones) is coming."

5. A collective noun takes a singular verb when the group is considered as one; it takes a plural verb when the group is considered as individuals; as, " The committee *was* holding a meeting," and " The committee *were* leaving the building one by one."

6. When such expressions as " along with," " in addition to," and " as well as " follow a singular subject, the predicate is singular. For example, in

the sentence, " The boy, as well as the girl, *was* interested in the lecture," the subject is " boy " and takes a singular predicate. The expression, " as well as the girl," is parenthetical and does not make the subject compound.

7. When a sentence begins with the word " there," the subject generally follows the verb. Both the subject and the predicate must be in the same number. For example, in " There *are* several men waiting in the office," the subject is the noun " men "; since it is plural, the predicate must be plural. In the sentence, " There is only one Golden Rule," the predicate is singular because the subject is singular.

When " there " introduces a sentence and does not give the idea of a definite place, as the adverb " there " does, it is called an expletive.

8. The expression, " They don't want to go," is a contraction of " They do not want to go." Since the subject is plural, the verb is plural. If a singular subject is used, the expression becomes, " He doesn't want to go." " Don't " is plural and demands a plural subject. Never say, " He don't want it," for that means " He do not want it," and such language shows rank ignorance. This is a very serious blunder which is inexcusable. If the subject is singular, as " he," " she," " the girl," etc., use " doesn't."

DIRECTIONS. *A.* Write the following sentences, filling the blank in each with one of the verbs found in parentheses at the end of the sentence. Underline the simple subject and the simple predicate.

1. —— you ever in San Francisco? (was, were)
2. Every one of the pupils —— doing excellent work. (is, are)
3. The little boy —— want to go to bed. (don't, doesn't)
4. There —— two books lying on the library table. (was, were)
5. Each of the men —— for the same company. (work, works)
6. We —— invited to go to the theater. (was, were)
7. The jury —— discharged by the judge. (was, were)
8. Every pupil who joins the class —— to work hard. (expect, expects)
9. Mr. Jones, Mr. Smith, and Mr. Brown —— the committee chosen to investigate the plan. (was, were)
10. When —— you at my house? (was, were)
11. Each of them —— to be earnest. (seem, seems)
12. There —— only three words in that sentence. (is, are)
13. The furniture, which consisted of a table, a couch, and two chairs, —— sold at an auction. (was, were)
14. A basket of apples —— put on the table. (was, were)
15. That wonderful collection of paintings —— sold yesterday. (was, were)
16. The title of the book —— "The Just So Stories." (is, are)
17. I thought you —— at home. (was, were)
18. A boy from each of the rooms —— to the office for announcements. (go, goes)
19. Neither the coat nor the hat —— mine. (is, are)
20. Each went home and not one of them —— referred to the matter since. (has, have)

B. Listen to the speech of those about you and collect fifteen sentences in which the subject does not agree with the predicate. After each incorrect expression give the correct form.

XVI. Exercise 2. *Do you ever confuse the past participle with the past tense? Are you always able to use these forms correctly?*

EXPLANATION. In *Problem XV* we learned that verbs have three principal parts: the present, the past, and the past participle. The past participle is always used in forming the perfect tenses and can never be used without some form of the auxiliary " have." The past tense is often confused with the past participle, and as a result many very serious mistakes are made. For example, the past participle of " see " is used for the past tense; this results in the expression " I seen " for " I saw."

A person should make a determined effort to eliminate such expressions from his speech, for they indicate a very great ignorance of his own language. In order to be absolutely certain that you are using the correct forms, learn the principal parts of the verbs given in *Exercise 3* of *Problem XV* and then watch carefully every expression you write or say. In this way you will eventually acquire the habit of speaking correctly.

DIRECTIONS. *A.* Write the following sentences, filling the blank in each with one of the verbs found in parentheses at the end of the sentence. Underline the entire verb.

1. Some one has —— that glass. (broke, broken)
2. I —— my lesson last night. (did, done)
3. She has not —— him for years. (saw, seen)

4. This morning I —— all the way to school. (ran, run)
5. The man —— to tell us a story. (began, begun)
6. The little girl has —— home. (went, gone)
7. She has —— her dress. (tore, torn)
8. The boys —— their lessons quickly. (did, done)
9. Is that chair ——? (broke, broken)
10. How many glasses of milk have you ——? (drank, drunk)
11. When I —— into the building, I —— a most peculiar sight. (came, come; saw, seen)
12. After I had —— her, I unexpectedly —— her husband. (saw, seen)
13. Has the bell ——? (rang, rung)
14. The men —— their work too hurriedly. (did, done)
15. Have you —— to read that essay? (began, begun)
16. The girl has already —— once, but she will sing again. (sang, sung)
17. Although he had —— only a short distance, he was very tired. (went, gone)
18. I —— that play when I was a little girl. (saw, seen)
19. No one —— them as they entered the building. (saw, seen)
20. The child —— a woman's work. (did, done)

B. Write sentences containing the past tense and the past participle of the following verbs:

see	begin
do	ring
come	sing
go	drink
run	break

XVI. Exercise 3. *Do you know the verbs that are always intransitive and those that are always transitive? Can you use these verbs correctly?*

Explanation. There are some verbs that are always intransitive and others that are always transitive. They are so alike in form that they are often used incorrectly. To confuse these verbs and use a transitive verb for an intransitive verb is a very serious mistake. In this exercise we shall try to master each of these verbs and its various forms so that our expressions will be free from such errors.

The most familiar group is " lie " and " lay." The verb " lay," which means " to put " or " to place," is always transitive. Its principal parts are:

Present	lay
Past	laid
Past participle	laid

This verb must have a receiver of the action; generally the receiver is the object. Notice the different forms of the transitive verb " lay " in the following sentences:

1. I *lay* the clean *clothes* away every Tuesday.
2. She *laid* the *books* on the table.
3. They *have laid* the *baby* on the bed.

The verbs in these sentences are the three forms of " lay." Notice that each verb has an object, and therefore is transitive.

The principal parts of " lie," meaning " to recline," are:

Present	lie
Past	lay
Past participle	lain

" Lie " is always intransitive and must never have an object. Notice the use of the different forms of " lie " in these sentences:

1. I *lie* down every afternoon.
2. Yesterday I *lay* on the couch for an hour.
3. She *has lain* there many hours.

Do not confuse these two verbs. Remember that " lie " has no form that contains the letter " d," and that " lay " is the past tense of " lie."

A second group of verbs that is often confused is " sit " and " set." " Sit " is always intransitive and must never have an object; " set " is always transitive and must have an object that receives the action. Notice the use of the two verbs:

Intransitive " sit "	Transitive " set "
1. I *sit* here every day.	1. I *set* the *dishes* here every day.
2. I *sat* there for a long time.	2. I *set* the *vase* there.
3. They *have sat* there long enough.	3. They *have set* the *food* in the cupboard.

Note that the transitive verbs have objects and the intransitive verbs have none. The principal parts of these verbs are:

Present	Past	Past participle
sit	sat	sat
set	set	set

A third group of transitive and intransitive verbs is " awake " and " wake." " Awake " is always intransitive, and "wake" is always transitive. Their principal parts are as follows:

Present	Past	Past participle
awake	awoke	awaked
wake	woke	waked
	waked	

Since "awake" is intransitive, it must not have an object; but "wake" must always have a receiver of the action. Note the use of these verbs in the following sentences:

Intransitive	*Transitive*
1. I *awake* early every morning.	1. I *wake* my *brother* every morning.
2. She *awoke* at six o'clock.	2. She *woke* (waked) *me* at six o'clock.
3. I think she *has awaked*.	3. I think she *has waked* the *baby*.

One other group of verbs that must not be confused is "raise" and "rise." "Raise" is transitive and "rise" is intransitive. "Rise" should never have an object, and "raise" must always have a receiver of the action. Their uses are illustrated in the following sentences:

Intransitive	*Transitive*
1. I always *rise* when I hear the national anthem.	1. I *raise* the *curtains* every morning.
2. She *rose* to go to the door.	2. She *raised* the *curtain* to let the light in.
3. He *has risen*.	3. He *has raised* the *window*.

Study these four groups of words carefully. Learn which are the intransitive verbs and never use any form of the transitive verb for the intransitive verb. To confuse these groups results in serious errors. The best way to test your verb is this:

1. Is the verb transitive or intransitive?
2. If it is transitive, it must have a receiver of the action. Generally this is the object.
3. If it is intransitive, it must not have an object.

DIRECTIONS. *A.* Write the following sentences, filling the blank in each with the correct form of one of the verbs found in parentheses at the end of the sentence.

1. How long has he —— there? (lie, lay)
2. Will you —— and recite? (rise, raise)
3. I —— on the couch last evening and slept until Henry —— me. (lie, lay; awake, wake)
4. I was surprised to see him —— on the floor. (lie, lay)
5. She has —— all those things away. (lie, lay)
6. Around the table —— three men. (sit, set)
7. They —— the curtain. (rise, raise)
8. To the left of us —— a beautiful farm. (lie, lay)
9. They let the book —— on the grass all night. (lie, lay)
10. The books were —— where we —— them. (lie, lay)
11. I will —— and say what I think. (rise, raise)
12. As the men —— the sail, the wind ——. (rise, raise)
13. The poor old man was —— on the grass and near him —— a hungry dog. (sit, set; lie, lay)
14. When I had —— my sewing away, I —— down to take a nap. (lie, lay)
15. She —— her heavy burden on the ground and then —— down to rest. (lie, lay; sit, sat)

16. Shall I —— this basket on the table?   (sit, set)
17. The tide has —— since we came here.   (rise, raise)
18. The city —— to the west of us.   (lie, lay)
19. Why do you —— there before you have —— your
   bundle down?   (sit, set; lie, lay)
20. I was —— there when the little child came up to
   me, —— his hand on my face, and —— me.   (lie,
   lay; awake, wake)

B.   Write sentences containing the following words:

laid	lying
lain	laying
rose	awoke
risen	set
raised	sat
woke	lay (past of lie)
awaked	

XVI. Exercise 4.   *Do you understand the use of the
auxiliary verbs " shall " and " will "?   Can you use them
correctly?*

EXPLANATION.   Compare the two groups of sentences
that follow:

1. I *shall* do the work.   1. I *will* do the work.
2. You *will* do the work.   2. You *shall* do the work.
3. He *will* do the work.   3. He *shall* do the work.

There is a decided difference in the meaning of these
two groups of sentences, and the difference lies in the
meaning of *shall* and *will*.

When a person says, " I shall do the work," he is making a statement that merely means," In the future I expect
to do the work."   But should he say, " I will do the work,"
he means that he fully intends to do the work, has made

up his mind to do it; he has, in fact, exerted his will. The first statement refers to simple future time; the second expresses determination or volition. These illustrations show that *shall* in the first person expresses simple future time, while *will* in the first person expresses volition.

In the second and third persons the verbs are reversed; *will* expresses simple future time and *shall* expresses determination. For example, your mother expresses determination when she says, "I will not go away"; "You shall study"; "He shall stay at home this evening."

An outline may help to show the correct use of these auxiliaries.

	Simple futurity	*Volition*
First person	I shall	I will
Second person	You will	You shall
Third person	He will	He shall

In questions always use *shall* with the first person. In the second and third persons use *shall* if *shall* is expected in the answer, and *will* when *will* is expected in the answer. For example,

First Person
    Simple Futurity Shall we go? (We shall)

Second Person
    Simple Futurity Shall you go? (I shall)
    Volition Will you go? (I will)

Third Person
    Simple Futurity Will he go? (He will)
    Volition Shall he go? (He shall)

Suppose some one made the statement, "I shall be glad when Christmas comes," and you wish to quote that remark. There are two ways in which you could do this. You could quote the exact words; as, " He said, ' I shall be glad when Christmas comes.' " Or you could give his thought but not his exact words; as, " He said that he should be glad when Christmas comes." This second method of quoting is known as an indirect quotation since the direct words of the speaker are not given.

When a direct quotation that contains *shall* is changed to an indirect quotation, use *shall* or *should* in the indirect quotation; if the direct quotation contains *will*, use *will* or *would* in the indirect quotation. The following illustrations may make this matter clear:

> *Direct:* I *shall* come tomorrow.
> *Indirect:* She said that she *should* come tomorrow.

> *Direct:* He *will* be away for a week.
> *Indirect:* They said that he *would* be away for a week.

We have learned four rules in this exercise that will eliminate errors in the use of *shall* and *will,* provided, of course, we keep them in mind constantly. It may be of value to have these facts summarized:

1. To express simple future time use:
   Shall in the first person
   Will in the second person
   Will in the third person
2. To express volition use:
   Will in the first person
   Shall in the second person
   Shall in the third person
3. In questions use:
   Shall in the first person

Shall in the second and third persons when *shall* is
    expected in the answer

Will in the second and third persons when *will* is
    expected in the answer

4. In indirect quotations use:

Should or *shall* when *shall* was used in the direct
    quotation

Would or *will* when *will* was used in the direct
    quotation.

DIRECTIONS. *A*. Write the following sentences filling
the blanks with *shall* or *will, should* or *would*. Tell
whether simple futurity or volition is expressed.

1. I hope that we —— be friends.
2. He says that he —— be fifteen years old next week.
3. When —— you return to New York?
4. How —— we be able to find his house?
5. I —— not trouble you.
6. —— I telephone the doctor?
7. They —— not go until their lessons are finished.
8. You —— surely fail if you do not study.
9. —— you go to the mountains with us?
10. How soon —— Harry leave?
11. —— they wait there until noon?
12. They —— see that I can succeed.
13. Harry said that he —— be glad to go with us. (What
     were Harry's words before they were changed to
     an indirect quotation?)
14. —— we take these magazines home?
15. Mother said that Harry —— accept the position.
     (What were Mother's exact words?)

16. You —— wait here until I allow you to go.
17. How much —— you contribute to the fund?
18. We —— not go until he arrives.
19. He says he —— not read that book under any condition.
20. When —— you be twenty years old?

B. Write sentences containing the following. Explain the meaning of each.

1. *Shall* in the first person.
2. *Will* in the first person.
3. *Shall* in the second person
4. *Will* in the third person
5. A question in the first person with *shall*
6. A question in the second person with *shall* or *will*
7. A question in the third person with *shall* or *will*
8. An indirect quotation with *would* or *will*
9. An indirect quotation with *should* or *shall*

XVI. Exercise 5. *Do you know when and how to use the subjunctive mood?*

EXPLANATION. In *Problem XV* we learned that a verb is in the subjunctive mood when it is used to express a wish, a condition contrary to fact, or something that is uncertain.

The forms of the subjunctive mood of all verbs except " be " are the same as those of the indicative mood except that the third person singular of the present and present perfect tenses do not end in " s." The subjunctive forms of " be " are very different from those of the indicative and should be reviewed.

Directions. *A.* Write the following sentences, filling the blanks with the correct forms of " be." State the reason for your choice of the indicative or subjunctive form. Remember that the subjunctive mood is used in expressing a wish or a condition contrary to fact.

1. If you —— I, should you buy this hat?
2. I wish that she —— coming tonight.
3. If she —— not so proud, I should be glad to help her.
4. I use her car as if it —— my own.
5. I wish I —— going with you.
6. If he —— well, we should like to have him go on the fishing trip.
7. He would come if he —— asked.
8. We wished he —— there with us.
9. If he —— here now, he would help us.
10. If I —— wealthy, I should try to be unselfish.

B. Write the following sentences using the correct forms of the verb " be ":

Three sentences expressing a condition contrary to fact
Three sentences expressing a wish
Three sentences expressing a condition not contrary to fact

XVI. Exercise 6. *Can you use infinitives correctly?*

Explanation. We have learned that when a verb is used as a noun, it is called an infinitive. There are two kinds of infinitives: infinitives in " ing " and infinitives with " to."

The one important thing to remember about infinitives in " ing " is that the noun or the pronoun that modifies such a verbal noun must be in the possessive case. For example, it is incorrect to say, " She talked of John going to Europe." This sentence should be: " She talked of *John's* going to Europe."

A few simple rules govern the use of infinitives with " to." The most important for your work are these:

1. An adverb or a phrase should never separate an infinitive from its sign. It is incorrect to say, " I want *to* thoroughly *understand* this work." Instead one should say, " I want *to understand* this work thoroughly." When a word or a phrase separates an infinitive from its sign, it is called a split infinitive. Do not allow yourself to use split infinitives.

2. The subject and the complement of an infinitive should be in the objective case; as,

    (1) She wants *me* to be secretary.

    (2) I believe the thief to be *her*.

3. One should guard against the use of " and " with the infinitive. For example, it is not correct to say, " I shall try *and* do good work." The sentence should be, " I shall try *to do* good work." When the coördinate conjunction " and " connects two verbs, they should be of equal value; that is, they should be two predicates or two infinitives or two participles. An infinitive must never be joined to the predicate by " and."

4. The present infinitive should be used unless the action of the infinitive took place prior to that of the predicate. In that case, the perfect infinitive is used. For example, in the sentence, " I intended to go," the present infinitive is used because the " going " took place after the " intending." One rarely needs to use the perfect infinitive.

DIRECTIONS. *A.* Write the following sentences correctly by

1. Inserting in the correct place the word found in parentheses at the end of the sentence, or by
2. Filling the blanks with the correct form found in parentheses at the end of the sentence.

1. I hope to use correct English. (some day)
2. She will try —— work more conscientiously. (and, to)
3. It is my aim to finish my course. (soon)
4. My mother told me to fight. (never)
5. We tried to rest, but that was impossible. (quietly)
6. Are you willing to contribute money or time? (either)
7. It is a good thing to sit and think. (quietly)
8. Do not attempt —— jump across that stream. (to, and)
9. I like to read my books. (silently)
10. He desired to purchase that ring. (secretly)
11. I had not thought of —— coming before Christmas. (him, his)
12. I hoped —— her. (to see, to have seen)
13. I expect the visitor to be ——. (she, her)
14. The old lady does not like to be disturbed. (suddenly)
15. We had not thought of —— being responsible for the fire. (Jim, Jim's)

B. Write five sentences illustrating the rule for the possessive modifier of an infinitive in " ing."

C. Write three sentences to illustrate each rule that governs the use of an infinitive with " to."

XVI. Exercise 7. *Do the participles in your sentences always modify some word?*

EXPLANATION. When we were studying the various forms of verbs, we learned that a participle is a verbal adjective that must always modify some word. People who are ignorant of the rules of correct English often use participles that are not modifiers. Since such constructions do not belong to any word in the sentence, they are called " dangling " or " hanging."

The sentence, " Opening the window, there was a terrific explosion," is incorrectly expressed because the participial phrase " opening the window " does not modify any word in the sentence. This is a dangling participle and is a serious mistake. To correct the sentence, an antecedent for the participle must be supplied. When this is inserted, the sentence becomes, " Opening the window, I heard a terrific explosion." A still better way to correct such an expression is to change the participial phrase to a dependent clause. Then the sentence will be: " As I opened the window, I heard a terrific explosion."

Note the position of the participial phrase in " I heard a strange sound walking in the garden." The idea seems to be that the sound was walking in the garden; this, of course, is impossible. The phrase modifies " I " and should be placed at the beginning of the sentence near to its antecedent. If the phrase is changed into a dependent clause, it may stand where it is.

A comma is used to set off a participial phrase that comes at the beginning of a sentence.

DIRECTIONS. *A.* Write ten sentences containing participial phrases. Punctuate each correctly. Do not confuse a participial phrase with a sentence. Remember that a participle is a modifier and not the predicate. The participle in "ing" is a modifier, while the infinitive in "ing" is a verbal noun.

B. Rewrite each sentence in A, changing the participial phrase to a dependent clause.

C. Read the following sentences and make a list of those that are correct. Make another list of the incorrect sentences and tell why they are incorrect.

1. I was able to catch my hat, running down the street.
2. There sat my dear brother, nursing a little sick kitten.
3. We saw a wonderful sight, standing on the mountain top.
4. Opening the window, I heard a cry of distress.
5. Entering the attic, the stairs were steep and winding.
6. Having slept for only a few minutes, it seemed as if an hour had passed.
7. Standing on the mountain top, we saw a wonderful sight.
8. Running down the street, I was able to catch my hat.
9. I fell and broke my ankle, coming home from school.
10. Entering the attic, we climbed the stairs that were steep and winding.

XVI. Exercise 8. *Are you able to choose the correct tense and voice for your verbs? Do you shift from one tense to another when you write a story?*

EXPLANATION. What do you notice about the verbs in the following paragraph?

Yesterday I went to see my grandmother. When I arrive there, she asks me to pick some cherries for her.

I was glad to do this. I get the ladder and climb up to the top of the tree. Before I knew it, I had a quart of big red cherries for her. When these are shown to her, she is happy. So was I a little later, for she makes them into a pie for me.

A person has no difficulty in knowing that the fault in these sentences is the constant changing of the tenses. The first verb is in the past tense; the next two are in the present tense. Then comes one in the past tense, and this is followed by two in the present tense. Such writing, of course, is unworthy of high school students, but some high school students do not seem to be able to do much better.

When you are writing a letter, a composition, or a paper for some class, be sure that the verbs agree in tense unless the meaning demands a change. Decide at the beginning what tense you intend to use, and use it constantly. This will result in what is known as unity, a quality that every letter and composition should possess.

It would be wise at this time to read again *Exercises* 4 and 5 of *Problem* XV. These deal with the tenses of verbs. Remember that each tense denotes some special time. Since this is so, one should not change from one tense to another unless the meaning demands it.

The same rule holds true with the voice of verbs. Do not shift from active to passive and vice versa unless the meaning demands it. In the paragraph quoted above notice the sentence, " When these are shown to her, she is happy." All the verbs in the preceding sentences are in the active voice; " are shown " is in the passive voice. There is no reason why it should be. The sentence would be better expressed if the voice had not been changed; then the unity of the voice of the verbs would not have been violated. Reread *Exercise 2* of *Problem* XV to review the important facts about voice.

DIRECTIONS. *A.* Write the paragraph in the explanation, changing all verbs so that they will agree in tense and voice unless the meaning demands a change. Underline the verbs that are predicates.

B. Write a paragraph of eight or ten sentences telling what you did last Saturday. Underline all verbs. Decide upon the tense you intend to use, and then use it throughout the paragraph unless the meaning demands a change.

XVI. Exercise 9. *Do you always use verbs correctly? Do you understand the exact meaning of verbs?*

EXPLANATION. A few verbs must be studied individually since they often cause trouble.

1. " Ought " is not a participle; therefore it cannot be used with " had " or " have." It is correct to say, " I ought to do that work "; but it is never correct to use such an expression as, " I had ought " or " She hadn't ought."

2. " Got " is not an auxiliary; consequently it cannot be used with another verb; as, " The dog got shot." Say, " The dog was shot." " Got " should not be used to express possession; as, " I have got an apple " or " I got a new dress." These sentences should be: " I have an apple " and " I have a new dress."

3. It is never correct to say " ain't." It is sometimes used as a contraction of " are not," " am not," and

"is not" by very illiterate people. These sentences are correct.

I *am not* going. (There is no contraction for "am not")

She *is not* going. (She *isn't* going.)

Are you *not* going? (*Aren't* you going?)

Am I *not* going? (There is no contraction.)

They *are not* going. (They *aren't* going.)

To use "ain't" shows that one is exceedingly ignorant of correct English.

4. "Of" is sometimes used for "have." For example, the sentence, "I might have gone," is written "I might of gone." This mistake occurs when a person is careless about his pronunciation. If you have acquired this habit, get rid of it at once.

5. The two verbs "let" and "leave" are often confused and used incorrectly. "Let" means to allow; "leave" means to depart or to let remain; as, "I am leaving today," or "I shall leave the book here." Observe their meaning when you use them. Never say, "Leave me do it." Say, "Allow me to do it" or "Let me do it."

6. Two other verbs that are often used incorrectly are "can" and "may." "Can" denotes power and ability, while "may" denotes permission. They cannot be interchanged. Say, "May I go?" not "Can I go?" Watch your speech to see that you use these verbs correctly.

There are other errors that are made in the use of verbs, but they are minor ones and need not be listed here. Watch your speech and written expressions constantly; do not allow yourself to use any form of a verb that is incorrect. If you are in earnest about this matter, you will eventually acquire the habit of speaking correctly, and unconsciously you will choose the correct word.

DIRECTIONS. *A.* Write the following sentences, filling each blank with the correct form. State the reason for your choice.

1. You —— to read so late at night. (hadn't ought, ought not)
2. That poor little boy ——. (got hurt, was hurt)
3. She —— gone. (could have, could of)
4. He —— afraid of that engine. (ain't, isn't)
5. Mother, please —— me have a dollar for my books. (leave, let)
6. My father says I —— go to the beach for a week. (can, may)
7. —— she a dear little child? (isn't, ain't)
8. I —— do this work easily. (can, may)
9. Mary —— a beautiful new bookcase. (has, has got)
10. You —— to tease those little children. (hadn't ought, ought not)
11. —— I read this book, Miss Smith? (can, may)
12. Several men —— when the tank burst. (got burned, were burned)
13. —— a member of the club? (ain't I, am I not)
14. I —— not go until I have finished my work. (can, may)
15. If she —— the test, she —— passed. (had of taken, had taken; would of, would have)
16. Harry —— a new suit of clothes. (has got, has)
17. My teacher —— me do that for her. (will let, will leave)

18. I suppose I —— to talk in this way. (hadn't ought, ought not)
19. —— he going to the picnic. (ain't, isn't)
20. —— a good student? (ain't I, am I not)

B. Write three correctly expressed sentences to illustrate each rule that is given in the explanation.

XVI. Exercise 10. *How well can you use verbs?*

EXPLANATION. All of the important facts about verbs have been explained in the preceding exercises. It would be wise for you to read over the explanation in each exercise, in order to be certain that you understand every point. When you are writing or speaking, remember these facts:

1. The predicate of a sentence agrees with the subject in person and number.
2. The past participle is used in forming every perfect tense and never stands alone. The past tense is never used with the auxiliary " have " or " had." It always stands alone.
3. Certain verbs are always transitive and must have a receiver of the action. This is generally the object complement. Other verbs are always intransitive, and must never have an object.
4. *Shall* and *will* have very definite meanings and cannot be interchanged.
5. The subjunctive mood is used to express a wish or a condition contrary to fact. The form of the subjunctive mood of the verb *be* is very irregular.
6. Infinitives must never be split.
7. An infinitive must be in the present tense unless the meaning demands the perfect tense.

8. The subject and the complement of an infinitive must always be in the objective case.

9. Participles that do not modify any word in a sentence should never appear in one's expressions.

10. The tense and the voice of the verbs in a letter or a composition should not be changed unless the meaning demands it.

11. Certain improper expressions must not be used; such as, " hadn't ought," " got hurt," " ain't," etc.

You should make it a point to master each of these facts before you attempt to write the assignment.

DIRECTIONS. *A.* Listen to the speech of those about you and make a list of fifteen errors in the use of verbs. Write the sentence containing the error and then correct the expression. State the reason for your correction.

B. Write the following sentences, filling each blank with one of the words found in parentheses at the end of the sentence. State the reason for your choice.

1. —— you happy when you saw your mother? (wasn't, weren't)

2. One of the boys in that club —— very talented. (is, are)

3. There —— a few blossoms on the trees. (is, are)

4. Some one has —— that dish. (broke, broken)

5. When a jury —— in a verdict, —— discharged immediately. (hand, hands; they are, it is)

6. Every one of the students —— a reason for his choice. (has, have)

7. They —— the carpet on the floor. (lay, laid)

8. He expected her ——. (to call, to have called)

9. When —— you in Chicago? (was, were)

10. I wish he —— here now. (was, were)

11. When a person like you —— such a story, I am inclined to think it is true. (believe, believes)

12. Any one that can remain calm at such a time —— worthy of praise. (is, are)

13. They —— in the grass all night. (laid, lay)

14. A little girl, accompanied by her nurse and three friends, —— just left. (has, have)

15. When they spoke of —— being president, I was too surprised to say a word. (me, my)

16. I will try ——. (to never fail, never to fail)

17. Each of them —— trying to speak correct English. (is, are)

18. —— you call for Mother this afternoon. (shall, will)

19. John, as well as James and Henry, —— coming here for the holidays. (is, are)

20. There is no danger of —— running away. (his, him)

21. If I —— you, I should not buy so expensive a hat. (was, were)

22. I —— do that whether she is here or not. (shall, will)

23. The committee —— a meeting every Tuesday evening. (hold, holds)

24. I had hoped —— him. (to see, to have seen)

25. —— I go to the city, Mother? (can, may)

26. Shall I —— here? (set, sit)

27. The papers of every student —— returned when they are corrected. (is, are)

28. I did not think that I —— enjoy the party, but Mother said that she ——. (should, would)

29. That is one of the saddest stories that —— ever been written. (has, have)

30. Where —— you when I called? (was, were)

31. When I was —— on the ground, Dash —— down beside me. (lying, laying; laid, lay)

32. There she —— absolutely helpless. (lay, laid)

33. —— your basket down and then come and —— with me. (sit, set)

34. They began to come, and immediately I —— to prepare dinner. (have, had)

35. He —— like to have his mother go away. (don't, doesn't)

36. What —— we do if we cannot find a garage? (shall, will)

37. There —— to be a doubt in your mind. (seem, seems)

38. —— you at the concert yesterday? (was, were)

39. She —— to act so foolishly. (hadn't ought, ought not)

40. Each pupil in this class —— to be studious. (seem, seems)

41. My brother sat down and —— me all about the party. (tells, told)

42. If I —— going, I should be glad. (was, were)

43. —— you study French next year? (shall, will)

44. We hope——. (to soon be at home, to be at home soon)

45. Poor old Towser! He has —— on the damp porch all night. (laid, lain)

46. —— I telephone you tomorrow? (shall, will)

47. She —— when the glass broke. (got hurt, was hurt)

48. The idea of —— renting a machine had not occurred to us. (John, John's)

49. —— I be excused to go to the game, Mr. Lane? (can, may)

50. He said he —— be glad to accept the invitation. (should, would)
51. She —— her work well. (did, done)
52. I will try —— get my work done early. (and, to)
53. Mother will not —— me go. (leave, let)
54. I —— them when they drove past in a big machine. (saw, seen)
55. —— you see him in the morning? (shall, will)

THE CORRECT USE OF VERBS AND PRONOUNS

Purpose of Study

We have said that our aim in taking this course is to learn to write and speak English that is absolutely correct. The only way we can accomplish our goal is to know the rules that govern the use of words, and then have so much drill in applying these rules that we shall eventually speak and write correctly from mere force of habit.

Nearly all the mistakes in the use of words are made with pronouns and verbs. We shall be satisfied with nothing less than the absolute mastery of these words. Since this is our desire, the purpose of *Problem XVII* is to give more drill in the correct use of these words.

Exercises

1. Selecting the correct pronoun and verb
2. Selecting the correct pronoun and verb
3. Selecting the correctly written sentence
4. Selecting the correctly written sentence
5. Revising the incorrect forms
6. Revising the incorrect forms

XVII. Exercise 1. *Can you always select the correct verb or pronoun?*

EXPLANATION.   Since this problem is for the purpose of drilling on the facts learned in *Problems XIII, XIV, XV,* and *XVI,* it is unnecessary to repeat the information given there.   Consult those problems whenever you are in doubt.

DIRECTIONS.   Write the following sentences, filling each blank with one of the words found in parentheses at the end of the sentence.   State the reason for your choice.

1. Each of the boys —— left —— books at home. (has, have; their, his)
2. The man —— you want is not here.   (who, whom)
3. Who ever heard of —— running for Governor! (John, John's)
4. Tell —— and —— the story.   (she, her; I, me)
5. We —— the children playing in the water.   (saw, seen)
6. It is ——.   (I, me)
7. Is it —— —— —— hurt when the boiler ——? (him, he; who, whom; got, was; bursted, burst)
8. They —— that song many times.   (sang, sung)
9. I —— into the house before I knew that Mr. Jones was there.   (ran, run)
10. I do not know —— to ask.   (who, whom)
11. I tried —— as I went up the stairs.   (to quietly walk, to walk quietly)
12. The little child fell into the water and was ——. (drowned, drownded)
13. I intend to select the person —— you think will be satisfactory.   (who, whom)
14. The jury —— dismissed after —— had given —— verdict.   (was, were; it, they; its, their)
15. His report on electrical appliances, especially those used in homes, —— very interesting.   (was, were)

16. She said that she —— try to go. (should, would)
17. —— do you want to see? (who, whom)
18. When —— you at my house? (was, were)
19. Is that —— —— gave the interesting lecture? (she, her; who, whom)
20. Please —— the books where they are supposed to ——. (lie, lay)

XVII. Exercise 2. *How well can you select the correct verb or pronoun?*

EXPLANATION. If there was any sentence in *Exercise 1* that caused you difficulty, make sure that you master that subject now. It is possible for you to use these forms correctly at all times if you will give this problem careful study.

DIRECTIONS. Write the following sentences, filling each blank with one of the words found in parentheses at the end of the sentence. Make any other changes that are necessary. State the reason for your choice.

1. —— —— and Mildred play with —— children? (can, may; I, me; them, those)
2. I had never heard of —— having traveled abroad. (his, him)
3. I rewarded the child —— I believe had done the best work. (who, whom)
4. That tank has ——. (burst, bursted)
5. I do not know —— he is. (who, whom)
6. —— and my sister like to read good books. (I, myself, me)
7. —— me go with John and ——. (leave, let; her, she)

8. —— I —— the table? (shall, will; sit, set)

9. If I —— going, I should wear a heavy coat. (was, were)

10. —— do you think that big man is? (who, whom)

11. She —— know —— you are. (don't, doesn't; who, whom)

12. I thought you —— at home. (was, were)

13. —— you give Mary and —— a ride? (can, may; me, I)

14. Goodness! That is —— —— took the watch. (himself, he, him; who, whom)

15. I expect the stranger to be ——. (she, her)

16. —— you come tomorrow? (shall, will)

17. The boys —— first; the men followed. (came, come)

18. When the boys have ——, we —— do the work. (went, gone; shall, will)

19. I —— fall unless one of you men —— me. (shall, will; help, helps)

20. He expected —— the prize. (to win, to have won)

XVII. Exercise 3. *Can you distinguish correctly written sentences from sentences that contain incorrect expressions?*

Explanation. If you understood every sentence in *Exercise 2*, you are ready for *Exercise 3*. Master each exercise before you go on to the next one. This is the only way you will master the entire subject.

Directions. Each of the following groups contains two sentences: one is correctly written; the other contains words that are used incorrectly. Select the correct sentence from each group and tell why it is correct by giving the rules that govern the words that are used correctly.

1. (*a*) If you were I, what should you do?
   (*b*) If you was me, what should you do?
2. (*a*) Was it him who bought the umbrella?
   (*b*) Was it he who bought the umbrella?
3. (*a*) Did you hear about his asking for a copy of that book?
   (*b*) Did you hear about him asking for a copy of that book?
4. (*a*) To who will we send invitations?
   (*b*) To whom shall we send invitations?
5. (*a*) I will be glad to see yourself and your friend at my home Tuesday afternoon.
   (*b*) I shall be glad to see you and your friend at my home Tuesday afternoon.
6. (*a*) I saw a funny sight today.
   (*b*) I seen a funny sight today.
7. (*a*) Each of them boys have lost their locker key.
   (*b*) Each of those boys has lost his locker key.
8. (*a*) I and Mary was so tired that we laid down to rest.
   (*b*) Mary and I were so tired that we lay down to rest.
9. (*a*) I will try to do my work carefully.
   (*b*) I will try and carefully do my work.
10. (*a*) When he had finished his work, he laid his books away.
    (*b*) When he had finished his work, he lay his books away.
11. (*a*) Is there any danger of him coming tonight?
    (*b*) Is there any danger of his coming tonight?
12. (*a*) John, the boy who sells fruit, he got hurt today.
    (*b*) John, the boy who sells fruit, was hurt today.

13. (a) Can you learn me how to speak correctly?
    (b) Can you teach me how to speak correctly?
    > *Note:* We have not discussed " learn " and
    > " teach " in any problem. Consult the dic-
    > tionary to learn their meanings. Then you
    > will have no difficulty in knowing which
    > sentence is correct.

14. (a) Did you expect her to be I?
    (b) Did you expect her to be me?

15. (a) Nothing can ever come between you and I.
    (b) Nothing can ever come between you and me.

16. (a) He tried to quietly tell me where he had lain
    the book.
    (b) He tried to tell me quietly where he had laid
    the book.

17. (a) Where were you when I telephoned? Was you
    lying down?
    (b) Where was you when I telephoned? Was you
    laying down?

18. (a) When I saw her coming, I ran around the corner
    and into the house.
    (b) When I seen her coming, I ran around the corner
    and into the house.

19. (a) Do you know whom each of them boys are?
    (b) Do you know who each of those boys is?

20. (a) We looked as if we were ready to lie down and
    never rise.
    (b) We looked as if we were ready to lay down and
    never raise.

XVII. Exercise 4. *How well can you distinguish correctly written sentences from sentences that contain incorrect expressions?*

EXPLANATION. It is impossible to list all the mistakes that are used with pronouns and verbs. Especially is this true of those mistakes that are made because one does not know the meaning of a word. Take, for example, the words "learn" and "teach." If a person consults a dictionary, he will not use these incorrectly. It would be wise for you to have a dictionary of your own. Keep it with you so that you can consult it when in doubt. If you persist in this habit, you will eventually gain a large vocabulary that will be of great value to you. Furthermore, you will not make mistakes that arise from not knowing the meaning of words.

DIRECTIONS. Each of the following groups contains two sentences: one is correctly written; the other contains words that are used incorrectly. Select the correct sentence from each group and tell why it is correct by giving the rules that govern the words that are used correctly.

1. (a) Have you heard of his being given the position of postmaster?
   (b) Have you heard of him being given the position of postmaster?
2. (a) She don't seem to want to go.
   (b) She doesn't seem to want to go.
3. (a) Us boys like to go on fishing trips.
   (b) We boys like to go on fishing trips.
4. (a) If she was here, she would enjoy the new house.
   (b) If she were here, she would enjoy the new house.
5. (a) You ought not to let your mother work so hard.
   (b) You hadn't ought to let your mother work so hard.
6. (a) Each one of them seem to be anxiously waiting for an opportunity to speak.

    (*b*) Each one of them seems to be waiting anxiously for an opportunity to speak.

7. (*a*) Is it me who you want to see?
  (*b*) Is it I whom you want to see?

8. (*a*) When I had lain my bundles on the table, I set down to rest.
  (*b*) When I had laid my bundles on the table, I sat down to rest.

9. (*a*) Have you saw her recently?
  (*b*) Have you seen her recently?

10. (*a*) Is it him whom you think is coming?
   (*b*) Is it he who you think is coming?

11. (*a*) My friend and I shall call tomorrow.
   (*b*) Me and my friend will call tomorrow.

12. (*a*) She has not drunk any water for a week.
   (*b*) She has not drank any water for a week.

13. (*a*) I wish I was going with them boys.
   (*b*) I wish I were going with those boys.

14. (*a*) I finally caught my hat, running down the street.
   (*b*) Running down the street, I finally caught my hat.

15. (*a*) I awoke suddenly and then ran to wake my brother.
   (*b*) I waked suddenly and then ran to awake my brother.

16. (*a*) Listen to him playing. Ain't it beautiful!
   (*b*) Listen to his playing. Isn't it beautiful!

17. (*a*) Was you glad when the team won?
   (*b*) Were you glad when the team won?

18. (*a*) How many of them dishes have you broke?
   (*b*) How many of those dishes have you broken?

19. (*a*) When can you send some groceries to her and I?
   (*b*) When can you send some groceries to her and me?

20. (a) Who do you suppose the visitor is?
    (b) Whom do you suppose the visitor is?

XVII. Exercise 5. *Are you able to recognize the mistakes in an incorrectly expressed sentence? Can you restate the sentence in correct form and give the reason for each change?*

EXPLANATION. In the preceding exercises we have always had the possibility of choosing the correct form. Now we shall see how well we can correct sentences without having this choice.

DIRECTIONS. Many of the following sentences contain grammatical errors. Revise those that are incorrectly written, and give the reason for each change.

1. I was so sleepy that I laid down for an hour.
2. Will you be here Monday?
3. I seen a man which looked like my uncle.
4. When I saw those boys help theirselves to the refreshments, I ran to catch them.
5. Can you tell me whom that tall man is?
6. Leave me go.
7. Do you think us boys would do such a thing?
8. No one among those people want to give away everything they own.
9. Some one called while you was away.
10. Me and John asked them boys to go with us.
11. Don't he sing beautifully!
12. I am as old as her, but that is known only to you and I.
13. There was so many people in the hall that we was unable to easily walk.

14. If she was older, I think she could do the work easily.
15. Give Harry and I some money.
16. Is it her whom they think have the keys?
17. Can we have these books for an hour?
18. My mother and myself often read aloud in the evening.
19. Each of the rooms were painted white.
20. Yourself and your friends are invited to spend the evening with my mother and I.

XVII. Exercise 6. *How well can you recognize the mistakes in incorrectly expressed sentences? How well can you restate the sentence in correct form and give the reason for each change?*

EXPLANATION. If there is any sentence in *Exercise 5* that you do not fully understand, return to it before you go on with *Exercise 6*. Do not be satisfied with just guessing at the correct expressions; know definitely why one form is correct and why another is incorrect. Pay special attention to the reasons that you write.

DIRECTIONS. Many of the following sentences contain grammatical errors. Revise those that are incorrectly written and give the reason for each change.

1. There was only two items that they didn't mention.
2. They must of been here while we was away.
3. Mr. Jones, who sings in our choir, he has a beautiful voice.
4. Either Mrs. Hamilton or Mrs. Reed are intending to bring the ice cream.
5. Uncle Joe brought Janet and I gifts from abroad.
6. We hadn't ought to leave grandma alone in the house.

7. I shall never be so thoughtless again; of that I am certain.
8. He done his work hurriedly, for me and him was going away.
9. Set down and talk with me.
10. The little child was laying on the grass.
11. He said that he would return as soon as possible.
12. I insist that the boys will not interrupt the speaker.
13. Can Johnny play with me and Jim?
14. John has got a new car what runs very easily.
15. Neither the boy nor the girl were ready to start.
16. I know one who I shall ask, but it won't be her.
17. No one seen them except I.

   (*Note:* What part of speech is " except " ?

18. I and John hoped to have seen Edgar when we was in Boston.
19. Each of us were eager to hear the new organ.
20. My mother will not hear of me being out so late.

A STUDY OF THE FORMS AND USES OF ADJECTIVES AND ADVERBS

Purpose of Study

People who are careless in their speech often use adjectives when they should use adverbs, and they also use adverbs when they should use adjectives. The use of adjectives and adverbs is governed by certain very definite rules which we must know if we are to use these words correctly. After we have learned the rules, we must have drill in applying them. This is the purpose of *Problem XVIII*.

Exercises

1. Recognition of adjectives and adverbs
2. Correct use of adjectives and adverbs
3. Recognition of the degree of adjectives and adverbs
4. Correct use of adjectives and adverbs in the three degrees
5. Recognition of double negative
6. Correct placing of modifiers
7. Recognition of adjectives as subjective complements
8. Some special uses of adjectives and adverbs
9. Selecting the correct adjective and adverb

10. Distinguishing correctly written sentences from incorrectly written sentences
11. Recognition and revision of incorrect expressions

XVIII. Exercise 1. *Are you able to distinguish adverbs from adjectives?*

EXPLANATION. We have learned that an adjective is a word that modifies a noun by describing or limiting it.

The two uses of adjectives are illustrated in the following sentences:

1. The *little* boy ran to his mother. (" Little " is a modifier of the noun " boy.")
2. The girl is *little*. (" Little " is a subjective complement.)

Adverbs are modifiers also, but they never modify nouns or pronouns. Instead they modify verbs, adjectives, or other adverbs. They are easily recognized by asking the questions: how, when, where, or why. The only word that can answer any of these questions is an adverb.

Many adverbs are formed by adding " ly," to an adjective. For example, notice the following lists:

Adjectives	*Adverbs*
quick	quickly
immediate	immediately
diligent	diligently
silent	silently
interesting	interestingly

Whenever you wish to know whether a word is an adjective or an adverb, decide what the word does. If it modifies a noun or a pronoun, it is an adjective; if it modifies a verb, an adverb, or an adjective, it is an adverb.

Directions. *A*. Make a list of the adjectives and another list of the adverbs that you find in the following sentences:

1. Did you lose your new glasses there?
2. I seldom go into those little stores.
3. She learns her English lessons easily.
4. Those orange trees have grown very rapidly.
5. Marian was the best speller in the class.
6. This red apple tastes sweet.
7. We really want to learn to use correct English.
8. Do you feel bad?
9. The boy looked at the closed door angrily.
10. She was sick in the night.
11. That boy is very good.
12. The rose smells sweet.
13. She is very happy about that business transaction.
14. The boy looked angry.
15. He does his work well every day.
16. Try to write and speak correctly.
17. The dish felt hot.
18. Did he speak respectfully to his teacher?
19. An exceedingly brilliant boy entered the contest.
20. He suddenly became sick.

B. 1. Write sentences containing the following adjectives:

good	quick
sick	well
fine	merry
sweet	distinct
angry	rapid

2. Write sentences containing the following adverbs:

sweetly	rapidly
angrily	boldly
quickly	clearly
distinctly	thoroughly
well	merrily

XVIII. Exercise 2. *Do you ever use an adverb for an adjective, or an adjective for an adverb?*

EXPLANATION. In *Exercise 1* we learned that adjectives modify nouns, and that adverbs modify verbs, adjectives, and other adverbs. People who are careless about their written or spoken expressions often confuse these words. Let us look at some of the most common errors that arise from confusing adjectives and adverbs.

1. The expression, " He is a real fine singer," is incorrect, for " real " is an adjective meaning " genuine," and can not be substituted for the adverb " very " or " exceedingly." The speaker should have said, " He is a very fine singer," or " He is an exceedingly fine singer."

2. The adjective " real " must not be used for the adverb " really," which means " actually," or " in truth." It is correct to say, " We really tried to do our best."

3. " Sure " is an adjective and is incorrectly used in such an expression as, " I sure did have a good time." The correct form is, " I surely did have a good time."

4. Adjectives ending in " y " or " ly " are often confused with adverbs. For example, in the sentence, " She dresses gaudy," " gaudy " should be changed

to the adverb because it tells how she dresses. When it is corrected the sentence reads, "She dresses gaudily."

5. "Almost" and "most" do not have the same meaning. "Almost" means "nearly," while "most" is the sign of the superlative degree and means "in the highest degree." We may say, "She is most patient with children;" but we must not say, "We are most home."

6. A very serious error is made when the adverbs "there" and "here" are used to modify a noun; as, "I don't own this here book." Never use such an expression in anything you write or speak.

7. Another example of the confusion of an adverb and an adjective is seen in the use of the adverb "near-by." We may say, "The store is near-by;" but we must not use this word as an adjective and say, "We went to a near-by store." Such an expression must be changed to, "We went to a store that was near-by."

8. "Near" is not an adverb and must not be used for one. Therefore we cannot say, "I was near starved." The sentence should be, "I was nearly starved."

These illustrations show a few of the errors that are made in the use of adverbs.

DIRECTIONS. *A.* Write the following sentences, filling the blank in each with one of the words found in parentheses after the sentence. State the reason for your choice.

1. He's a —— friendly man. (real, very)
2. I was —— as hungry as he. (most, almost)

3. —— lady has a camera.   (that, that there)
4. How —— she dances!   (pretty, prettily)
5. She was —— dead when they found her.   (near, nearly)
6. We visited a —— church.   (near-by, that was near-by)
7. Is —— picture yours?   (this, this here)
8. She —— is a bright little child.   (sure, surely)
9. He —— always helps his mother with the work.   (most, almost)
10. Have you been a —— good boy.   (real, very)
11. I —— wish I had that car.   (sure, surely)
12. I am —— exhausted.   (near, nearly)
13. We can —— always find something to do to help others.   (almost, most)
14. A meeting was held in a —— hall.   (near-by, neighboring)
15. He's —— good to the children.   (real, very)
16. I was —— delighted to see my cousin.   (most, almost)
17. I am —— tired out.   (almost, most)
18. He is a —— interesting speaker.   (most, almost)
19. I —— do like that book.   (surely, sure)
20. Do you like to see a person dress ——?   (gaudy, gaudily)

B. Write sentences to illustrate each of the points explained in this exercise.

XVIII. Exercise 3. *Can you recognize the various forms of adjectives and adverbs?*

EXPLANATION. Notice the italicized words in the following sentences:

1. The fruit is *sweet*.
2. The cake is *sweeter*.
3. The candy is *sweetest*.

In these sentences we learn that the fruit and the cake and the candy have the quality of sweetness, but that they do not possess it in the same degree. The cake, for example, is *sweeter* than the fruit, and the candy is the *sweetest* of the three. This change is called comparison. There are three different degrees of comparison: the positive, the comparative, and the superlative.

The positive degree denotes the simple quality; as, " The fruit is *sweet*." The comparative degree denotes more of the quality; as, " The cake is *sweeter*." The superlative degree denotes most of the quality; as, " The candy is the *sweetest*."

If you will notice again the sentences given at the beginning of the explanation, you will see that the comparative of " sweet," which is " sweeter," is formed by adding " er " to the positive degree; the superlative, " sweetest," is formed by adding " est " to the positive.

Not all adjectives are compared in this way. Note the italicized words in the following sentences:

1. The picture is *beautiful*.
2. This picture is *more beautiful*.
3. That picture is *most beautiful*.

These sentences show that the adjective " beautiful " is compared by prefixing " more " to the positive to form the comparative, and " most " to form the superlative.

Most adjectives are compared by one of these two methods. There are, in addition, a few adjectives that are compared irregularly. Notice the irregular comparison of the adjective " good " in the following sentences:

1. Mary does *good* work.
2. John does *better* work.
3. James does the *best* work.

The preceding illustrations show three ways of comparing adjectives. Let us summarize them:

1. Adjectives are compared by adding " er " and " est." These are added to adjectives of one syllable and to a few of two syllables.
2. Adjectives are compared by prefixing " more " and " most." These words are used in comparing adjectives of three syllables and some adjectives of two syllables.
3. Some adjectives are compared irregularly; they change their form for the comparative and superlative degrees.

Sometimes one wishes to give the idea that an object possesses a certain quality in a less degree than some other object. This descending scale of comparison is made by prefixing the adverbs " less " and " least " to the positive to form the comparative and superlative; as, " She is less anxious to go than I," or " She is the least anxious of all."

Adverbs also have the property of comparison. The rules that govern the comparison of adjectives also govern the comparison of adverbs.

Some adjectives and adverbs can not be compared at all. The sense of an expression determines whether the quality expressed by the word can have the different degrees. For example, we cannot say, " This plant is more dead than that one." Such an expression is ludicrous and impossible.

The following list contains the comparison of the most common adjectives and adverbs that are compared irregularly.

Positive	Comparative	Superlative
good, well	better	best
ill, bad	worse	worst
many, much	more	most
little	less	least
far	farther, further	farthest, furthest
late	later, latter	latest, last
old	older, elder	oldest, eldest
	former	foremost, first

DIRECTIONS. *A.* Make a list of the adjectives and the adverbs in the following sentences. After each word tell whether it is an adjective or an adverb and state its degree. If the word cannot be compared, do not give its degree.

1. She does her work more thoroughly than I.
2. How well he sings!
3. I could scarcely recognize an object in the dark room.
4. Please be more thoughtful when you enter the house.
5. He is the taller of the two boys.
6. This is the best handwriting in the class.
7. The largest girl in the class is also the youngest.
8. She has more money than I.
9. That is the saddest story I have ever read.
10. John ran fast and caught the stage.
11. The smaller children played more merrily than the larger ones.
12. He was a very stern man.
13. The first boy in that row is a cousin of mine.
14. Come back sooner this time.
15. She is more beautiful than Helen.

16. He spoke more respectfully to his mother than he did to his father.
17. She is the last person whom I expect to see today.
18. I was less nervous about the meeting than she was.
19. Mary sings well, but Mildred sings better.
20. This lesson is less difficult than some that we have had.

B. Write ten sentences, each containing an adjective or an adverb in the comparative or superlative degree. Illustrate each kind of comparison.

XVIII. Exercise 4. *Do you know how to use adjectives and adverbs in the three degrees?*

EXPLANATION. In the last exercise we learned that many adjectives denote different degrees of a quality. Errors are sometimes made in the choice of the degree, for the three degrees can not be used indiscriminately. Note the following sentences:

1. The boy is taller than the girl.
2. She is the tallest person in the room.

In sentence 1 two individuals are compared, and the comparative degree is used. In the second sentence more than two persons are compared, and the superlative degree is used.

These sentences illustrate the use of the comparative and superlative degrees. If two persons or objects are compared, the comparative degree is used; if more than two persons or objects are compared, the superlative degree is used.

The sentence, " He is the oldest of the two," is incorrect, for " oldest " is the superlative degree. Since only two persons are mentioned, the comparative degree must be used. The sentence should be, " He is the older of the two."

The same rule is true of adverbs. In " He walks more slowly than I," the comparative degree is used because only two persons are mentioned.

Watch everything you write and speak. Do not allow yourself to make errors in the choice of the degree of an adjective or an adverb.

DIRECTIONS. *A.* Write the following sentences, filling the blank in each with one of the words found in parentheses after the sentence. State the degree and the reason for your choice.

1. Which is the —— book, " Rab and His Friends " or " The Call of the Wild? " (better, best)
2. Which is ——, John or Henry? (taller, tallest)
3. She is the —— of all the girls. (livelier, liveliest)
4. Who walked ——, you or Harry? (farthest, farther)
5. Of her two children, John is the ——. (stronger, strongest)
6. Which of the two children is —— careful in his work? (more, most)
7. Which of your hands is the ——? (cleaner, cleanest)
8. Marian is the —— of the two, is she not? (older, oldest)
9. Do you know who the —— pupil in this school is? (younger, youngest)
10. That is the —— joke in the paper. (funnier, funniest)
11. William is the —— courteous of all the young men. (most, more)
12. Which of the two men is the —— likely to be elected? (more, most)

13. Which is the —— way to Chicago, the Canadian Pacific or the Union Pacific? (cheaper, cheapest)

14. There is not much difference between the two boys except that John is the ——. (taller, tallest)

15. Which is the ——, Mt. Rainier, or Mt. Whitney? (higher, highest)

16. I shall buy the —— expensive of those two coats, for I like it ——. (less, least; better, best)

17. This room is —— comfortable, for the other has no large windows. (more, most)

18. She is the —— agreeable of the two sisters. (more, most)

19. That is the —— sight I have ever seen. (lovelier, loveliest)

20. I had several pencils, but I have lost the —— one. (better, best)

B. 1. Write sentences containing the comparative degree of the following words:

good	well
much	little
far	beautiful
late	careful
old	first

2. Write sentences containing the superlative degrees of the words listed in *B.* 1.

XVIII. Exercise 5. *Do you ever use two negative words in the same sentence?*

EXPLANATION. People who are uneducated often use two negative words in a sentence. This is a very serious mistake which one should never make.

In addition to the words *not* and *no*, which express negation, *scarcely, but,* and *only* also make a statement negative. This second group of words should never be used with the first group. For example, one should not say, " She hadn't but two friends in the world," for the sentence contains two negatives. To correct the error, one of the negatives must be omitted. Then the sentence will be, " She had but two friends in the world," or " She had not more than two friends in the world."

This mistake rarely appears in one's written expression, but it is often heard in speech. Do not allow yourself to be ranked as ignorant and uneducated because you use more than one negative in a sentence.

DIRECTIONS. *A.* Rewrite the following sentences correctly, allowing only one negative to appear in each. Underline the negatives.

1. No one never told me about that accident.
2. Never give me no more of that medicine.
3. Nobody should never fight.
4. I can't hardly hear you.
5. She didn't have but three cents when I left the store.
6. I didn't have only one.
7. I don't want no lunch.
8. I couldn't scarcely hear a sound.
9. I don't think it won't rain.
10. I didn't hardly expect her to come.
11. I never can see nothing that I want to see.
12. They didn't hardly intend to stay so late.
13. Why hasn't he done none of those problems?
14. I don't never want him to come here again.
15. They hadn't heard only one or two songs when the fire broke out.

16. Haven't you done none of your work yet?
17. I haven't but three pounds of flour.
18. You couldn't hardly imagine a more discouraging talk.
19. Won't you never speak to me again?
20. Aren't you never going to stop?

B. Write eight sentences containing the following words:

1. hardly
2. scarcely
3. but (negative)
4. only

C. Listen to the speech of those about you and collect ten illustrations of double negatives. Write the correct expression after each incorrect sentence.

XVIII. Exercise 6. *Do you know how to place modifiers correctly?*

EXPLANATION. Every modifier should be placed as close as possible to the word it modifies. This is especially true of such adverbs as *only, merely, almost, ever, just, quite, scarcely, also.*

Notice the difference that the place of the modifier " only " makes in the following sentences:

1. *Only* yesterday I saw her.
2. Yesterday I *only* saw her.
3. Yesterday I saw *only* her.

It is not necessary to explain the differences of meaning; they are apparent when you read the sentences. They show, however, how necessary it is to place the modifier correctly. This error appears more often in written work

than in oral expressions. Look over everything you write
to see that there are no misplaced modifiers in your sentences.

DIRECTIONS. *A.* Write eight sentences containing the
following adverbs:

1. only	5. almost
2. quite	6. hardly
3. nearly	7. ever
4. just	8. also

B. Rewrite the following sentences, improving the arrangement by changing the adverbial modifiers:

1. He had seen only her once.
2. They had entered just the room where the girl
   fainted.
3. There are two ways only of securing good results.
4. Have you heard a wild cat scream ever?
5. They nearly were starved when the boat landed.
6. She lost almost her footing as she stepped on the
   narrow plank.
7. He nearly remembered all of the poem.
8. I gave also the old coat away.
9. I only had a few pennies.
10. We were so busy that we could only write a few
    lines to the family at home.
11. John asked him merely a civil question.
12. Send me also some bananas and oranges.
13. The old woman was exhausted quite from the heat.
14. When I was in the store yesterday, I saw one bar-
    gain only.
15. When ever shall we finish this work?
16. I can only go shopping on Monday.
17. I only need three dollars.

18. Harry had reached almost the top of the house when his mother saw him.

19. Do you ever remember to have been here before?

20. I only saw him once before.

XVIII. Exercise 7. *Do you understand adjectives and adverbs well enough to use an adjective and not an adverb as the subjective complement?*

Explanation. A common error in written and spoken English is to use an adverb as the subjective complement. For example, we should say, " The woman feels bad," not " badly," because " bad " is the subjective complement that describes the subject " woman." For the same reason we should say, " The rose smells sweet," not " sweetly." Since the verb " smells " expresses a state of being rather than an action, there can be no word to describe the action.

The verbs *be* and *become* are generally completed by a predicate adjective or a predicate noun as the subjective complement. There are other verbs that may take a predicate noun or adjective, or be modified by an adverb; the most common of these are: *look, grow, appear, smell, feel, taste, sound.*

In order to be sure whether you should use an adjective or an adverb, study the word to see what it does in the sentence. If it completes the verb and describes the subject, it is a predicate adjective; if it modifies the verb, it must be an adverb.

Do not confuse the adjective " good " with the adverb " well." " Good " is always an adjective. " Well " may be an adverb or an adjective; it is an adjective when it has the meaning of " being in good condition " or " not ill." One should say, " I feel well " not " good," when one wishes to give the impression of being in good health.

Directions. *A.* Write the following sentences, filling the blank in each with one of the words found in parentheses at the end of the sentence. State the reason for your choice by telling whether the word is a predicate adjective or an adverbial modifier.

1. He feels ——. (bad, badly)
2. How —— that rose smells. (sweet, sweetly)
3. This maple sugar tastes ——. (good, well)
4. The child felt ——. (bad, badly)
5. The old man looked ——. (angrily, angry)
6. This cherry tastes ——. (bitter, bitterly)
7. That little baby looks ——. (happy, happily)
8. How —— that music sounds. (sweet, sweetly)
9. I can feel those keys ——. (easy, easily)
10. The old man looked at us ——. (angry, angrily)
11. How —— that lily smells. (fragrant, fragrantly)
12. He has been looking —— for some time. (queer, queerly)
13. He becomes —— as he grows older. (noisier, more noisily)
14. She feels —— tonight. (finely, fine)
15. He treats the child very ——. (gently, gentle)
16. Those flowers grew ——. (quick, quickly)
17. He spoke very —— about the woman. (uncharitable, uncharitably)
18. The air from the orange trees smells ——. (sweet, sweetly)
19. My little girl is feeling —— this afternoon. (good, well)
20. The road felt —— to his bare feet. (rough, roughly)

B. 1. Write sentences containing a predicate adjective with each of the following verbs:

be	smell
become	feel
look	taste
grow	some
appear	well

2. Write sentences containing the following verbs modified by adverbs:

taste	smell
grow	well
appear	sound
look	feel

XVIII. Exercise 8. *Do you understand the correct use of adjectives and adverbs?*

EXPLANATION. In addition to the facts we have learned about adjectives and adverbs in the preceding exercises of this problem, there are a few special points that should be noticed.

1. There are no such adverbs as *anywheres, nowheres, somewheres, someplace*. The correct forms are as follows:

   anywhere for anywheres
   nowhere for nowheres
   somewhere for somewheres and someplace

2. The expression, " I do not like those kind of chairs," is incorrect, for the noun " kind " is singular and the adjective " those " is plural. The sentence should be, " I do not like that kind of chairs." Singular nouns must be modified by singular adjectives. For that reason the singular nouns *kind,*

class, and *sort* must be modified by *this* and *that,* not by *those* and *these.*

Say	Do not say
(1) I like this kind.	I like these kind.
(2) I like that kind.	I like those kind.

3. *Somewhat* is an adverb and must not be confused with the adjective *some.* The sentence, " He is some better," is incorrect because an adjective modifies an adjective. Correct the sentence by using the adverb *somewhat;* as, " He is somewhat better."

4. The articles *the, a,* and *an* sometimes cause errors. *The* is used to point out a definite object, and *a* or *an* are used to point out an indefinite object. For example, we say, " I bought the book," and " I bought a book." " *The* book " means that the speaker had some definite book in mind; " *a* book " shows that he did not buy any particular book. Careful writers always notice the difference in the meaning of these two articles.

Articles are often omitted when they should be expressed. The article must always be repeated when we wish to denote more than one person or thing. For example, we must not say, " I saw a man and child sitting on the porch," for this means that the man and child were one person, and that, of course, is impossible. The sentence should be, " I saw a man and a child sitting on the porch."

We may omit the second article in such an expression as, " The secretary and treasurer was chosen by the president," if we mean that the secretary and the treasurer are one person. The sentence, " She has a red and white ribbon " is correct if the speaker means that the ribbon was red and white. If, however, there were two ribbons, the sentence must be, " She has a red and a white ribbon."

DIRECTIONS. *A.* Write the following sentences, filling the blanks in each with one of the words found in parentheses at the end of the sentence. State the reason for your choice.

1. She looked —— for her hat. (everywheres, everywhere)
2. My father is —— better. (some, somewhat)
3. I gave some money to —— beggar who was sitting on the street. (the, a)
4. —— student of Latin can read French easily. (the, a)
5. I saw —— dog and —— boy running down the street. (the, a)
6. —— poet and his friend often sat under that maple tree. (the, a)
7. Do you like —— style of coats? (those, that)
8. Did you see —— old woman as you entered the building? (the, an)
9. My eyes feel —— better now. (some, somewhat)
10. Some day we shall forget —— trouble we have had. (the, a)
11. I don't like —— kind of people. (those, that)
12. —— secretary and —— president were not able to attend the meeting. (the, a)
13. —— kind of melons is the sweetest. (this, these)
14. I prefer —— kind of melons. (those, that)
15. I must have put my purse —— in this drawer. (somewhere, someplace)
16. To —— studious person —— kind of examples is not tiresome. (the, a; those, that)
17. I wish I had —— book to read. (the, a)

18. My brother wants —— sort of stamps for his collection. (these, this)
19. She will not read —— kind of books. (those, that)
20. Your child must be —— in this building. (somewheres, someplace, somewhere)

B. Write two sentences to illustrate each point that is given in the explanation.

XVIII. Exercise 9. *Are you able to select the correct form of an adjective and an adverb?*

EXPLANATION. We have studied the most important rules that govern the use of adjectives and adverbs. In order to acquire the habit of using these words correctly, we should have considerable drill in applying the rules that we have learned. This we shall do in the last three exercises of this problem.

DIRECTIONS. *A.* Write the following sentences, filling the blank in each with one of the words found in parentheses at the end of the sentence. State the reason for each choice.

1. Which do you like ——, the beach or the mountains? (better, best)
2. People —— always like to play. (most, almost)
3. He is the —— runner on the team. (faster, fastest)
4. Mildred is —— than Mabel. (beautifuller, more beautiful)
5. It was a —— pleasure to talk with her. (real, very)
6. I —— am glad to see you. (sure, surely)
7. —— knife is sharp. (this, this here)
8. They were —— dead when they were found. (near, nearly)

9. He spoke his piece ———. (good, well)
10. The girls looked ——— in their pretty white dresses. (beautifully, beautiful)
11. Go ———. (slow, slowly)
12. She doesn't like ——— kind of shoes. (those, that)
13. That tree has grown ———. (rapid, rapidly)
14. Henry is the ——— of the two. (strongest, stronger)
15. I want to go away ———. (somewheres, somewhere)
16. He hasn't ——— of my pencils. (none, any)
17. Are you ——— ready to leave? (most, almost)
18. He studies ——— every night. (considerable, considerably)
19. How ——— he walks. (heavy, heavily)
20. I shall take three of ——— kind. (these, this)

B. Write ten sentences illustrating the points that you consider most important in *Problem XVIII.*

XVIII. Exercise 10. *Can you distinguish a correctly written sentence from one that is incorrectly written?*

EXPLANATION. If you understand every sentence in *Exercise 9,* you are ready for *Exercise 10.* Before you attempt to work this lesson, you should read over the explanations given in the preceding exercises of this Problem.

DIRECTIONS. Each of the following groups contains two sentences: one is correctly written; the other contains words that are used incorrectly. Select the correct sentence from each group and tell why it is correct by giving the rules that govern the words that are used correctly.

1. (*a*) He surely does speak well.
   (*b*) He sure does speak good.
2. (*a*) This machine goes very slow.
   (*b*) This machine goes very slowly.

3. (*a*) Those kind is best.
   (*b*) This kind is best.
4. (*a*) He is the richest man in the world.
   (*b*) He is the most richest man in the world.
5. (*a*) He has done his lesson good.
   (*b*) He has done his lesson well.
6. (*a*) She learns her lessons quick.
   (*b*) She learns her lessons quickly.
7. (*a*) The milk in that bottle is near gone.
   (*b*) The milk in that bottle is nearly gone.
8. (*a*) He is the older of the two.
   (*b*) He is the oldest of the two.
9. (*a*) I lost my book in the store somewhere.
   (*b*) I lost my book in the store someplace.
10. (*a*) You are doing good now.
    (*b*) You are doing well now.
11. (*a*) Which of the two boys should receive more credit?
    (*b*) Which of the two boys should receive most credit?
12. (*a*) The horse is the most intelligent of all animals.
    (*b*) The horse is the most intelligent of all other animals.
13. (*a*) We couldn't find the watch nowhere.
    (*b*) We couldn't find the watch anywhere.
14. (*a*) Do not look at us so angrily.
    (*b*) Do not look at us so angry.
15. (*a*) He is a real good man.
    (*b*) He is a very good man.
16. (*a*) Which is the tallest, you or your brother?
    (*b*) Which is the taller, you or your brother?
17. (*a*) I sure will try to help the child.
    (*b*) I surely will try to help the child.

18. (a) She is most considerate than all the other girls.
    (b) She is more considerate than all the other girls.
19. (a) I saw a man and woman on the street.
    (b) I saw a man and a woman on the street.
20. (a) I am feeling real good today.
    (b) I am feeling very well today.

XVIII. Exercise 11. *How well can you recognize errors? Can you revise a sentence that contains an error and rewrite it so that it is expressed correctly?*

EXPLANATION. You should have no difficulty in using adjectives and adverbs correctly. If you have worked all the exercises conscientiously, you should have absolute mastery of the subject. Do not be satisfied with less.

DIRECTIONS. Many of the following sentences contain grammatical errors. Revise those that are incorrectly written and give the reason for each change.

1. Did you sleep good last night?
2. The boat goes real rapid.
3. John sure does his work good.
4. She didn't hardly notice me.
5. Please don't walk so slow.
6. I just have told Mary about the fire.
7. Do you like these kind of ties?
8. She most knocked me down.
9. Of the two Janet is the most obliging.
10. Which of you two girls can eat the most candy?
11. How beautifully the sky looks tonight.
12. New York is larger than any city in the United States.
13. They didn't have but one dollar between them.

14. She is a real interesting person.
15. He looked guiltily, but he never said anything to nobody.
16. I feel some better this afternoon.
17. How softly that plush feels!
18. I will try to be good every day.
19. You couldn't hardly tell what the woman was saying.
20. She hadn't only one friend.

THE CORRECT USE OF PREPOSITIONS AND CONJUNCTIONS

Purpose of Study

We have had one aim before us as we have worked the exercises in these problems; namely, to learn to write and speak English that is absolutely correct. With that goal before us we shall now study the uses of prepositions and conjunctions, for they sometimes cause trouble.

This problem finishes our drill in correct usage. We should continue to watch carefully everything we write and say in order to acquire the habit of using words correctly. This ability will come only after much thought and drill and persistent effort. Let us not be satisfied with anything less than absolute mastery in our English work.

Exercises

1. Recognition of the meanings of various prepositions
2. Recognition of redundant prepositions
3. A study of prepositions that cannot be omitted
4. Correct use of conjunctions and correlatives
5. A study of the conjunction *and*
6. Selecting the correct form
7. Recognition of correctly written sentences
8. Recognition and revision of incorrectly written sentences

XIX. Exercise 1. *Do you understand the meanings of various prepositions?*

Explanation. Since we wish to speak correct English, we must learn the meaning of certain prepositions and avoid errors in their use. Study the following prepositions so that you can use them accurately.

1. *Among* and *between .*

> *Between* refers to only two persons.
> *Among* refers to more than two persons.
>> Mother divides the work *between* us two girls.
>> Mother divides the work *among* us four girls.

2. *By* and *with*

> *By* refers to the doer of an action.
> *With* refers to the instrument with which the action was performed.
>> The deer was shot *by* the hunter.
>> He shot it *with* a rifle.

3. *In* and *into*

> *In* conveys the idea of presence within.
> *Into* conveys the idea of motion.
>> I sat *in* the office for two hours.
>> I walked *into* the office.

4. *At* and *in*

> *In* is used when we speak of a country, a city, or a state.
> *At* is used when we speak of a small town or village.
>> We stopped *in* Chicago and New York.
>> We stopped *at* many small towns in California.

5. *At* and *to*

> *At* conveys the idea of being in a place.
> *To* conveys the idea of going to a place.

I shall stay *at* home today.

Are you going *to* school now?

6. *Beside* and *besides*

Beside means by the side of.

Besides means in addition to.

I sat *beside* Helen.

Is anyone here *besides* you?

Some words require special prepositions to express certain meanings; as,

He agreed *with* Mr. Harding.

She agreed *to* the plan.

This side corresponds *to* (or *with*) that side.

I correspond (exchange letters) *with* her sister.

My plan is different *from* yours.

The children parted *from* their mother.

The woman parted *with* her jewels.

I waited *for* Mary at the station.

I will not let you wait *on* me, for I am not sick.

She died *of* diphtheria. (not *with*)

He fell *off* the horse. (not *off of*)

He looked *out* the window. (not *out of*)

Please do not be angry *with* me. (not *at*)

I shall have this work finished *within* an hour.

The boy climbed *upon* the roof of the burning house. (not *onto*)

She stepped *on* the wet grass. (not *onto*)

Study these prepositions until you are familiar with the differences in their meaning and use. Remember that good English requires the correct use of prepositions as well as the correct use of pronouns and verbs. Watch your written and spoken expressions.

DIRECTIONS. *A.* Write the following sentences, filling the blank in each with the correct preposition:

1. Why should there ever be any trouble —— you and me?
2. Is any one —— your friend coming?
3. Where were you when you fell —— the car?
4. We are waiting —— James, who has just gone —— the store.
5. He walked —— the room without knocking.
6. She was angry —— me.
7. Please go —— that room.
8. Can you open this can —— your knife?
9. Are you angry —— me?
10. Do you know any one in this city —— me?
11. We went —— the office.
12. This is different —— what I expected to see.
13. She died —— pneumonia.
14. —— the three men there was a friendly feeling.
15. He fell —— the well.
16. They were waiting —— the car.
17. May I sit —— you?
18. The Capitol is located —— Washington.
19. The hat will be finished —— an hour.
20. I correspond —— many people.
21. Is there harmony —— you three girls?
22. When we lost our money, I had to part —— my jewelry.
23. The tramp was killed —— a train.
24. When you are —— Paris, buy me a new gown.
25. Mildred is different —— me in many ways.
26. When I have an appointment with a person, I do not like to wait —— him.

27. On the Fourth of July we hang the flag —— the window.
28. She said she could not agree —— the plan.
29. Johnny, don't put your head —— the window.
30. Why are you angry —— her?
31. He took it —— the shelf and put it —— the vase.
32. There will be five guests —— Aunt Anna.
33. Did you ever stop —— the little town of Chester?
34. —— five minutes she was telling me the joke.
35. He is different —— his brother in that he enjoys being in the mountains.
36. How can you agree —— such a ridiculous plan?
37. Does my plan correspond —— yours?
38. He sat down —— me.
39. At that time Mr. Johnson was living —— Buffalo.
40. I wish some one —— me could go to the store.

B. Write sentences to illustrate each preposition mentioned in the explanation.

XIX. Exercise 2. *Do you ever use prepositions that are superfluous?*

EXPLANATION. In the sentence, " I don't know where the book is at," the preposition " at " is entirely unnecessary and should be omitted from the sentence. In " I should like for you to study," the preposition " for " is unnecessary and makes the sentence incorrect. Such superfluous words are known as redundant words. A correctly written sentence never contains a redundant word or expression.

Each of the incorrect sentences that follows contains a redundant word. Notice the correct way of expressing the thought.

Incorrect	*Correct*
Where is it at?	Where is it?
Where are you going to?	Where are you going?
He got off of the car.	He got off the car.
The dinner ended up with ice cream.	The dinner ended with ice cream.
I'll borrow a pencil off of Mary.	I'll borrow a pencil of Mary.
I wanted for him to come.	I wanted him to come.
Let's divide the candy up into four parts.	Let's divide the candy into four parts.
Please sit near-by me.	Please sit near me.
Are you going later on?	Are you going later?
I did not look out of the window.	I did not look out the window.
Mrs. Smith sat opposite to me.	Mrs. Smith sat opposite me.
An hour passed by before he said a word.	An hour passed before he said a word.
The table is in back of the door.	The table is back of the door. (Or — The table is behind the door.)

DIRECTIONS. *A.* Rewrite the following sentences, omitting the redundant prepositions:

1. I took it off of the table.
2. Where is she going to?
3. Where is your hat at?
4. She threw the paper out of the window.
5. Why can't you sit opposite to me?
6. Must you leave later on?
7. Can you divide that line up into two parts?
8. She wants for you to speak to her.

9. When I got off the car, I saw Mr. Hamilton.
10. I shall be glad when the picnic ends up.
11. A second passed by, and then every one began to laugh.
12. I don't know where my book is at.
13. I sat near-by my friend.
14. John, where is James going to?
15. Why don't you ask for him to come?
16. A certain rich man divided his money up among the poor.
17. The little boy stood near-by the policeman.
18. Who sat opposite to you at the banquet?
19. Mrs. Dow sat in back of us.
20. I wish I knew where my purse is at.

B. Listen to the speech of those about you and collect twenty sentences that contain redundant words. After each sentence give the correct form.

XIX. Exercise 3. *Do you ever omit prepositions that must be expressed?*

EXPLANATION. A preposition should never be omitted when it is necessary to the grammatical structure of a sentence. Especially is this true of expressions that indicate the time of an occurrence. For example, one should say, " He was born *on* the twenty-third of December," for " twenty-third " is the object of the preposition " on," which must be stated.

For the same reason say:

(1) Why do you write *in* that way? not — Why do you write that way?

(2) We shall leave *on* the fifth of November; not — We shall leave the fifth of November.

(3) I shall stay *at* home tonight; not — I shall stay home tonight.

(4) It's *of* no use to write to him; not — It's no use to write to him.

(5) *In* the preceding month he traveled in France; not — The preceding month he traveled in France.

(6) They can find some wire *of* that size; not — They can find some wire that size.

It is just as necessary to use these prepositions as it is to omit redundant prepositions. Make a decided effort to become familiar with these expressions so that you will not omit the necessary prepositions.

DIRECTIONS. *A.* Rewrite the following sentences, inserting necessary prepositions:

1. It's no use to talk about the affair.
2. When will he be home?
3. My mother was born the sixteenth of September.
4. Did you stay home last night?
5. Why do you act that way?
6. Did Columbus discover America the fourteenth of October?
7. It's no use to write to him.
8. Can you buy some rope that size?
9. The last year he made fifty thousand dollars.
10. Is it any use to send them an invitation?
11. I wish you would not act that way.
12. The preceding summer I went to Alaska.
13. Try to buy some cloth that weight.
14. He left the sixth of August.
15. I shall stay at home all summer.

B. Write two original sentences to illustrate each of the six correct sentences given in the explanation.

XIX. Exercise 4. *Can you use conjunctions correctly?*

EXPLANATION. We have learned that a conjunction is a word that connects words, phrases, or clauses. A few conjunctions are used in pairs and when so used are called correlatives. Notice the correlatives in the following sentences:

1. The boy has *both* education *and* ability.
2. He will *either* buy the book *or* borrow it from the library.
3. She can *neither* cook *nor* sew.
4. I do not know *whether* he intends to stay in the office *or* go to the club.
5. She is *not so* old *as* you are.
6. She is *as* old *as* you are.
7. I am *so* tired *that* I cannot read.
8. I *not only* saw Mrs. Snyder *but* I *also* talked with her.

Notice that the correct correlatives are *either-or* and *neither-nor*. It is incorrect to say, " She can neither sing or play." The sentence should be, " She can neither sing nor play."

Notice, too, that the correlatives *so* and *as* are used with a negative; as, " She is *not so* strong *as* he." The correlatives *as-as* are used with an affirmative statement; as, " She is *as* strong *as* he."

There are three words that are often used incorrectly as conjunctions. They are *without, except* and *like*.

The word *like* is never a *conjunction*. It is always a

verb or a preposition, and therefore must introduce a phrase and not a clause. The sentence, " She acted like she owned the house," is incorrect, for " like " does the work of a conjunction. The idea should be expressed in this way: " She acted as if she owned the house." It is correct to say, " She looks like you," for " like," in this sentence, is a preposition.

Without is an adverb or a preposition, but never a conjunction. Do not make the mistake of using the preposition " without " for the conjunction " unless." For example, it is correct to say,

    1. I will not go unless you stay at home.
    2. I will not go without you.

It is incorrect to say,

    I will not go without you stay at home.

Except is a preposition but is often used incorrectly for the conjunction *unless*. The sentence, " He cannot go except he does his work," should be, " He cannot go unless he does his work."

Guard against the misuse of any of the words listed in this exercise. Watch everything you write and speak to make sure that you do not violate the correct usage of these words.

Directions. *A.* Write the following sentences, filling the blank in each with the correct conjunction or correlative:

    1. She bakes the bread —— she enjoyed the work.
    2. John is not —— strong as he was in the fall.
    3. He acts —— he had lost his way.
    4. I wish I could play on the piano —— Mildred can.

5. Either be quiet —— run outside to play.

6. He is not —— tall as I am.

7. —— I go now, I shall be late.

8. The boys are —— studious —— the girls.

9. He will go either to France —— to Italy.

10. You will never be able to succeed —— you spend some effort.

11. The team did not play —— well this year —— it did last year.

12. That poor man can neither read —— write.

13. I can not go —— you go with me.

14. It seems —— she is always busy.

15. I have not yet decided whether I shall go to college —— stay in the city and work.

16. Mother bought not only a coat —— a hat.

17. I will spare neither money —— time to locate that boy.

18. I wish I could either play —— sing.

19. This house looks just —— it did ten years ago.

20. You are not —— tired as she is.

B. Write original sentences containing the correlatives and conjunctions listed in this exercise.

XIX. Exercise 5. *Do you always use the coördinate conjunction " and " correctly?*

EXPLANATION. The coördinate conjunction *and* should connect words or groups of words that have the same grammatical value. For example, two simple subjects may be changed to a compound subject by *and;* as, " *John and Mary* are working every day." Two phrases may be joined, as, " He walked *on the porch and into the house.*" Two independent clauses may be joined by *and* to make a compound sentence; as, " The *boys played and the girls served.*"

In such a sentence as, " They brought us several boxes of peaches and pears and which mother canned," " and " should be omitted, for the two clauses are not independent. The clause, " which mother canned," is dependent and cannot be joined to the independent clause by a coördinate conjunction.

To join two elements that do not have the same grammatical construction, is a sign of carelessness. Mistakes of this kind can be corrected in three ways: (1) omit the conjunction, (2) change the dependent clause to an independent clause, or (3) insert a dependent clause before the conjunction. For example, let us take the sentence, " While in San Francisco, we saw many tourists from all parts of the United States and who were very much pleased with the West." Notice the three different corrections:

1. While in San Francisco, we saw many tourists from all parts of the United States, who were very much pleased with the West. (The conjunction is omitted.)

2. While in San Francisco, we saw many tourists from all parts of the United States, and they were very much pleased with the West. (The dependent clause has been changed to an independent clause.)

3. While in San Francisco, we saw many tourists who had come from all parts of the United States, and who were very much pleased with the West. (A dependent clause has been inserted.)

Directions. *A.* Rewrite the following sentences, making the coördinate conjunction connect only those elements that have the same grammatical value:

1. I read articles about Marconi and Edison, and who are very interesting men.

2. Night descended on the silent forest, and Stephen heard the solemn cry of the owls and which frightened him exceedingly.

3. He looked pitifully at the stern face, but saw that he would receive but little sympathy from the Indian and who had captured him.

4. When Bob awoke in the morning, he told his mother about his dream and which amused her very much.

5. The fire had recently been replenished with green wood, and which made a dense smoke.

6. John laughed, partly from relief, and partly from joy.

7. He bought some books about electricity, and which were very interesting.

8. The old man looked about for some weapon, but could find nothing better than his cane and which he seized.

9. This is the man who called yesterday, and who owns the house that is for sale.

10. I am trying to sell the property, and which is located in the business district.

11. Mrs. Jones induced her husband to buy a house, and which was located in a beautiful residential district.

12. Mr. Pearson, soon after his arrival at the hotel, went into a conference with Mr. Simmons and who told him the cause of the failure of the bank.

13. Mr. Houston said the lumber would be brought in boats, and which the company owned.

14. The building, and which has been carefully planned, will contain ten rooms.

15. The thermometer registered as high as ninety-five degrees, and which was the highest point it has reached this year.

16. The exhibition, and which was opened Saturday night, was one of the most elaborate ever attempted in the United States.

17. The manager of the factory investigated Mr. Vose, and who was able to give much valuable information.

18. The athletes wish to have an opportunity to know the men and who will have charge of selecting the team.

19. We had a good crop of wheat, and which is valued at several million dollars.

20. The manager of a dry goods store has advertised for a floor-walker, and who must have had at least five years' experience.

B. Look over the compositions and other papers you have written this term, and make a collection of sentences in which you have used " and " incorrectly.

XIX. Exercise 6. *Are you able to select the correct preposition or conjunction?*

EXPLANATION. People who use correct English are very careful about their choice of prepositions and conjunctions. Since we wish to speak and write correctly, we, too, shall use these words accurately.

DIRECTIONS. Write the following sentences, filling the blank in each with one of the words found in parentheses at the end of the sentence. State the reason for your choice.

1. The board is —— the door.　(in back of, behind)
2. I won't go —— you go.　(without, unless)
3. Can you get a pencil —— her?　(off of, of)
4. He is not —— young as he seems.　(as, so)

5. Neither John —— Harry can go. (nor, or)
6. A person should never be angry —— anyone. (with, at)
7. —— two hours the house was completely ruined. (within, inside of)
8. He doesn't play —— John does. (as, like)
9. The boys cannot go to the beach —— they do their work. (without, unless)
10. Do you know if John died —— diphtheria? (of, with)
11. I shall wait —— you until two o'clock. If you do not come then, I shall go home. (on, for)
12. She is different —— her sister. (than, from)
13. Who was that man sitting —— you? (beside, besides)
14. Don't jump —— the well. (in, into)
15. It broke his heart to part —— his sister. (from, with)
16. I wish I felt —— you do. (as, like)
17. Please put it —— the shelf. (onto, on)
18. There was a dispute —— the two men. (among, between)
19. Why did you sit —— the boys on the team? (between, among)
20. You act —— you are tired. (like, as if)

XIX. Exercise 7. *Can you distinguish a correctly written sentence from one that is incorrectly written?*

EXPLANATION. We cannot always give a grammatical reason for the use of the correlatives and many of the prepositions. For example, we " agree *to* a plan " and " agree *with* a person." There is no reason for this except that good usage makes this distinction. To use these prepositions differently would show ignorance of correct usage. It would be wise for you to memorize the correct forms before you work this exercise.

DIRECTIONS. Each of the following groups contains two sentences: one is correctly written; the other contains words that are used incorrectly. Select the correct sentence from each group and tell why it is correct by giving the rules that govern the words that are used correctly.

1. (a) Did you agree to Mr. Smith?
   (b) Did you agree with Mr. Smith?
2. (a) Did he sit near-by you?
   (b) Did he sit near you?
3. (a) The poor child fell off the roof.
   (b) The poor child fell off of the roof.
4. (a) I do not like to have any one sit besides me when I am studying.
   (b) I do not like to have any one sit beside me when I am studying.
5. (a) When are you going in the school?
   (b) When are you going into the school?
6. (a) I have waited on him long enough. Why doesn't he come?
   (b) I have waited for him long enough. Why doesn't he come?
7. (a) Are you intending to leave the tenth of this month?
   (b) Are you intending to leave on the tenth of this month?
8. (a) She never went without her work was finished.
   (b) She never went unless her work was finished.

9. (a) I cannot divide up this pie into three equal parts.
   (b) I cannot divide this pie into three equal parts.

10. (a) When did you part from your sister?
    (b) When did you part with your sister?

11. (a) She looked like she was very sad.
    (b) She looked as if she was very sad.

12. (a) He died with influenza.
    (b) He died of influenza.

13. (a) Why does she walk that way?
    (b) Why does she walk in that way?

14. (a) These sentences are not so hard as the others.
    (b) These sentences are not as hard as the others.

15. (a) Are you very different than your sister?
    (b) Are you very different from your sister?

16. (a) I can be there within an hour.
    (b) I can be there inside an hour.

17. (a) Mother cannot go except I do her work.
    (b) Mother cannot go unless I do her work.

18. (a) I'll try to get some money off of my father.
    (b) I'll try to get some money of my father.

19. (a) The party ended up with refreshments.
    (b) The party ended with refreshments.

20. (a) I wish you would not walk onto the lawn.
    (b) I wish you would not walk on the lawn.

XIX. Exercise 8. *How well can you recognize errors in the use of prepositions and conjunctions? Can you revise a sentence that contains errors and rewrite it so that it is expressed correctly?*

EXPLANATION. You should now be able to use prepositions and correlatives correctly. Do not attempt to write the assignment until you have memorized these words.

DIRECTIONS. Many of the following sentences contain grammatical errors. Revise those that are incorrectly written and give the reason for each change.

1. Why do you look out of the window so often?
2. My friends and I took a long hiking trip and which we enjoyed very much.
3. Is any one beside you going?
4. I told him that it's no use to try to influence Robert.
5. How long did you wait on John at the station?
6. My father is never angry at me.
7. I shall be going a little later on.
8. Please stay home tonight with me.
9. The girls cannot go without they have escorts.
10. That carpet looks like it had received hard usage.
11. I can neither eat or sleep.
12. Must I part with my mother?
13. When you go in the office, please telephone my sister.
14. I can never leave the first of September.
15. This building is not as large as the one we visited yesterday.
16. Have the boys thrown the books out of the window?
17. Who took my book off of the desk?
18. Her mother sat in back of us.
19. Will you be to home tomorrow?
20. The teacher often sat between the pupils in the class.

Review

Now that we have finished all of the problems which deal with the essentials that help us to express our thoughts in correct sentences, we should test our ability to construct perfect sentences. This is the purpose of *Problem XX*.

Exercises

1. An exercise in constructing perfect sentences
2. An exercise in constructing perfect sentences
3. An exercise in constructing perfect sentences

XX. Exercise 1. *Can you construct correct sentences?*

EXPLANATION. If there is any difficulty in the preceding problems that you have not mastered, return to it now and overcome it before you attempt to work the assignment.

DIRECTIONS. *A.* Rewrite the following sentences. Change incorrect forms to correct ones. Do not change the wording unless the expression is incorrect. Underline every word that you change and below the sentence give the reason for each change.

1. The man, whom I thought was a writer, asked Mary and I to buy some of his pictures.
2. Do you use these kind of pens?
3. It is necessary for you and I to go now.
4. If anyone disobeys the law, they should be punished.

5. Don't her child sleep good?
6. John is the best swimmer of the two, ain't he?
7. Every person that thinks they can do as they please will soon learn that this is impossible.
8. Me and Harry like to sit before the fire and talk.
9. I couldn't scarcely believe what they just had told mother and I.
10. Us boys planned to go to the mountains.
11. I have resolved to save my money and which I shall need next year.
12. Was it me who you sent for?
13. If any one calls, tell them I shall be back soon.
14. Which of you two girls worked the hardest?
15. I shall be satisfied with whomever you choose.
16. Must I divide my candy up between all the children in the class?
17. That is the man whom every one thought would be mayor.
18. Ain't she younger than him?
19. Everyone is going except she.
20. There was no thought of John winning the prize, for us boys knew that he couldn't hardly write a sentence correct.

B. Punctuate the following sentences. Number each mark and below the sentence give the reason for every mark.

1. When John and I returned to the front of the house we found that one of the windows had been partially opened
2. One of the guests a woman from New York told me that she had never seen the poet before

3. Just send a letter a post card or a note to this address and you will receive the story of a great institution

4. Inasmuch as all the instruction is carried on by mail it makes no difference where you live

5. I have earned the money that I needed and I know several women who want me to make more dresses for them

6. Among the members of the class are housewives mothers business women teachers girls at home and in school and girls in shops and stores and offices

7. As soon as we received our instructions which came in separate envelops we read all about the interesting facts regarding our work

8. The roomful of men stirred uncomfortably and one or two of them laughed awkwardly

9. She needed help desperately she needed money and friends and a home

10. We are here you dear fellow because we know and appreciate the melancholy which comes over one when he is far from home

11. The woman who was on the verge of crying checked herself and merely smiled at her accuser

12. Yes I will do that if you want me to mister

13. Why should he not be happy when justice and honor and fame had come to him

14. He paused on the threshold for outside the door he heard a loud voice calling him

15. There was no light in the alley all the backs of the blocks around it were entirely dark

16. A person who called himself a sculptor showed the audience some interesting paintings

17. Any person that will mistreat a little child is not really human

18. They often asked us where we were going but we did not wish to tell them

19. Did you see the balloon John

20. Have you ever read the biography of Charles Dickens the author of " David Copperfield "

XX. Exercise 2. *How well can you construct correct sentences?*.

EXPLANATION. If any sentence in *Exercise 1* caused you any difficulty, master the points involved before you work *Exercise 2*. Your aim should be complete mastery of sentences.

DIRECTIONS. *A.* Rewrite the following sentences, changing any words or expressions that you think are incorrect. Below the sentence give the reason for each change.

1. I might of known that they was coming tonight.
2. My little boy is feeling badly today.
3. This here paper is not numbered correct.
4. Have you got your purse with you?
5. How quiet she talks!
6. What fun we could have if she was here.
7. I hadn't but one dollar in my purse.
8. Will you set here besides me?
9. John is the most fastest runner on the team, but I don't hardly think he will be able to play.
10. How long shall the play last?
11. The little boys learned him how to swim.
12. I wish I could lay down for an hour.
13. Can I go to the park, mother?

14. I seen four men entering the store.
15. I run home last night as fast as I could go.
16. I don't know what I done with my purse.
17. Some one has broke my ink bottle.
18. Mr. Smith, with his wife and children, are taking a trip abroad.
19. Did he hurt himself bad?
20. I wish he was going to visit you and she.

B. Punctuate the following sentences. Number every mark of punctuation and give the reason for each below the sentence.

1. He took a glance into the street behind him and when he saw nothing he turned and went into the café
2. He stood erect for a moment and then his glance fell upon the small child at his side
3. Even if they had recognized him would they let others know that he was in the city
4. He will tell you the truth James
5. When Willie spoke his voice sounded as if it came from a weary and worn-out man
6. Again a faint smile crept from under the chief's gray mustache and his eyes became earnest and appealing
7. Well go out and see the game Willie but don't go down to meet the boat
8. From my desk I could see the stern-faced man who was in charge of those poor hungry children
9. As she thought of it later she knew it was right for her brother to go
10. Dearie I do not blame you but I would not do it again

11. We entered the machine which was upholstered in gayly flowered cretonne and sat down on the soft cushions

12. We explored the ten-cent store which had always been the children's favorite store and each child bought one little present

13. Miss Glynn a little elderly sweet-faced woman stood before the crowd of children

14. Attracted by the display of pink and white cakes we had our lunch in a stuffy little restaurant

15. The boys ordered what they liked and every one was supremely happy

16. When the girls said they wanted to go into the principal department store of the village the boys rebelled most strenuously

17. We had dinner with Mr. Johnson the senior member of the firm

18. I am going to town and I wonder if you would like to go with me

19. Lena sat down on the bed which she had just made and breathed a sigh of relief

20. Way up on the mountain side two old veterans who have not spoken to each other for years hold down an old and forsaken mine

XX. Exercise 3. *Have you mastery of the essentials of grammar and punctuation? Can you construct sentences that are correctly expressed and punctuated?*

Explanation. You should now be able to express your thoughts in correct sentences. Watch your speech and written work carefully. Do not allow yourself to fall into careless habits. Remember that the ability to use perfect

English is one of the greatest possessions that you can have. Be satisfied with nothing less than perfection.

DIRECTIONS. *A*. Rewrite the following sentences, changing any words or expressions that you think are incorrect. After each sentence state the reason for the changes.

1. Don't you lay down to rest every afternoon?
2. Do you know where she is going to?
3. It was her whom they wanted, but we couldn't hardly hear what they was saying.
4. The days are much more warmer now, and it is hard to always be studying.
5. Each of the boys were studying so much that they did not hear the bell.
6. The matter lays entirely between you and I.
7. The boys raised as the ladies entered.
8. He laid his long, friendly hand upon the older man's shoulder reaching forward from where he sat.
9. Me and him was not expecting to hear of father being elected.
10. He talked entirely of hisself and of him going to New York.
11. I cannot study without I have a better light.
12. Have you ever eaten those kind of figs?
13. I wish I was going with them boys.
14. Have each of the children their car-fare?
15. When we was going into the store, we seen a man and woman standing near the door.
16. Who is the youngest, John or James?
17. Mother cannot go except I help her.
18. He hadn't ought to expect me and her to do all of the work.

19. Nobody in the house does nothing to help mother and I.
20. We seen her when she done the work.

B. Punctuate the following sentences. Number every mark of punctuation and below the sentence give the reason for each mark.

1. Lady listen that man is the one who took your purse
2. When a person like him decides to do a thing he usually does it
3. Now that you are here and have finished your work won't you stay and talk with us
4. Oh Mr. Jones what are a few thousand dollars to a rich grateful generous man like you
5. A certain softness was coming into the man's proud face something almost kindly was twinkling in his eye
6. At first it hardly seemed that she had heard him for her mother held her attention so closely
7. As he passed along a close observer might have noticed the frown on his face
8. Well John we are out of luck today but we will make a success of this business yet
9. The elevator was not running at that time of night and Mr Thompson was forced to walk up the dark stairway to the offices
10. One thing is certain I will not be here tomorrow morning
11. Although he did not yet know how dangerous the situation was he was not entirely unaware of his danger
12. John pressed me hard for an immediate agreement but I would not yield I had no faith in the man's account

13. Her suit which she had wanted so much was now a source of trouble and annoyance to her

14. Since it was at least eight miles to the Glen the station agent advised me to hire a taxi

15. Fred's place the store around the corner was where we went and as we neared it we could hear some one talking loudly

16. As Charley spoke a vision flitted through his mind

17. In the company of Mr Blembery and Mr McKay fellow traders like himself Jim had gone to the restaurant for lunch

18. I'm interested in the story John I want to hear more of it

19. As the two men hurried toward the door Charley rose and thrust back his chair

20. He had not been at the office that morning nor had any one heard from him but Charley knew what he was doing

KEYS TO THE EXERCISES

Problem I — Exercise 1

A.

The groups that are sentences	The groups that are not sentences
1	2
4	3
7	5
9	6
12	8
14	10
16	11
17	13
19	15
	18
	20

B. Have your teacher or some one in the class help you to correct this part of the exercise. Select some one who you believe is a good judge of sentences.

Problem I — Exercise 2

A. The groups that do not express complete thoughts are:

1	8	13
3	9	14
4	10	17
5	11	18
6	12	19

B. *Note:* Since this part of the exercise is original, your teacher will help you to correct it.

Problem I — Exercise 3

A.

1. Where is my book?
2. Why has he gone away?
3. Please take me to the party.
4. I cannot find my cap.
5. Open that door for me.
6. Oh, that man is falling!
7. When did you come?
8. The children cannot go now.
9. Shall I see you this afternoon at the party?
10. Where has he gone?
11. Leave those books in this room.
12. Goodness, I have lost my necklace!
13. Sing me a song, John.
14. Will he come soon?
15. Be sensible, little boy.

B. Since this part of the exercise is original, your teacher or one of the pupils in the class will help you to correct it.

Problem I — Exercise 4

A. How should you like to have everything you touch turn to gold? That is what happened to an ancient king. Have you never read the story of Midas? This is it. Many years ago there lived in a foreign land a king and his little daughter. Their home was a beautiful palace built on the shore of the ocean where the king and his daughter could see the wonderful sunsets. About the palace was a beautiful garden in which there were all kinds of lovely flowers. The king had many servants who worked continually to keep his palace and gardens beautiful. King Midas was very rich. He owned a great city and a magnificent palace filled with costly furniture. He also had countless bags filled with gold coins and gold dust. Did he enjoy all this wealth and beauty? He did not. He rarely looked at the ocean and the gorgeous sunsets. Seldom did he go into his gardens and enjoy the beauty of the flowers. There was only one thing that he really enjoyed. That was to count his coins and run the gold dust through his greedy fingers. He had only one desire. That was to gain more gold to give to his daughter. Sometimes the little girl would beg her father to look at a sunset. Every time he did this he wished he could turn the gold of the clouds into coins. Occasionally he would go into the garden with his child. Then he would wish that he could turn the roses into gold. How foolish he was not to enjoy the beauty of nature! One day his wish to have more gold was granted. Everything he touched turned to gold. Did that bring happiness? It did not. It brought only misery and suffering. Do you wish to know the rest of the story of King Midas? Ask the librarian for it. You will find that it is very interesting.

> B. *Note:* You may have stated your answers for *B* in different words, but the meaning will be the same as expressed here.

I have learned by studying *Problem I* that

1. A sentence is a group of words that express a complete thought.
2. Every sentence begins with a capital.
3. Every sentence ends with a mark of punctuation which is decided by the meaning of the sentence.

(1) A sentence that states a fact is followed by a period.

(2) A sentence that expresses a command or entreaty is followed by a period.

(3) A sentence that asks a question is followed by a question mark.

(4) A sentence that expresses sudden thought or strong feeling is followed by an exclamation mark.

2. These facts will help me to express my thoughts in correct sentences, and whatever I write will be easily understood.

Problem II — Exercise 1

A.   *Predicates*

1. saw
2. sent
3. returned
4. drank
5. went
6. made
7. read
8. did
9. rang
10. worked.
11. sang
12. came
13. go
14. see
15. told
16. took
17. knew
18. fastened
19. lay
20. brought

B. Have your teacher help you to judge these original sentences. If there is some one in the class who uses correct English, let him look over this work.

Problem II — Exercise 2

A.   *Simple Predicates*

1. may take
2. must see
3. will learn
4. have brought
5. has laid
6. was seen
7. may see
8. have learned
9. should have taken
10. has been gone
11. has stolen
12. should have come
13. have broken
14. am studying
15. were struck
16. had been taken
17. will lie
18. has drunk
19. can win
20. will have been done

B. Have some one in the class help you to correct this part of the exercise. Select a person who does excellent work.

Problem II — Exercise 3

A.   *Simple Predicates*

1. had forgotten
2. had been trained
3. did recognize
4. could make
5. could be frightened
6. had been eaten
7. will return
8. had seen
9. will bother
10. have taken
11. shall hear
12. had collected
13. had gone
14. shall consider
15. must have seen
16. had been living
17. had feared
18. must go
19. can tell
20. has lost

B. Have your teacher or some pupil in the class help you to correct this part of the exercise.

Problem II — Exercise 4

A. Simple Predicate	Simple Subject	Simple Predicate	Simple Subject
1. found	he	11. come	(you)
2. ate	men	12. ran	child
3. have been returned	books	13. shall go	I
		14. take	(you)
4. must come	you	15. will stop	storm
5. can learn	pupil	16. do like	you
6. walked	children	17. did find	she
7. saw	we	18. have read	I
8. bought	man	19. sing	(you)
9. does lose	person	20. came	Dick
10. sing	birds		

B. Have your teacher or some pupil help you to correct this part of the exercise.

Problem II — Exercise 5

A. Simple Predicate	Simple Subject	Complete Subject
1. had poked	vessel	a war vessel
2. put	labor	a few hours' labor of the men
3. were eaten	tips	the tender tips of the fallen palms
4. kept	Borckman	Borckman
5. beheld	eyes	many eyes
6. uprose	rain	a glittering, glistening rain of tomahawks
7. would have resented	heart	Jerry's heroic little heart of courage
8. eat	(you)	(you)
9. could win	John	John

10. had eaten	savages	the wild savages
11. had made	he	he
12. had increased	interest	his interest in that line of work
13. did receive	dog	the little dog
14. take	(you)	(you)
15. has gone	child	that child

B. Have your teacher help you to correct this part of the exercise.

Problem II — Exercise 6

A. Simple Predicate	Simple Subject	Complete Subject	Complete Predicate
1. yelped	Jerry	Jerry	yelped eagerly at the recognition of Skipper's voice
2. whimpered	dog	the little dog	whimpered like a lost child in the loneliness of the dark
3. was lifted	he	he	was lifted out of the sea into the boat then with amazing abruptness
4. did walk	dog	the poor little dog	did not just calmly walk overboard
5. were grouped	boys	the boys	were grouped in a semi-circle about the fire
6. shall set	we	we	shall set the baskets of fruit where
7. were brought	flowers	the flowers in the vase	were brought to me yesterday
8. open	(you)	(you)	open all the windows in this room
9. looked	boy	the little boy	looked how miserable
10. could have made	man	the man	could have made the attempt only for love of his child

| 11. knew | they | they, having lived in savagery all their lives | knew naught else |
| 12. called | Anna | Anna, hearing the commotion upstairs | called for her father at that moment |

B. Have some one in the class help you to correct this part of the exercise.

Problem II — Exercise 7

Simple Predicate	Simple Subject	Complete Subject	Complete Predicate
1. sat	mother	my dear mother	sat in the dark and dreary room
2. became	boy	that interesting boy	became the brightest student in his class at college
3. gave	you	you	gave a very fine address today
4. have seen	I	I	have never before seen such a beautiful sunset
5. came	messenger	a messenger from the king	came in the morning of the third day
6. brought	mother	my mother	brought us many beautiful things from Italy
7. made	he	he	made a collection of rare paintings in this way
8. do fear	(you)	(you)	do not fear the strange man
9. studied	Henry	Henry	studied foreign languages for two years
10. came	children	two dear little children	came down the stairs silently
11. did awake	he	he	did not awake until two hours later
12. play	boys	the little boys on our street	play ball every evening

Problem III — Exercise 1

A. Number 9 is the only group that is a sentence as it stands. All other groups must be completed.

Note: Since this work is largely original, the teacher or one of the pupils in the class will help you to correct the exercise.

B. Have some one who understands this exercise help you to correct these original sentences.

Problem III — Exercise 2

A. Groups 2, 4, 7, and 10 are sentences. All other groups are incomplete and must be completed by having independent clauses added.

B. Note: Have your teacher or some pupil who does excellent work help you to correct the original sentences in A and B.

Problem III — Exercise 3

A. Correct your papers for sentences and end punctuation. Do not bother about the commas. They are placed here to make the paragraph complete.

A farmer called on Earl Fitzwilliam to tell him that his crop of wheat had been seriously injured in a field adjoining a certain wood where the earl and his friend had hunted during the winter. He said that the young wheat had been so cut up and destroyed that in some places he could not hope for any produce. When the lord heard this he said he should be glad to repay the injury that his horses and hounds had made. Anticipating the earl's consideration and kindness, the farmer had a friend assist him in estimating the damage. Believing that the crop was entirely destroyed, they thought fifty pounds would cover the loss. As the harvest approached the wheat grew, and in those parts of the field which were most trampled the wheat was strongest and most luxuriant. The farmer went again to the earl and told him that he had come to speak about the wheat in the field adjoining the wood. Earl Fitzwilliam immediately remembered the circumstance, and asked if he had not given enough to cover all losses. The farmer then told the earl that he had not had any losses. He explained that where the horses had most cut up the land the crop was most promising. Having told all these facts, the farmer then returned the fifty pounds to the earl. The nobleman was greatly pleased to see such great honesty. He entered into a conversation with the farmer, asking him several questions about his family, his children, and the age of each. His lordship then went into another room. On returning, he presented the farmer with a cheque for one hundred pounds. Being an independent man, the farmer did not wish to take the gift. The earl then told him to give it to his eldest son when he had become of age. He also asked him to relate to the young man the event which had produced the money. This the farmer promised to do.

B. 1. A phrase is a group of closely related words that has no subject or predicate and does not express a complete thought. A sentence is a group of words having a subject and a predicate. It expresses a complete thought.

2. Have some one in the class correct these original sentences.

3. A clause is a group of words having a subject and a predicate.

4. A dependent clause does not express a complete thought, but an independent clause gives a complete idea.

5. Have some one in the class correct these original sentences.

Problem IV — Exercise 1

A. Nouns

1. man, wood, branch, brushwood
2. attention, children
3. beauty, living
4. boy, girl, education
5. schools, parts, city
6. Mr. Smith's, address, enthusiasm
7. plan, buildings
8. boy, candy, cookies, toys
9. stove, room
10. girl
11. Christmas, tree, master, mistress, house, hands, servants, hymns, pine
12. bell, morning
13. Rose, Uncle Alex, advice
14. minister, pulpit, company
15. children, blackberries, bushes, road, soldiers

B. Have some pupil help you to correct this part of the exercise.

Problem IV — Exercise 2

A.

1. The President spends much time at the White House.
2. I am sorry Helen could not attend the meeting of the Ebell Club.

3. One of the largest cities in the eastern part of this country is Chicago.
4. John does not want Mary to go to the party because she is so small.
5. Richard and Robert are very good to their mother.
6. When will Jane return from New York?
7. The Higgens Building is on Second Street.
8. Mildred came running up the stairs, laughing about Howard's good fortune.
9. I want to go to Oregon on *The Yale.*
10. I have read many books by Dickens and Scott.
11. Did Aunt Stella send her pictures from France and Italy?
12. Oh, my father is coming home tonight!
13. Many times fathers and mothers are too absorbed in business and housekeeping to study their children.
14. Do you often read the Atlantic Monthly?
15. I am sure that Uncle Fred will stay at a quiet hotel.
16. He is attending East High School and enjoys his work very much.
17. The President of the United States has more power than the King of England.
18. They had not seen Judge Allen for many years.
19. Two days later the Campbells went home, a larger party than when they came.
20. There is one street in New York that I can always find, and that is Broadway.

B. Have some pupil help you to correct this original work.

Problem IV — Exercise 3

A. Pronouns

1. he, your, you
2. I, who, he
3. mine, I, them, her
4. yours, it, hers
5. they, her, their
6. he, them, they, his
7. their
8. those, my
9. they
10. I, whom, my
11. she, it, you
12. I, she
13. who, their
14. I, they, their
15. you, him, he, his, yours

B. Have some one in the class who understands this work help you to correct this part of the exercise.

Problem IV — Exercise 4

A. Verbs

1. had found, could go
2. did say, was, cried
3. wished, could have, enjoyed, possessed
4. went, filled
5. had lifted, carried
6. will work, eat
7. secured, started
8. must have walked, came
9. watched, studied
10. stood, looked

11. is
12. was, commanded
13. cast, poled
14. had sprung, would have been
15. did stagger, fall
16. is
17. were looking, heard, was
18. went, feasted
19. should do
20. has been, has worn

B. Have some one in the class help you to correct this work.

Problem IV — Exercise 5

A. Nouns	Adjectives
1. books	those, interesting
girl	the, little, Spanish
2. Mr. Jones	
home	a, fine, new
3. success	unexpected
task	the, hard
4. candle	the, small
light	a, clear, steady
5. affairs	household
6. man	that
condition	a, miserable
effort	greater
7. hours	
sea	a, calm
8. workmanship	such
boys	most, English
time	much
work	manual

9. story   a, long
   travel   foreign
10. man   a, strange
    door
    money   a, little
    food   some, warm
11. lady   a, happy, old
    grandchildren   little
    candy   some, pink, white
12. Jack
    warrior   a, interesting, little
    mustache   a, great, black
    mouth   rosy

B. Since this part of the exercise is original, have your teacher or one of the pupils help you to correct it.

Problem IV — Exercise 6

A.   Adverbs (*and the words they explain*)

1. slowly   (entered)   7. quietly   (wait)
   silently   (entered)   8. there   (lay)
2. how (rapidly) rapidly (flies)   away   (ebbed)
3. soon   (will come)   9. when   (will put)
4. quickly   (looked)   down   (will put)
   then   (asked)   10. early   (went)
   immediately (show)   there   (met)
5. first   (found)   11. always   (remembers)
   then   (ran)   quietly   (speak)
   swiftly   (ran)   12. scarcely   (had taken)
   very   (safe)   very   (old)
6. away   (ran)   hurriedly (enter)
   never   (was seen)
   again   (never)

B. Have your teacher or one of the pupils help you to correct these sentences.

Problem IV — Exercise 7

A. Conjunctions

1. and
2. unless
3. or
4. but
5. as
6. as if
7. but
8. although
9. neither, nor
10. but
11. as
12. because
13. since
14. till
15. for
16. and, and
17. if
18. before
19. if
20. as

B. Have some pupil in the class look over these sentences.

Problem IV — Exercise 8

A. Phrases and Prepositions

1. *with* his dog
2. *down* the dusty road, *on* a stone, *by* the edge, *of* the road
3. *on* the walls
4. *into* the room, *about* the president
5. *from* Japan, *on* it
6. *with* a little dish, *of* clay
7. *at* the beach, *in* the rocks
8. *at* that time, *in* my diary
9. *into* our home, *of* us
10. *to* me, *from* you
11. *of* her child's voice, *to* him, *in* children's voices
12. *through* a mutiny, *in* the prison yard, *with* Gatling guns, *upon* them, *with* pick handles, *by* brawny guards

B. Have your teacher help you to correct these sentences. Be sure that you can recognize prepositions before you go to the next exercise.

Problem IV — Exercise 9

A. You can easily correct this part of the exercise by referring to the preceding explanations.

B.

1. *pro.* *adj.* *n.* *v.* *adv.* *v.* *prep.*
My poor grandmother has scarcely recovered from
art. *n.* *pro.* *v.* *prep.* *art.* *n.*
the fall she received in the winter.

2. *adj.* *adj.* *adj.* *n.* *v.* *adj.* *n.* *n.*
This beautiful little girl is some man's child.

3. *pro.* *v.* *prep.* *art.* *adj.* *n.* *prep. n.* *pro.* *v.*
He thought about the long years of toil which had
v. *v.* *prep.* *n.* *conj. prep. n.*
been spent in camps and in mines.

4. *art.* *n.* *prep. art. adj.* *adj.* *n.* *v.* *prep.* *art.*
A woman in a soft, pretty gown came through the
n. *prep.* *art.* *n.*
gate from the bungalow.

5. *art.* *n.* *v.* *prep. pro.* *n.* *conj.* *v.* *adv.*
A tramp scrambled to his feet and stood watchfully
conj. *adv.*
and awkwardly.

6. *pro.* *v.* *prep.* *pro.* *adv.* *v.* *art.* *n.*
He looked about him irresolutely, climbed the fence,
v. *art.* *n.* *conj.* *v.* *prep.* *art.* *n.*
crossed the bridge, and slouched along the road.

7. *art. adj.* *n.* *v.* *pro.* *prep. art. adj.* *n.* *prep. art.*
A few steps brought him into the main street of the
n.
village.

C. Have your teacher look over these sentences so that you will be sure you understand the various parts of speech.

Problem V — Exercise 1

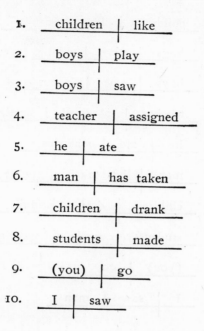

1. children | like
2. boys | play
3. boys | saw
4. teacher | assigned
5. he | ate
6. man | has taken
7. children | drank
8. students | made
9. (you) | go
10. I | saw

Note: Look at your paper again, keeping in mind these questions:

1. Does the line that separates the subject from the predicate in each sentence cut the sentence line? (Your diagrams are not correct unless this is done, for every sentence has two parts.)

2. Have you shown that the subject of "go" in sentence 9 is "you" understood?

Problem V — Exercise 2

1. children | like | candy

2. boys | play | ball

3. boys | saw | circus

4. teacher | assigned | lesson

5. he | ate | cherries

6. man | has taken | purse

7. children | drank | milk

8. students | made | speeches

9. (you) | go

10. I | saw | man

Note: Examine each of your diagrams with these questions in mind:

1. Does the line that separates the complement from the verb divide the sentence line? It must not, because there are only two main divisions to every sentence.
2. Does the line that separates the subject from the predicate divide the sentence line? It must, because there are two parts to every sentence.

Problem V — Exercise 3

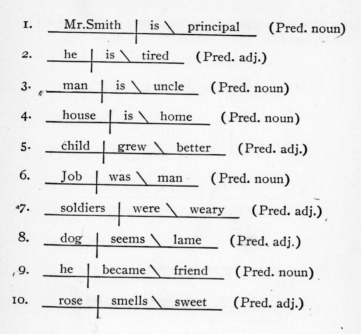

1. Mr. Smith | is \ principal (Pred. noun)

2. he | is \ tired (Pred. adj.)

3. man | is \ uncle (Pred. noun)

4. house | is \ home (Pred. noun)

5. child | grew \ better (Pred. adj.)

6. Job | was \ man (Pred. noun)

7. soldiers | were \ weary (Pred. adj.)

8. dog | seems \ lame (Pred. adj.)

9. he | became \ friend (Pred. noun)

10. rose | smells \ sweet (Pred. adj.)

Note: In each sentence look at the line that separates the complement from the verb; does it slant toward the subject? It must, for the subjective complement tells something about the subject. Does it cut the sentence line? It must not, for there are only two main divisions in each sentence.

Problem V — Exercise 4

A. This diagram does not show the real relation of the words " three old men," because " three " is made to modify " old " when it is really a modifier of " men."

B.

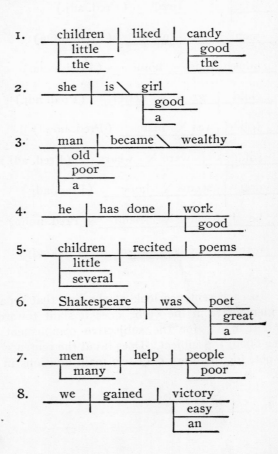

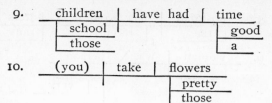

9.
children | have had | time
school | good
those | a

10.
(you) | take | flowers
pretty
those

Note the following points:

1. Look once more at the complement lines. Do you know the difference between the object and the subjective complements? Have you shown this difference?

2. Do you know what the modifiers of the subjects and the complements are? Have you shown this correctly, or have you diagramed them like A?

3. Have you shown that the subject of sentence 10 is " you " understood?

Problem V — Exercise 5

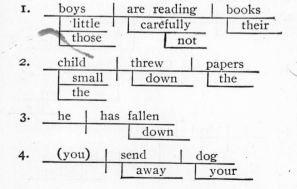

1.
boys | are reading | books
little | carefully | their
those | not

2.
child | threw | papers
small | down | the
the

3.
he | has fallen
down

4.
(you) | send | dog
away | your

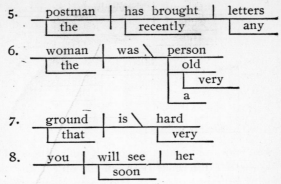

5. postman | has brought | letters
the | recently | any

6. woman | was \ person
the | old
very
a

7. ground | is \ hard
that | very

8. you | will see | her
soon

Note the following points:

1. The complement lines in sentences 6 and 7.
2. The adverb " very " in sentence 6.
3. The lack of an object complement in sentence 3. Nothing receives the action expressed by the verb.

Problem V — Exercise 6

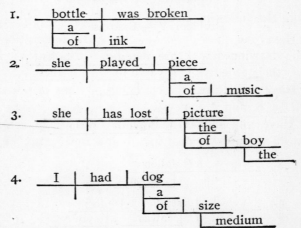

1. bottle | was broken
a
of | ink

2. she | played | piece
a
of | music

3. she | has lost | picture
the
of | boy
the

4. I | had | dog
a
of | size
medium

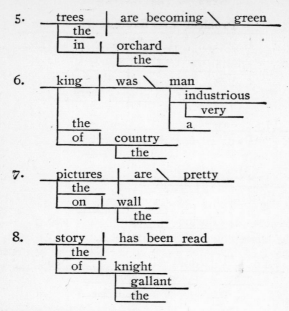

5. trees | are becoming \ green
   the
   in | orchard
        the

6. king | was \ man
                 industrious
                    very
   the   a
   of | country
        the

7. pictures | are \ pretty
   the
   on | wall
        the

8. story | has been read
   the
   of | knight
        gallant
        the

Note the following points:

1. Have you shown the objects of the prepositions by drawing lines that separate prepositions from their objects?

2. Have you drawn the complement lines in sentences 5, 6, and 7 correctly?

3. Have you made the adverb "very" in sentence 6 modify "industrious" and not "man"?

Problem V — Exercise 7

1.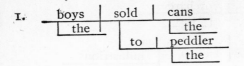

2.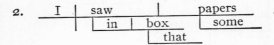

3.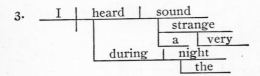

4.

5.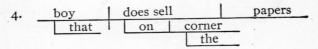

6.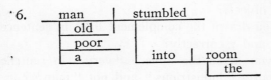

7.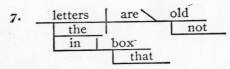

8.

```
story    |  is \  interesting
    the   |         |    very
    of    |  Beautiful Joe
```

Problem V — Exercise 8

art.   n.   prep. art. adj.   n.   v.   v. prep.
1. The pictures in the front room were painted by

art. n.   prep. art. adj.   n.
a pupil of a great artist.

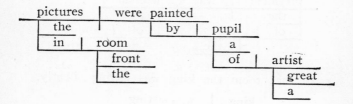

v.   art.   adj.   n.   v.   art.   n. prep.
2. Does the kindergarten teacher tell the story of

art. adj.   n.   prep. pro.   n.
the three bears to her pupils?

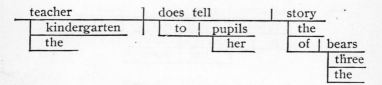

prep. pro.   adj.   n.   v. art.   n.   prep.
3. For your English lesson write a composition about

n.
Columbus.

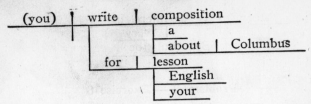

The (you) write composition / a / about Columbus / for lesson / English / your

art.   n.   prep. art.   n.   v. art.   n.   prep. adj.

4. The president of the club was a woman of great

n.

ability.

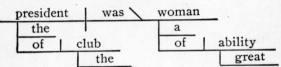

president | was \ woman / the / a / of club / of ability / the / great

prep. adj.   n.   art.   n.   v.   v.   adv.

5. In that room the king was sitting silently.

king | was sitting / the / silently / in room / that

A.   **Problem VI — Exercise 1**

1.

children | sent | books / those / x sister / many / in house / sick / that / their

2.

he | brought | boxes / x her / three / of pens

3.

(you) | give | pencils / x me / those

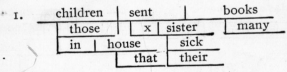

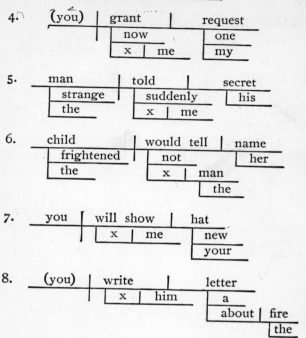

4. (you) | grant | request
now | one
x | me | my

5. man | told | secret
strange | suddenly | his
the | x | me

6. child | would tell | name
frightened | not | her
the | x | man
the

7. you | will show | hat
x | me | new
your

8. (you) | write | letter
x | him | a
about | fire
the

B. Have some one in the class look over these sentences. Select a person who will know whether they are correct or not.

Problem VI — Exercise 2

A.

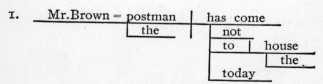

1. Mr. Brown = postman | has come
the | not
to | house
the
today

2.

```
Crisis = book | is \ interesting
     The    a          | very
            by | Churchill
```

3.

```
Mrs.Smith = president | gave | tickets
              the       | x | children | to | concert
              of | club     several         the
                    the
```

4.

```
Auditorium = building | has been bought
    the        a        | by | Mr.Jones = man
               in | Chicago           wealthy
                                        very
                                       a
```

5.

```
book | was given
   a   | to | Mr.Smith = winner
                   the
                   of | prize
                         the
```

6.

```
they = children | had been \ hungry
      poor        |   always
      those
```

7.

```
you | will send | book = Jungle
       x | me      the    The
       tomorrow
```

8.

```
brother = George | became \ educator
    my              |          noted
                               a
```

B. Have a pupil who does excellent work help you to correct these sentences.

Problem VI — Exercise 3

A. The direct object, or the object complement, completes the verb by naming the person or thing that receives the action of the verb. A noun in direct address names the person addressed.

B.

1.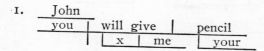

2.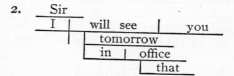

3.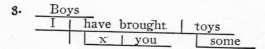

4.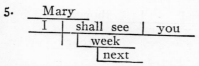

5.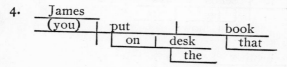

Note: In this sentence you will see that " week " is a noun used like an adverb, for it tells when. Such a noun is called an adverbial noun. Like any other noun it is modified by an adjective. The same is true of " afternoon " in sentence 8.

6.
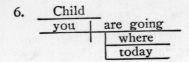

7.
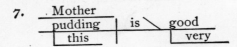

8.
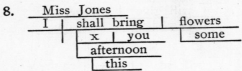

C. Let some one in the class help you to correct these sentences.

Problem VI — Exercise 4

1.
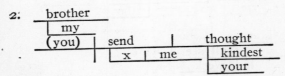

2.
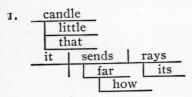

3.

Note: Can you tell why "grocer" is in apposition with "Mr. Brown"? Why is "Mr. Brown" not a noun in direct address?

4.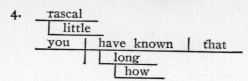

5.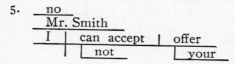

6.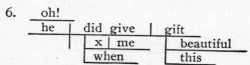

7.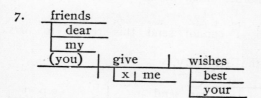

8.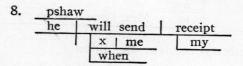

Problem VI — Exercise 5

A. A noun in apposition is a noun that is another name for the word it explains. An independent element is a word that is not necessary to the meaning of a sentence. It is not an explanatory word.

B.

 Int. *pro.* *v.* *adv.* *v.* *pro.* *art.* *adj.* *n.*
1. Oh, he has not given her the right package.

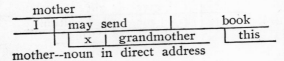

    her--indirect object

   n.   *v.* *pro.* *v.*   *n.*   *adj.* *n.*
2. Mother, may I send grandmother this book?

   mother--noun in direct address

 adv. *pro.* *v. adv.* *v.* *adj.* *n.* *prep.* *n.*
3. No, I cannot send this report to Mrs. Price,

 art.   *n.*
 the secretary.

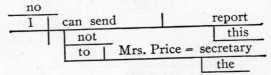

   secretary--noun in apposition

 pro. *adj.* *n.* *pro.* *v.* *adv* *adj.* *n.*
4. My dear child, you look very happy today.

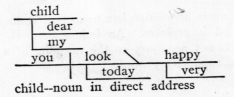

  child--noun in direct address

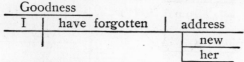

       n.   *pro.* *v.*   *v.*   *pro.* *adj.*   *n.*
5. Goodness! I have forgotten her new address.

Goodness--exclamatory noun

Problem VII — Exercise 1

A.

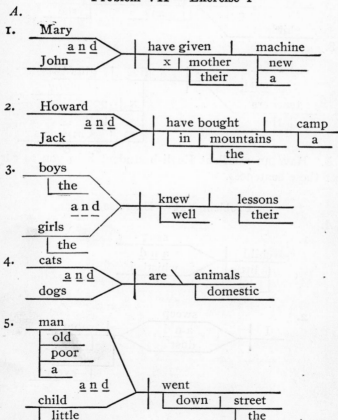

6.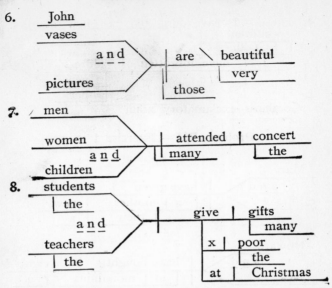

7.

8.

B. Have an excellent English student help you to correct these sentences.

Problem VII — Exercise 2

A.

1.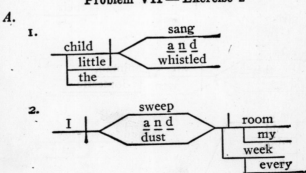

2.

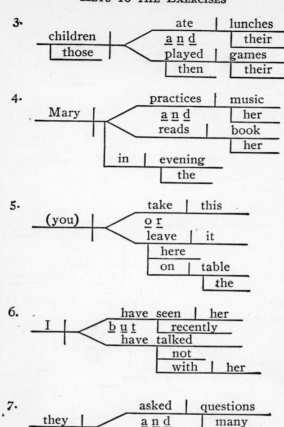

3.
children / those
ate | lunches
<u>a</u> <u>n</u> <u>d</u> | their
played | games
then | their

4.
Mary
practices | music
<u>a</u> <u>n</u> <u>d</u> | her
reads | book
her
in | evening
the

5.
(you)
take | this
<u>o</u> <u>r</u>
leave | it
here
on | table
the

6.
I
have seen | her
<u>b</u> <u>u</u> <u>t</u> | recently
have talked
not
with | her

7.
they
asked | questions
<u>a</u> <u>n</u> <u>d</u> | many
went
then
off
without | answer
an

8.

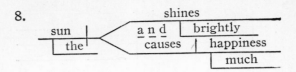

B. Have an excellent English student look **over these** sentences.

Problem VII — Exercise 3

A.

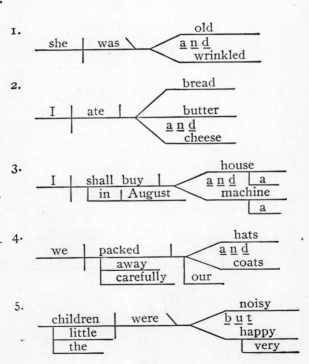

6.
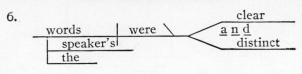

7.
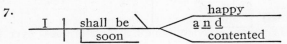
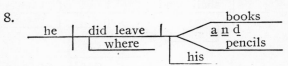

8.
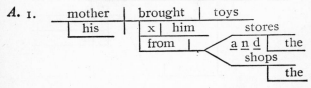

B. Have your teacher correct these sentences.

Problem VII — Exercise 4

A. 1.
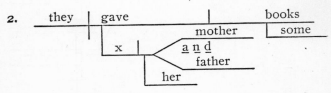

2.

3.
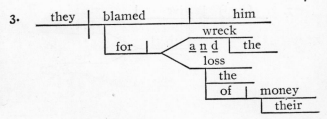

4.

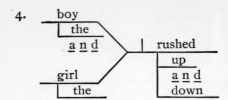

5.

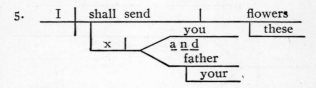

6..

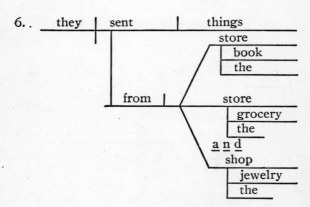

7.

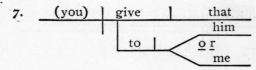

8.

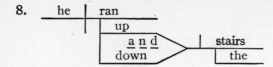

B. Have your teacher correct these sentences.

Problem VII — Exercise 5

1.

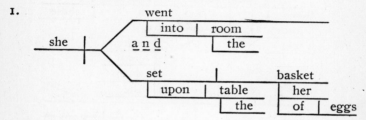

2.

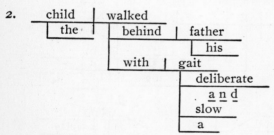

3.

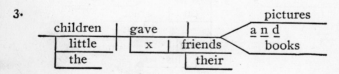

4.

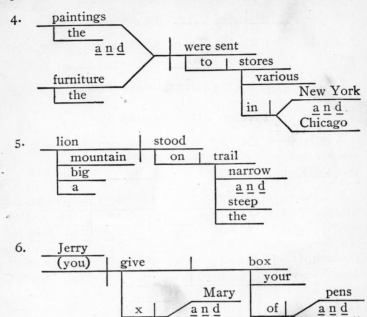

5.

6.

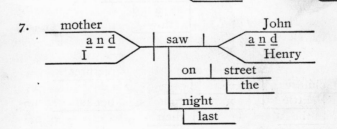

7.

8.

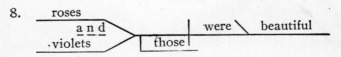

Problem VIII — Exercise 1

A. The four kinds of sentences according to their use are:

       1. Declarative
       2. Interrogative
       3. Exclamatory
       4. Imperative

Note: Since the illustrations are original, have your teacher or one of the pupils in your class help you to correct them.

B. Have you ever read the biography of Guglielmo Marconi, the inventor of the wireless? It is as fascinating as any story of adventure that was ever written. Let me tell you a few interesting things that the author tells about this remarkable man. Marconi was born into a home of wealth in Italy. He never lacked money for an education which could fit him for his wonderful work. In addition he was always able to buy any apparatus that was needed for his experiments. What do you suppose he invented first? When he was five years old, he made an indelible ink from wild berries. With this he marked his clothes. Then for eleven years he made no more discoveries. Are you wondering why he stopped so suddenly? Like all children, he wanted the appreciation of his mother, and when she did not seem to appreciate this first attempt at invention the little child was too discouraged to try anything else. At the age of sixteen he began to experiment with a crude apparatus which he had made himself. When he was twenty-one Marconi took out his first wireless patent. How he was ridiculed at first! But did he stop his work because of this? No, he went on as though nothing had been said. By the time he was twenty-four years of age, he had shown the world that messages could be transmitted without wires. He soon became world famous. His fame seemed to make as little impression upon him as did the ridicule that he had received earlier in his life. He continued to be simple in his tastes and unassuming in his actions. Do you want to know more about this man? Read his biography.

Note: Correct your paper for end punctuation only. Do not be concerned about the punctuation within the sentences.

Problem VIII — Exercise 2

A.

1. Dr. Marks called at 3 P.M.
2. Mrs. Price has gone to see her sister Miss Hunt.
3. If I do not order the groceries by 9 A.M., I shall not get them until afternoon.
4. Messrs. Jones and Allen are thinking of buying that hotel.
5. Columbus discovered America in 1492 A.D.

B. Since this part of the exercise is original, have your teacher or one of the pupils in the class help you to correct it.

Problem VIII — Exercise 3

A.

1. John, I wish you would bring me that book.
2. Which house did you visit, Mary?
3. I saw you, sir, as you came into the house.
4. Boys, here is my brother.
5. Doctor, will you come in?

6. It seems to me, my friend, that your advice is very timely.
7. I like your boat, Captain.
8. How do you like my hat, Mary, and my new cape?
9. Nancy, you should behave differently.
10. Mr. Grant, there must be a package here for me.
11. You funny girl, don't you know who I am?
12. Surely, John, you can come and help me a little.
13. Poor little boy, have you lost your mother?
14. Never mind, sonny, she will be here soon.
15. Look here, Buddy, you must go with me.

B. Since this part of the exercise is original, have your teacher or one of the pupils in the class help you to correct it.

Problem VIII — Exercise 4

A.

1. They talked about operations, a topic of interest to many people.
2. In this attitude of thankfulness I went home to my castle, a tent on the shore of the lake.
3. I once knew a man, a peculiar old fellow, who would not wear a collar.
4. My friends, Mary and Jane, came to see me every day until I was well.
5. Abraham Lincoln, the famous president of the United States, was once a country boy.
6. He is the son of Mr. Snyder, the Mayor.
7. I tried to lift the gun, a heavy antique thing.
8. Howard Smith, a resident of San Francisco, was a passenger on the boat.
9. We arrived in Albany, the capital of New York.
10. Joe, the grocery boy, has a remarkable memory.

11. My hearth, an open place filled with square tiles, was the center of my new home.

12. Mr. Smith's daughters, Eunice and Eurina, will go to Canada next summer.

13. Before I could publish the document, Colonel House, President Wilson's associate, arrived in London.

14. Mr. Steele, a leading newspaper man, returned to Chicago early in the winter.

15. Tolstoy, a great Russian writer, desired universal peace.

B. Have your teacher or one of the pupils in the class help you to correct these sentences. Select some one who writes correct English.

Problem VIII — Exercise 5

A.

1. He traveled through Washington, Oregon, and California.

2. I had lost my boat, my gun, and my dog.

3. He rang the bell, waited a moment, looked through the window, and finally opened the door.

4. My dog and my cat and my parrot were now my only friends.

5. Day after day, week after week, month after month, he worked without a thought for himself.

6. He sold butter and cheese and milk.

7. I went up the hill to see how the shore lay, how the current set, and how the boat could leave the channel.

8. He carried in his belt a saw, a hatchet, and two powder pouches.

9. At my back I carried my basket, on my shoulder I had my gun, and over my head I raised a great, clumsy, ugly goat's-skin umbrella.

10. I listened, I looked around me, I could hear nothing, and I could see nothing.

11. I lay down and slept soundly and awoke much refreshed.

12. I should like to visit Norway, Holland, and Italy.

13. I took with me six candles, a tinder-box, a gun, and some biscuits.

14. I had two little goats, several parrots, and many tame sea-fowls.

15. He visited us in January, in March, and in August.

B. Have your teacher or one of the pupils in the class help you to correct these sentences.

Problem VIII — Exercise 6

A.

1. Yes, I can do this for you.
2. My, but she plays beautifully.
3. Goodness! how she does cry.
4. No, he cannot go.
5. Alas! I have lost my English paper.
6. Well, I will do what I can for you.
7. Heavens! she is alone on that raft!
8. Home! how I wish I were there!
9. Oh, my child is not here!
10. Hey, can't you hear me?

B. Have your teacher or some one of the pupils in the class help you to correct these sentences.

Problem VIII — Exercise 7

1. Send your bill,[1] Mr. Nash,[2] to my daughter,[3] the treasurer of the association.[5]

    1. Direct address   3. Direct address
    2. Abbreviation   4. Appositive
          5. Declarative sentence

2. Eat less candy,[1] drink more milk, and sleep more at
night.[3]

    1. Series of clauses   2. Series of clauses
         3. Declarative sentence

3. Hark![1] I hear some one at the door,[2] John.[3]

    1. Interjection   2. Direct address
         3. Declarative sentence

4. Yes,[1] I will send your name to Mr.[2] Jones,[3] the real
estate agent.[4]

    1. After yes   3. Appositive
    2. Abbreviation   4. Declarative sentence

5. I like cheese and crackers and sardines.[1]

    1. Declarative sentence

6. A boomerang,[1] the weapon used by the natives of
Australia,[2] was sent to me by my nephew.[3]

    1. Appositive   2. Appositive
         3. Declarative sentence

7. I did not know that Dr.¹ Smith,² John's friend,³ had been here.⁴

    1. Abbreviation
    2. Appositive
    3. Appositive
    4. Declarative sentence

8. Jane,¹ Mrs.² Smith,³ your cousin,⁴ visited us last night.⁵

    1. Direct address
    2. Abbreviation
    3. Appositive
    4. Appositive
    5. Declarative sentence

9. Open the desk,¹ take out the paper,² and write me a letter.³

    1. Series of clauses
    2. Series of clauses
    3. Imperative sentence

10. Aha!¹ I caught you this time,² you little rascal.³

    1. Interjection
    2. Direct address
    3. Declarative sentence

Problem IX — Exercise 1

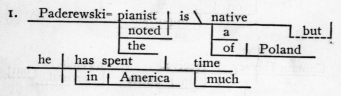

3.
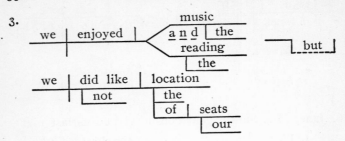

we | enjoyed | < music
                  a n d | the
                  reading
                        | the
                                    ⌐but⌐

we | did like | location
        | not | the
                  of | seats
                        | our

4.
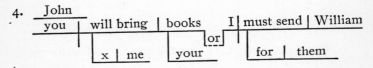

John
you | will bring | books
        | x | me | your
                  or
I | must send | William
        | for | them

5.
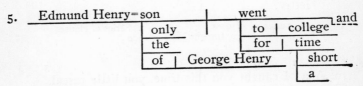

Edmund Henry=son   went   ⌐and
                  | only | to | college
                  | the | for | time
                  | of | George Henry | short
                                          | a

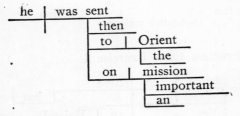

he | was sent
        | then
        | to | Orient
                  | the
        | on | mission
                  | important
                  | an

6.
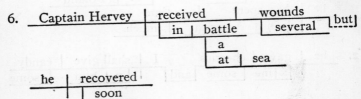

Captain Hervey | received | wounds
                  | in | battle | several   ⌐but⌐
                        | a
                        | at | sea

he | recovered
        | soon

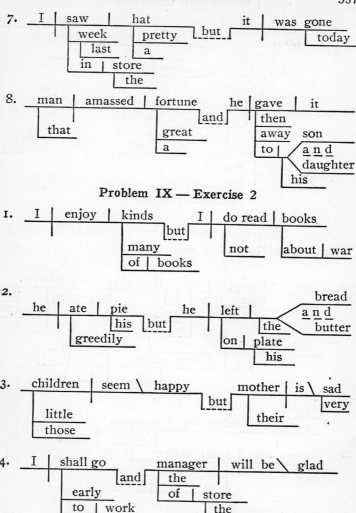

Problem IX — Exercise 2

5.

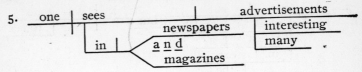

6.

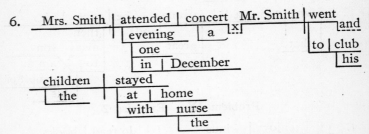

Note: The group of words "one evening in December" is understood to modify each verb.

7.

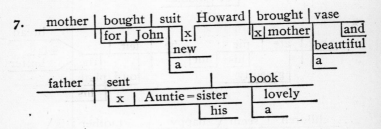

8.

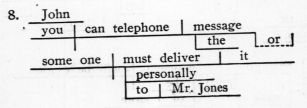

1.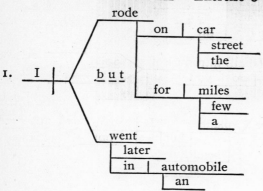

I | rode
but
on | car / street / the
for | miles / few / a
went / later / in | automobile / an

2.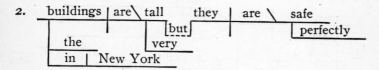

buildings | are \ tall [but] they | are \ safe
the / very / perfectly
in | New York

3.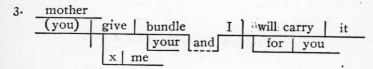

mother
(you) | give | bundle / your [and] I | will carry | it
x | me / for | you

4.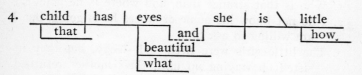

child | has | eyes [and] she | is \ little
that / beautiful / how
what

5.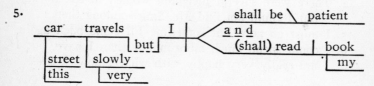

car | travels [but] I | shall be \ patient
street / slowly / and / (shall) read | book
this / very / my

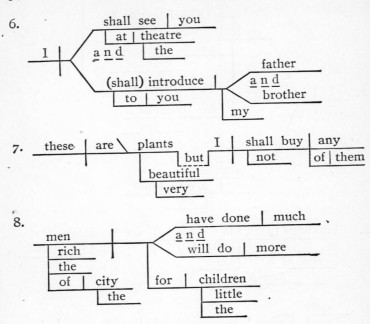

6.

7.

8.

Problem IX — Exercise 4

A.

1. Who is that strange man, and where is he going?
2. I do not know his name or where he is going, but I am willing to ask him.
3. The little girls were tired and sleepy, but they insisted on staying up until their mother returned.
4. There were several men and women in the library, but I could not find Mr. Smith among them.
5. I must go now, but sometime I'll come back again.
6. I could spend much more money than I have, but I am really very happy with what I now possess.

7. Our childhood days are our happiest ones, but one seldom knows it at the time.

8. At four o'clock a special edition of the paper is sold, and every one buys it most eagerly.

9. I once went through the southern part of Iowa with a two-horse covered sleigh, and the trip lasted two whole months.

10. We invaded Denver, and our traveler, Charley Cranston, took an order from a Denver bookseller for several hundred volumes of standard poems.

11. Dr. Hornaday was one of the world's foremost naturalists, and his last book came with authority from a man of ability.

12. I was a boy just out of college, and Mr. Allison appeared to me to be a person of great age and dignity.

13. The football team won every game, but the baseball team was not so successful.

14. He may have put limitations upon himself, but he never shrank from doing his duty.

15. Mr. Allison did not stand in the class with Lincoln, but he did belong to that class of statesmen who made possible the success of representative government.

16. I came here intending to open a shoe store, but it was impossible to find a vacant room.

17. Buildings were going up by the hundred, and the noise of the hammer was ceaseless.

18. Mr. Robertson also started a shoe business, and we supplied shoes to all the inhabitants of our little village.

19. The discomforts of life on the frontier were numerable, but many men and women endured them.

20. After breakfast we talked business, and the old men gave a larger order.

B. Have your teacher correct these sentences.

Note to student: In this exercise you have learned that a comma must precede the conjunction in a compound sentence. If the sentence contains clauses that are very short, the comma may be omitted except when the conjunction is *for*. In the sentence, " He went down the street whistling for his mother had just given him a dollar," a comma is needed before the conjunction as an aid to rapid reading. With the comma inserted the meaning of the sentence is clear at a glance, — " He went down the street whistling, for his mother had just given him a dollar."

When *for* is a conjunction, it is always preceded by a comma. In the sentence, " He whistled for his dog," no comma is needed because *for* is a preposition. Whenever you write a sentence containing *for*, determine whether it is a conjunction or a preposition. If it is a conjunction, precede it by a comma. If you think that you need a little practice in writing sentences containing *for*, write five sentences in which *for* is a conjunction and five in which *for* is a preposition. Your teacher will be willing to look these over.

Problem IX — Exercise 5

A.

1. I will study and finish my work; I won't be a failure.

2. It is hard to leave off old customs; it is harder to go against one's own will.

3. America is the melting pot of God; it is the great melting pot where all races are fusing and re-forming.

4. An honest man is a great man; he is beautiful, great, and strong.

5. The largest and noblest and most valuable qualities of manhood are not showy; the largest and noblest of men are alike unshowy.

6. Every day is a new life; every sunrise is but a new birth.

7. We have committed the golden rule to memory; now let us commit it to life.

8. There is only one real failure possible; that is not to be true to the best one knows.

9. Pessimism leads to weakness; optimism leads to power.

10. Hypocrisy desires to seem good rather than to be so; honesty desires to be good rather than to seem so.

11. Nothing great is achieved without the severest discipline of heart and mind; nothing is well done that is done easily.

12. We measure a man's intellect by his achievements; we measure his achievements by his difficulties.

13. The Government should help the farmers to get a start; it should not tax them to begin.

14. A camel can easily carry a weight of one thousand pounds on its back; this is four times as much as a horse can carry.

15. The camel begins work at the age of four years and is useful for half a century; the horse is generally played out at fifteen years of age.

16. This is the best day in the year; every day is the best of all days.

17. Wealth has no power to produce happiness; it takes away the spur of necessity, which is a man's great developer.

18. None knew what the sign meant; no one dared to ask.

19. There is no table talk like laughter at meals; it is the great enemy of dyspepsia.

20. Her heart lived always in the summer; the winter of age could touch only her body.

B.   Have your teacher correct these sentences.

Problem IX — Exercise 6

1. Do not become discouraged; always keep your enthusiasm.

2. Our little daughter has work she does every morning; then she plays as she wishes the rest of the day.

3. He felt that he was becoming very useless; therefore he decided to spend more time in study.

4. The world is full of opportunities; all gates open to him who can use them.

5. I have my health and my friends; what more do I want?

6. All our worries were needless, and not a single thing occurred to mar the happiness of all.

7. I will send him all that I can; moreover I will not let him repay it.

8. He has read the story, and he has seen the author; still he insists that he has no remembrance of either.

9. There are twenty ways of going to a point, but there is always one that is the shortest.

10. I know he was in the city last week; here is the letter in which he says so.

11. Look up and not down; look forward and not back.

12. I slept very late; in fact, it was noon before I awoke.

13. The chairman made the statement that every man and woman in the audience was selfish; then there began a veritable combat of words.

14. He made no pretense of liking the house; he showed clearly that he thought it was no place for him and his family.

15. At eight o'clock we retired to our berths; thus we failed to see their departure.

16. First you mix your eggs and milk, and then you let them boil for five minutes.

17. The boys are far more systematic about their football practice; they make more of a business of it.

18. I expressed a wish to see the institution; therefore John sent me an invitation to visit them for a week.

19. We hurriedly ate lunch, put on our hats, rushed out of the door, and then remembered that we had forgotten the cat.

20. Any place is a home where children dwell and are loved, and no place is a home if no children are ever there.

Problem IX — Exercise 7

A. Have your teacher help you to correct these sentences.

B.

1. She brought me a lovely fan from Italy[1]; from India she sent Mary some jade beads[2].

   1. Independent clauses without co-ordinate conjunction.
   2. Declarative sentence.

she	brought	fan	she	sent	beads

x | me   x   x | Mary   jade
from| Italy   lovely   from|India   some
   a

2. He had promised her a gown from Paris; therefore he sent it.²

    1. Independent clause without co-ordinate conjunction.
    2. Declarative sentence.

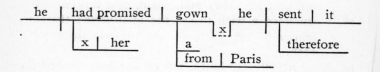

3. My son was happy in his work and did much for others.¹

    1. Declarative sentence.

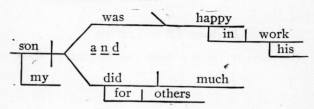

4. A man should think first of his character,¹ and then he can consider his condition.²

    1. Two independent clauses with co-ordinate conjunction.
    2. Declarative sentence.

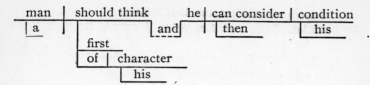

5. Many times he asked for flowers,[1] but the days were cold and dreary,[2] and we could find none in the fields and pastures.[3]

   1. Independent clauses with co-ordinate conjunction.
   2. Independent clauses with co-ordinate conjunction.
   3. Declarative sentence.

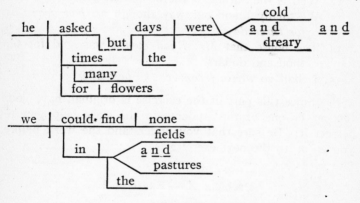

Problem X — Exercise 1

A.

Note: The dependent clauses are italicized and the conjunctions are in heavy type.

   1. He looked **as if** *he were hungry.*

2. I gave **him** the picture **that** *I liked best.*

3. **Unless** *I see you tomorrow,* I cannot do your work for you.

4. The little lady, **whose** *purse you found,* is here.

5. I will read the article **if** *you ask me to.*

6. Where is the house **that** *he bought?*

7. They sent the child to a school **where** *he knew the teacher.*

8. I ate some candy **that** *James gave me.*

9. I wish I had a machine **that** *would run without gasoline.*

10. **When** *you came,* I was fast asleep.

11. The knight, **who** *won the prize,* went away suddenly.

12. Who is the author of the book **that** *you mentioned?*

13. We finally found our way **though** *we had been lost for three days.*

14. The house **that** *Mr. Ryan owned* was sold for ten thousand dollars.

15. I shall go **where** *I can get the best offer.*

B. Since this part of the exercise is original, have your teacher or one of the students in the class help you to correct it. Be sure that you understand the work before you go on to the next exercise.

Problem X — Exercise 2

A.

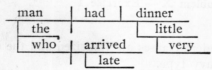

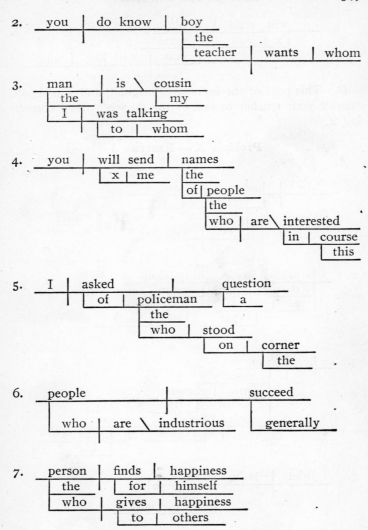

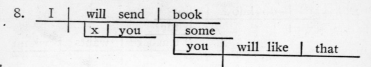

8.

B. This part of the exercise is original, and you should consult your teacher or one of the students when correcting it.

Problem X — Exercise 3

A.

1.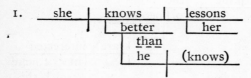

2.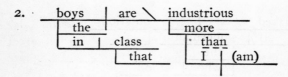

3.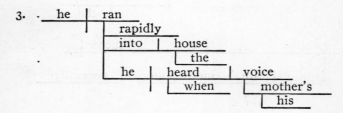

4.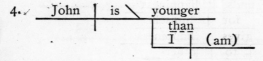

5.

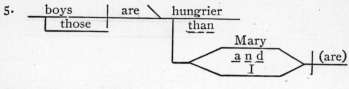

6.

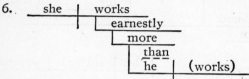

Note the following points:

1. The clause, "he knows" in sentence 1 modifies "better" and not "knows."
2. In sentence 3, the dependent clause is placed below the independent clause although it stands first in the sentence.

B. Since this part of the exercise is original, have your teacher or one of the pupils in the class help you to correct it. Be sure that you have mastered this exercise before you leave it.

Problem X — Exercise 4

A.

1.

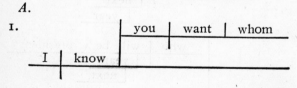

2.

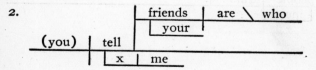

3.

		who	will be elected
you	do know		

4.

		he	is looking	
			for	whom
I	do know			
	not			

5.

		he	invited	whom
you	have forgotten			

B. Have your teacher or one of the pupils in the class help you to correct this part of the exercise.

Problem X — Exercise 5

A.

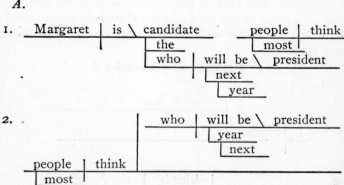

1. Margaret | is \ candidate
   the
   who | will be \ president
   next
   year
   people | think
   most

2. who | will be \ president
   year
   next
   people | think
   most

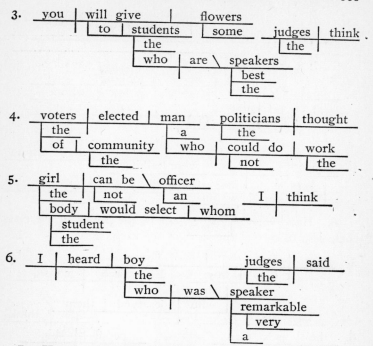

3.
```
you | will give | flowers
     | to | students | some | judges | think
          | the              | the
          | who | are \ speakers
                    | best
                    | the
```

4.
```
voters | elected | man           politicians | thought
the     |         | a            the
of | community | who | could do | work
     the         |      not      | the
```

5.
```
girl | can be \ officer
the   | not     | an              I | think
body  | would select | whom
  student
  the
```

6.
```
I | heard | boy                 judges | said
           | the                the
           | who | was \ speaker
                      | remarkable
                      | very
                    a
```

B. Have an excellent English pupil help you to correct these original sentences.

Problem X — Exercise 6

A.

1.
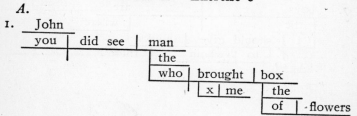
```
John
you | did see | man
              | the
              | who | brought | box
                    | x | me   | the
                                | of | flowers
```

2.

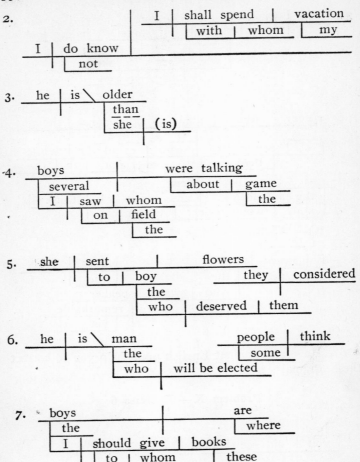

```
                      I | shall spend | vacation
                        |  with | whom | my
I | do know  |
  |  not
```

3.
```
he | is \ older
            than
            she | (is)
```

4.
```
boys          |        were talking
  several     |           about | game
  I | saw | whom              |  the
    |  on | field
          |  the
```

5.
```
she | sent   |        flowers
    | to | boy         they | considered
    |  the
    | who | deserved | them
```

6.
```
he | is \ man          people | think
         the             some |
         who | will be elected
```

7.
```
boys              |       are
  the             |         where
  I | should give | books
    |  to | whom      these
```

8.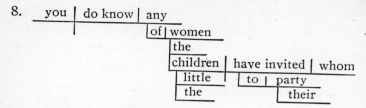

B. Have your teacher help you to correct this part of the exercise.

Problem XI — Exercise 1

A.

1. If he comes before I return, tell him to wait for me.
2. While he was sitting there, in walked his sister Jane.
3. When he heard his mother's voice, he ran into the next room.
4. While he sat there reading his book, the train left the station.
5. If you want me to do this work for you, say so.
6. While he was in Australia, he purchased many interesting souvenirs.
7. As soon as she came into the house, she made every one happy.
8. After he had been gone about a month, we heard that he was doing very well in his business.
9. While he was studying, his brother entered the room and took his hat.
10. When I go into a book store, I always want to buy something.
11. As soon as I saw him, he asked if mother was home.
12. When he saw us, he was very much surprised.
13. If you want to succeed in life, start at once to do your work to the best of your ability.

14. As soon as he went down, the elevator fell.
15. While the teacher was working at her desk, several visitors entered.
16. Although he was no financier, he was able to gain considerable wealth.
17. When he asked me for an opinion, I was very loath to give it.
18. After he had counted the votes, he posted the results.
19. When the telephone rang, I was talking with the laundry man.
20. Whenever she comes to my house, I am tempted to tell her the secret.

· *B.*   Have some one who understands this exercise help you to correct these original sentences.

Problem XI — Exercise 2

1. Mildred Smith, whose mother is a musician, cannot read a note of music.
2. All things that man has made will some day pass away.
3. The music that Handel composed is better than mine.
4. I saw the poor child, whom the truck had struck.
5. The clothes, which I put on the line last night, are not dry yet.
6. The boys that left the building early must remain later tonight.
7. The book, which I bought for mother, has been stolen.
8. The trip, which I chose for my vacation, costs too much for one of my means.
9. I made a great fire upon the hearth, which I had paved with some square tiles.

10. Mr. Spense, who cannot speak one word of French, is trying to carry on a conversation with a French-man.

11. I had my long sail boat, with which I could escape from my place of captivity.

12. The man that invented the telephone is my greatest benefactor.

13. All amusements that are really harmful should be prohibited.

14. I refuse to ride on any street car that is operated by one man.

15. Any man that is a gentleman will treat a lady with respect.

16. I know a place, where there is a hidden treasure.

17. The children that were present every day were given special recognition.

18. Here is Oscar, who won the prize for three years.

19. I will give a dollar to anyone that can answer this question.

20. James, who was ready to go, told the others to hurry.

B. Have your teacher help you to correct these sentences.

Problem XI — Exercise 3

A.

1. While he was studying, into the room walked his
mother and father.

    1. Dependent clause first   2. Declarative sentence

2. I have found my pearl necklace, which my brother
sent me from Japan.

    1. Non-restrictive clause   2. Declarative sentence

3. Just as I had set my mast and sail,[1] I saw some alteration of the current was near.[2]

    1. Dependent clause first   2. Declarative sentence

4. Shall the person that found your purse be rewarded?[1]

    1. Interrogative sentence (The dependent clause is restrictive.)

5. They that know what it is to be rescued from thieves may guess what my joy was.[1]

    1. Declarative sentence (The dependent clause is restrictive.)

6. The inlet,[1] which was as narrow as a brook,[2] was a beautiful place for a boating trip.[3]

    1.
    2. } Non-restrictive clause.   3. Declarative sentence

7. Robinson Crusoe was able to make a suit of clothes wholly of skins although he was not a tailor by trade.[1]

    1. Declarative sentence

8. When I had no need for my umbrella,[1] I could close it and carry it under my arm.[2]

    1. Dependent clause first   2. Declarative sentence

9. After he had resided on the island many years,[1] he returned to his native country.[2]

    1. Dependent clause first   2. Declarative sentence

10. When Mr. White returned from business,[1] he took a long trip around the world.[2]

    1. Dependent clause first   2. Declarative sentence

B. Have your teacher help you to correct these original sentences. Do not attempt to take a test on this work until you have mastery of the subject.

Problem XII — Exercise 1

A.

1. (*a-b*) Bob, John has sent Mildred and me a picture
   $^{n. (1)}$ $^{n.}$ $^{v.}$ $^{v.}$ $^{n.}$ $^{conj. pro. art.}$ $^{n.}$
   of his new home; it is very beautiful.
   $^{prep. pro. adj.}$ $^{n. (2)}$ $^{pro. v.}$ $^{adv.}$ $^{adj. (3)}$

    1. Noun in direct address
    2. Compound sentence without co-ordinate conjunction
    3. Declarative sentence

(c)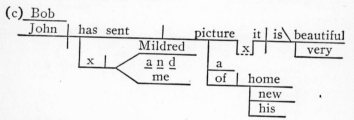

(*d*) Compound sentence
(*e*) Use of italicized words:
    Bob — noun in direct address
    me — indirect object
(*f*) Reason for capitalization:
    Bob — proper noun and the first word of the sentence
    John, Mildred — proper nouns

2. (*a-b*)
     v.   pro.   n. (1) pro.   v.   prep.   n. (2)   adj.
    Is your son, who lives in Chicago, older

    conj. pro. (3)
    than I?

       1 and 2 — non-restrictive clause; 3 — Interrogative sentence.

(*c*)

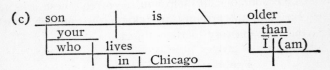

(*d*) Complex sentence
(*e*) Use of italicized words:
    who — subject of dependent clause
    I — subject of dependent clause
(*f*) Reason for capitalization
    Is — first word of the sentence
    I — when used as a word, is always capitalized

3. (*a-b*)
       pro.   v.   adv.   v. art. n.   prep. n (1)   art.
    We have just read a book by Kipling, the

    adj.   n. (2) conj. pro. v.   adv.   v.   pro. prep. art.
    English poet, but we have not returned it to the

    n.   (3)
    library.

    1. Appositive
    2. Appositive; two independent clauses connected by a co-
        ordinate conjunction
    3. Declarative sentence

(*c*)

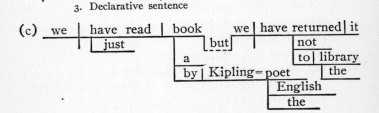

(*d*) Compound sentence

(*e*) Use of italicized words:

poet — noun in apposition

but — coördinate conjunction that connects two independent clauses

(*f*) Reason for capitalization:

We — first word of the sentence

Kipling — proper noun

English — proper adjective

4. (*a-b*)
    conj. *adv.* *pro.*   *v.*   *adv.* (1) *pro.* *v.*   *v.*   *pro.* *adj.*
When he comes here, I shall give him this
    n. (2)
magazine.

    1. Dependent clause standing first in a complex sentence
    2. Declarative sentence

(c)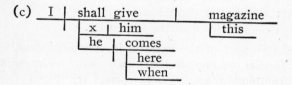

(*d*) Complex sentence

(*e*) Use of italicized words:

when — conjunctive adverb that introduces the dependent clause and connects it to the independent clause

him — indirect object

(*f*) Reason for capitalization:

When — first word of the sentence

I — when used as a word, is always capitalized

        v. pro. art.   adj.   n. (1) *pro. pro.   v.   v.*

5. (*a-b*) Is he the interesting man, who you said will

        v. prep. art.   n.   n. (2)

be at the hotel tonight?

    1. Non-restrictive clause
    2. Interrogative sentence

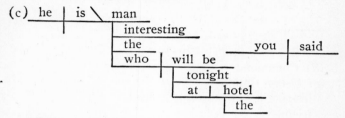

   (*d*) Complex sentence
   (*e*) Use of italicized words:
     man — subjective complement
     who — subject of dependent clause
   (*f*) Reason for capitalization:
     Is — first word of the sentence

B. This part of the exercise is very important. Have your teacher or one of the pupils, who understands the work thoroughly, help you to correct it.

Problem XII — Exercise 2

A.

          (1)   *n.*   (2) *art.*   *n.*   *prep.* *n.* (3) *v.*

1. (*a-b*) Mr. Wallace, the instructor in music, gave

    pro.   *n.*   *art. adj.*   *n.* (4) *pro.* *v.*   *conj.*   *v.*

his friends a rare treat; he played and sang

    pro. *prep. pro.*   *n.* (5)

many of his pieces.

    1. Abbreviation
    2. Appositive
    3. Appositive
    4. Two independent clauses without co-ordinate conjunction
    5. Declarative sentence

(c)

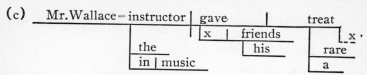

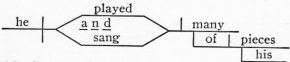

(d) Compound sentence
(e) Use of italicized words:
   instructor — noun in apposition
   friends — indirect object
(f) Reason for capitalization:
   Mr. — first word of the sentence; the abbreviation
   "Mr." is always capitalized
   Wallace — proper noun

        v.   *pro.*   *v.*   *adv.*   *conj.* *pro.*
2. (*a-b*) Are you going sooner than we?

(c)

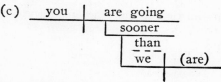

(d) Complex sentence
(e) Use of italicized words:
   than — subordinate conjunction that introduces the
   dependent clause and connects it to the independent clause
   we — subject of dependent clause
(f) Reason for capitalization:
   Are — first word of the sentence

         v.   *pro.*   *v.*   *prep.* *pro.*   *adj.*   *n.*   *v.*   *v.* (1)

3. (*a-b*) Do you know for whom that man is looking,

      n. (2)

    Mary?

      1. Noun in direct address
      2. Interrogative sentence

(*c*)   Mary

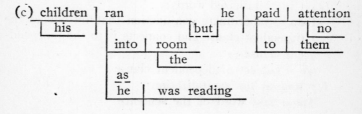

   (*d*) Complex sentence

   (*e*) Use of italicized words:

     whom — object of preposition

     Mary — noun in direct address

   (*f*) Reason for capitalization:

     Do — first word of the sentence

     Mary — proper noun

      conj. pro. *v.*   *v.* (1) *pro.*   *n.*   *v.* *prep.* *art*

4. (*a-b*) As he was reading, his children ran into the

     n.   *adv.* (2) *conj. pro.* *v.*   *adj.*   *n.*   *prep*

    room hurriedly, but he paid no attention to

     pro. (3)

    them.

      1. Dependent clause standing first
      2. Two independent clauses connected by co-ordinate conjunction
      3. Declarative sentence

(*c*) children | ran ... he | paid | attention

(*d*) Compound-complex sentence

(*e*) Use of italicized words:

as — subordinate conjunction that introduces the dependent clause and connects it to the independent clause

but — co-ordinate conjunction that connects two independent clauses

(*f*) Reason for capitalization:

As — first word of the sentence

5. (*a-b*) The man, whom you saw here, gave mother and me tickets to the lecture, but we cannot use them.

art. n. (1) *pro. pro. v. adv.* (2) *v. n.*
conj. pro. n. prep. art. n. (3) *conj. pro. v. adv.*
v. pro. (4)

1.
2. } Non-restrictive clause

3. Two independent clauses connected by co-ordinate conjunction

4. Declarative sentence

(c)

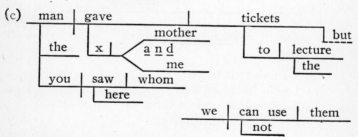

(*d*) Compound-complex sentence

(*e*) Use of italicized words:

whom — object complement of saw

me — indirect object

(*f*) Reason for capitalization:

The — first word of the sentence

Note: Look at the diagrams of sentences 4 and 5 again. Both consist of three clauses: in each there are two independent clauses and one dependent clause. Have you shown this?

B. Have your teacher or some one in the class help you to correct this part of the exercise. Be sure that you understand this work.

Problem XII — Exercise 3

⁓ *A.*

      art.   *n.* (1)   *pro.*   *art.*   *n.*   *v.* (2)
1. (*a-b*) The boys, whom the teacher recommended,
     v.   *v.*   *prep.* (3)   *n.*   *conj. pro.*(4)
    were rewarded by Mr. Smith and me.

      1. ⎱
      2. ⎰ Non-restrictive clause
      3. Abbreviation
      4. Declarative sentence

(*c*)

   (*d*) Complex sentence
   (*e*) Use of italicized words:
     whom — object complement of " recommended "
⁓   me — object of preposition

             n. (1)   *pro.*   *v.*   *pro.*   *v.*   *v.* (2) *conj. adv.*
2. (*a-b*) Goodness! I thought you had gone, but here
    pro.   *v.*   *adv.* (3)
    you are again !

      1. Exclamatory noun
      2. Two independent clauses connected by co-ordinate conjunction
      3. Exclamatory sentence

(c)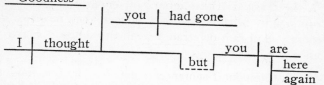

(d) Compound-complex sentence

(e) Goodness — exclamatory noun

you — subject of dependent clause

but — co-ordinate conjunction that connects two independent clauses

3. (*a-b*)
$\overset{adj.}{This} \overset{adj.}{pretty} \overset{n. (1)}{cloth,} \overset{pro.}{which} \overset{pro.}{she} \overset{v.}{will} \overset{v.}{make} \overset{prep.}{into}$
$\overset{n. (2)}{dresses,} \overset{v.}{was} \overset{art.}{a} \overset{n.}{gift} \overset{prep.}{from} \overset{n.}{Mildred} \overset{conj.}{and} \overset{pro. (3)}{me.}$

1.
2. } Non-restrictive clause

3. Declarative sentence

(c)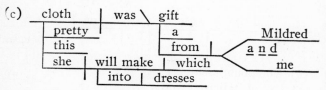

(d) Complex sentence

(e) Use of italicized words:

which — object complement

gift — subjective complement

me — object of preposition

4. (*a-b*)
$\overset{pro.}{He} \overset{adv.}{often} \overset{v.}{asked} \overset{pro.}{her} \overset{conj.}{and} \overset{pro.}{me} \overset{adj.}{strange} \overset{(n)}{questions,}$ 1.
$\overset{conj.}{but} \overset{pro.}{we} \overset{adv.}{never} \overset{v.}{answered} \overset{pro. (2)}{them.}$

1. Two independent clauses connected by a co-ordinate conjunction

2. Declarative sentence

(c)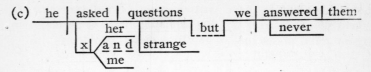

(*d*) Compound sentence

(*e*) Use of italicized words:

    her — indirect object

    but — co-ordinate conjunction that connects two independent clauses

             n. (1) *pro.* *v.*   *v.* *adj.*   *n.* *conj.*(2). *pro.* *v.*

5. (*a-b*) Mother, I will do this work, for you must

    v. *adv.* (3)

    rest now.

      1. Noun in direct address
      2. "For" as a conjunction
      3. Declarative sentence

(c)

Mother
I	will do	work	you	must rest
		this	for	now

(*d*) Compound sentence

(*e*) Use of italicized words:

    mother — noun in direct address

    for — co-ordinate conjunction that connects two independent clauses

B. Have your teacher help you to correct these original sentences.

Problem XII — Exercise 4

This is a very important exercise, for in writing letters and assignments for other lessons you will often use such sentences as you have written here. Have your teacher help you to correct it. Be sure that there is no doubt in your mind about any of the first eleven problems.

Problem XIII — Exercise 1

A.

	Number			*Number*
1. each	singular	10. either		singular
boys	plural	hats		plural
2. army	singular	11. yours		singular (or plural)
3. flock	singular	12. United States		singular
birds	plural	13. some one		singular
4. they	plural	his		singular
their	plural	14. army		singular
5. committee	singular	it		singular
6. everybody	singular	15. committee		plural
he	singular	their		plural
7. we	plural	16. you		singular (or plural)
our	plural	17. they		plural
8. nobody	singular	18. pupil		singular
9. every one	singular	his		singular

Notice these points:

1. " Committee " in sentence 5 is singular because the collection of individuals is considered as one group. In sentence 15 " committee " is plural because the group is considered as individuals.
2. " Yours " in sentence 11 may be singular or plural since the form is the same for both numbers.

B. Have your teacher or some one in the class help you to correct this part of the exercise.

Problem XIII — Exercise 2

A.	*Number*	*Gender*	*Person*
1. each	singular	masculine	3
boys	plural	masculine	3
his	singular	masculine	3
sister	singular	feminine	3
2. she	singular	feminine	3
her	singular	feminine	3
3. no one	singular	common	3
4. any one	singular	common	3
5. I	singular	common	1
book	singular	neuter	3
6. teacher	singular	common	3
7. army	singular	neuter	3
individuals	plural	common	3
8. my	singular	common	1
it	singular	neuter	3
9. We	plural	common	1
your	singular (plural)	common	2
10. anybody	singular	common	3
11. neither	singular	feminine	3
12. some	plural	common	3
I	singular	common	1

B. Have some one in the class correct this part of the exercise.

Problem XIII — Exercise 3

A.	*Use*	*Case*
1. he	subject of " has left "	Nominative
2. we	subject of " are " understood	Nominative

A.	Use	Case
3. who	subjective complement of " is "	Nominative
she	subject of " is "	Nominative
4. she	subjective complement of " is "	Nominative
5. we	subject of " may go "	Nominative
6. he	subjective complement of " is "	Nominative
7. he	subject of " is " understood	Nominative
8. I	subjective complement of " is "	Nominative
9. who	subject of " will be "	Nominative
10. I	subjective complement of " was "	Nominative
who	subject of " spoke "	Nominative
11. we	subjective complement of " is "	Nominative
who	subject of " lost "	Nominative
12. we	subject of " voted "	Nominative

B. Have your teacher or some one in the class help you to correct this exercise

Problem XIII — Exercise 4

A.	Use	Case
1. me	indirect object of " gave "	Objective
2. whom	object complement of " do want "	Objective
3. me	object of preposition " between "	Objective
4. me	object of preposition " for "	Objective
5. whom	object complement of " saw "	Objective
6. me	indirect object of " send "	Objective
7. her	object complement of " drove "	Objective
8. him	object of preposition " between "	Objective
her	object of preposition " between "	Objective
9. I	subject of " shall do "	Nominative
me	object of preposition " to "	Objective
10. him	indirect object of " sent "	Objective
me	indirect object of " sent "	Objective

11. Who   subject of " had caused "   Nominative

12. whom   object complement of " do expect "   Objective

   B. Have your teacher or some pupil in the class help you to correct this part of the exercise.

Problem XIII — Exercise 5

A.	*Number*	*Case*
1. boy's	singular	Possessive
2. boys'	plural	Possessive
3. lady's	singular	Possessive
4. grocer's	singular	Possessive
our	plural	Possessive
5. weeks'	plural	Possessive
6. men's	plural	Possessive
7. children's	plural	Possessive
8. child's	singular	Possessive
9. yours	singular (or plural)	Possessive
10. ladies'	plural	Possessive
11. its	singular	Possessive
12. hers	singular	Possessive
13. women's	plural	Possessive

NOTE: In sentence 3 " grocer's " is in the possessive case because the meaning is " I am going to the grocer's store." Such expressions as " the butcher's," " the baker's," and " the grocer's," are in the possessive case though the noun to which they show possession is not expressed.

   B. Have your teacher or some pupil help you to correct these sentences. Be sure that you have written sentences that are punctuated correctly.

Problem XIII — Exercise 6

A	Use	Case
1. whom	object complement of " did see "	Objective
you	subject of " did see "	Nominative
2. she	subjective complement of " is "	Nominative
whom	object complement of " want "	Objective
3. whom	object complement of " selected "	Objective
they	subject of " selected "	Nominative
4. whom	object of preposition " at "	Objective
5. who	subjective complement of " is "	Nominative
6. its	shows possession of " foot "	Possessive
7. me	object of preposition " to "	Objective
8. whom	object complement of " selected "	Objective
9. me	object of preposition " for "	Objective
10. he	subject of " was " understood	Nominative
11. he	subject of " is " understood	Nominative
12. whom	object of preposition " to "	Objective
13. he	subjective complement of " is "	Nominative
who	subject of " will win "	Nominative
14. who	subject of " deserve "	Nominative
15. who	subjective complement of " can be "	Nominative

Note: In sentence 1 " whom " introduces a question and is therefore called an interrogative pronoun. Its case forms are the same as those of the relative pronoun " who." " Which " and " what " are also interrogative pronouns when they introduce questions.

B. Be sure that these sentences are corrected by some one who understands this work thoroughly. It is very important.

Problem XIII — Exercise 7

A.	Use	Case
1. me	object of preposition " for "	Objective
2. whom	object of preposition " to "	Objective
3. he	subjective complement of " was "	Nominative
4. me	object of preposition " on "	Objective
5. who	subject of " should be made "	Nominative
6. he	subjective complement of " is "	Nominative
whom	object complement of " know "	Objective
7. we	subjective complement of " is "	Nominative
whom	object complement of " asked "	Objective
8. us	object of preposition " to "	Objective
9. whom	object complement of " saw "	Objective
10. who	subjective complement of " is "	Nominative

B. Have your teacher or some one in the class help you to correct these sentences. Select a person whose spoken English is excellent so that no mistakes will be overlooked. This is very important work.

Problem XIII — Exercise 8

	No.	Gen.	Per.	Use	Case	Ante-cedent
1. he	sing.	mas.	3	subject of " went "	Nom.	
I	sing.	com.	1	subject of " went "	Nom.	
2. us	plur.	com.	1	indirect object of " send "	Obj.	

	No.	Gen.	Per.	Use	Case	Ante-cedent
3. she	sing.	fem.	3	sub. com. of "was"	Nom.	
who	sing.	fem.	3	sub. of "phoned"	Nom.	she
4. I	sing.	com.	1	sub. com. of "is"	Nom.	
5. who	sing.	mas.	3	sub. com. of "is"	Nom.	he
6. who	sing.	com.	3	sub. of "will be"	Nom.	person
7. she	sing.	fem.	3	sub. com. of "is"	Nom.	
who	sing.	fem.	3	sub. of "gave"	Nom.	she
8. whom	sing.	com.	3	obj. com. of "chose"	Obj.	
9. who	sing.	com.	3	sub. of "is coming"	Nom.	
10. me	sing.	com.	1	indirect obj. of "sent"	Obj.	

B. See that these sentences are written correctly. This is very important work and you cannot afford to make mistakes. Have your teacher help you to correct this part of the exercise.

Problem XIII — Exercise 9

A.

1. he — Use singular number and masculine gender because the antecedent "pupil" is in the singular number and common gender.

2. milliner's — Use possessive case, for it shows possession. The meaning is " the milliner's shop "

3. that — Use the relative pronoun " that " when referring to persons rather than " what " which never has an antecedent.

4. me — Use the objective case because " me " is indirect object of " sent."

5. whom — Use the objective case because it is object complement of " want."

6. his — The antecedent " one " is in the singular number and common gender; therefore the pronoun must be in the singular number and masculine gender.

7. hers — Use possessive case because ownership is shown. No apostrophe is used in the possessive of personal pronouns. (Notice that this is an exception to a rule we have had before. " Hers " is used as the subjective complement, but in form it is possessive. What is the case of the subjective complement ordinarily?)

8. he — The antecedent is in the singular number and common gender; therefore the pronoun must be in the singular number and masculine gender.

9. whom — Use objective case because " whom " is the object complement of " were discussing."

10. one's — It is possessive case because it shows possession.

he — The antecedent is in the singular number and common gender; therefore the pronoun is in the singular number and masculine gender.

11. lady's — Use " 's " because the word is in the singular number and possessive case.

12. she — Use the nominative case because it is the subjective complement of " is."

whom — Use the objective case because it is the object of the preposition " for."

13. father's — Use " 's " because the thought is possessive. (This is a peculiar combination, the object
of a preposition being in the possessive case.
What is the case of the object of a preposition
ordinarily? Read the note in number 7.)

14. her ⎫
    me ⎬— Use the objective case because these words
are the object of the preposition " for."

15. who — Use the nominative case because it is the subject of " will be."

B. Have your teacher or some one in the class help
you to correct this part of the exercise. Choose some one
who speaks correct English.

C. Your teacher will correct the parsing if she wishes
you to do it.

Problem XIV — Exercise 1

A.

1. *She* and *I* went to the city. (Subject, nominative
case)
2. Please give your books to Grace and *me*. (Object
of preposition, objective case)
3. Mother brought Mildred and *me* some interesting
books. (Indirect object, objective case)
4. When will you send *us* your plans? (Indirect object,
objective case)
5. Did you see John and *me* last night? (Object complement, objective case)
6. It is *I*. (Subjective complement, nominative case)
7. Was that *she* who called yesterday? (Subjective
complement, nominative case)

8. *We* boys want to go to the city. (Subject, nominative case)

9. My mother always prepares a good dinner for my sister and *me*. (Object of preposition, objective case)

10. It is a question between *him* and *me*. (Object of preposition, objective case)

11. Is it *we* who are to blame? (Subjective complement, nominative case)

12. *We* Americans love the name of Lincoln. (Subject, nominative case)

13. I have seen *him* and his daughter in the theater many times. (Object complement, objective case)

14. My father is sending my brother and *me* some books about Alaska. (Indirect object, objective case)

15. Will you please prepare the dinner for my mother and *me?* (Object of preposition, objective case)

16. *We* boys will go swimming after school. (Subject, nominative case)

17. He is not so tall as *she*. (Subject, nominative case)

18. Everything is over between *him* and *me*. (Object of preposition, objective case)

19. The teacher did not refer to Henry and *me*. (Object of preposition, objective case)

20. Some of *us* boys did not see the play. (Object of preposition, objective case)

21. Was it *they?* (Subjective complement, nominative case)

22. They sent us, Harry and *me,* to the warehouse. (In apposition with object complement, objective case)

23. You ought to consider *him* and his friends. (Object complement, objective case)

24. Did he send that to you and *me?* (Object of preposition, objective case)

25. Mother gave *him* and *me* some money. (Indirect object, objective case)

B. Discuss these errors and the correct forms with your classmates. Let your teacher look over the corrected sentences.

Problem XIV — Exercise 2

A.

1. I hope *you* and your guests will be able to call on my mother and *me*.
2. Did he hurt *himself* badly?
3. She threw *herself* on the bed.
4. The President *himself* was present at the convention.
5. The children can wash *themselves*.
6. The author *himself* (herself) revised the manuscript.
7. My brother and *I* visited our sister in Chicago.
8. We shall expect to see *you* and your mother next Tuesday.
9. This box of candy is for your brother and *you*.
10. He said the princess herself had given *him* the ring.
11. My friend and *I* shall go abroad next summer.
12. My cousin and *I* were invited to go to the theater.

B. Have your teacher or one of the pupils in the class help you to correct this part of the exercise. Be certain that you understand this work; otherwise you will use incorrect forms in your speech.

Problem XIV — Exercise 3

A.

1. I have asked *those* children to be quiet. (Adjective to modify noun)
2. The man gave *her* and *me* some oranges. (Indirect object, objective case)

3. My father and *I* will be there at noon. (Subject, nominative case; use personal pronoun)

4. *He* and *I* went to the city last night. (Subject, nominative case; state first person last)

5. Was that *she* who brought this lovely fruit to my mother and *me?* (she — subjective complement, nominative case; me — object of preposition, objective case)

6. His mother and *he* were expected to arrive last night. (Subject, nominative case; use personal pronoun)

7. *They* and their guests were badly frightened by the fire. (Subject, nominative case; use personal pronoun)

8. The little boy hurt *himself* while he was playing in the tree. (Reflexive pronoun for object complement; *himself* is the correct form)

9. *She* and her brother have often inquired about the price of the house. (Subject, nominative case; use personal pronoun)

10. Harry took *her* and *me* for a ride. (Object complement, objective case)

11. Where did you put *those* cakes? (Adjective to modify the noun)

12. Did your father send *those* books to your mother and you? (those — adjective to modify the noun; you — object of preposition, objective case; use personal pronoun)

13. *We* girls enjoyed our picnic at the beach. (Subject, nominative case)

14. Please send *her* and *me* to the store. (Object complement, objective case)

15. The minister *himself* swept the little church. (Intensive pronoun)

16. Give *him* and *me* some of your fruit. (Indirect object, objective case)

17. A lovely lady told an interesting story to *us* children. (Object of preposition, objective case)

18. My mother likes to have my friends come to our house. (It is not correct to repeat the subject.)

19. Mother, please read Mary and *me* a story about Indians. (Indirect object, objective case)

20. John and James and *I* are going away. (Subject, nominative case; state first person last)

B. Have some one in the class help you to correct these sentences.

C. Discuss these errors and the correct forms with your classmates. If there is any question as to the correct word, consult your teacher.

Problem XIV — Exercise 4

A.

1. I know the man *whom* you are looking for. (Object of preposition, objective case)
   (Better — I know the man *for whom* you are looking.)

2. That was *I whom* you saw on the street.
   (I — subjective complement, nominative case
   whom — object complement, objective case)

3. Was that *she who* called to you last night?
   (she — subjective complement, nominative case
   who — subject, nominative case)

4. Do you know *who* that man is? (Subjective complement, nominative case)

5. *Whom* do you want to talk to? (Object of preposition, objective case)
   Better — *To whom* do you want to talk?

6. Is it *I whom* they want?
   (I — subjective complement
   whom — object complement, objective case)

7. This check was sent to me by my brother, *who* you
   know is a very generous person. (Subject, nominative case)

8. Who do you think that man is?   (Subjective complement, nominative case)

9. They sent tickets to those, *who* they thought would
   enjoy the concert.   (Subject, nominative case)

10. They were very kind to my sister and *me, who* you
    know were alone in this city.
    (me — object of preposition, nominative case
    who — subject, nominative case)

11. *Whom* did they send?   (Object complement, objec-
    tive case)

12. The man *that* gave his last dollar to buy bread for
    the starving children was unselfish. (Restrictive
    clause introduced by "that." "Who" may have
    been used; subject, nominative case)

13. We are not so ambitious for fame as *they*. (Subject
    of " are " understood, nominative case)

14. She was kind to *us* men. (Object of preposition, ob-
    jective case)

15. Is it *we* boys who are to blame for what *those* girls
    did?
    (we — subjective complement, nominative case
    who — subject, nominative case
    those — adjective modifier of noun)

16. A large amount of money was left to *her* and her
    mother. (Object of preposition, objective case; use
    personal pronoun)

17. I was glad when I heard *whom* Mr. Smith had chosen for his new secretary. (Object complement, objective case)

18. Have you invited those *who* you know will be able to come? (Subject, nominative case)

19. I hope that nothing will ever come between *her* and *me*. (Object of preposition, objective case)

20. All the responsibility of the work rests upon you and *me*. (Object of preposition, objective case)

B. Have some one in the class help you correct these sentences. Select some one who uses excellent English.

Problem XIV — Exercise 5

A.

1. Each of the pupils did *his* work well. (Each is singular)

2. If anyone does not like this, let *him* say so now. (Anyone is singular)

3. Every pupil should show *his* loyalty by good scholarship. (Every is singular)

4. Each of the boys sent *his* mother some flowers. (Each is singular)

5. Every one who was present received *his* reward. (Every one is singular)

6. Five trains went by, each with *its* load of brave men. (Each is singular)

7. Each of them has *his* trials. (Each is singular)

8. No one would want to lose *his* way in this forest. (No one is singular)

9. They were told that each of the students would have to wait *his* turn. (Each is singular)

10. If anybody calls, tell *him* I shall be back soon. (Anybody is singular)

11. Has each of them fully decided to remain here during *his* vacation? (Each is singular)

12. On Sunday everybody puts on his best clothes. (Everybody is singular)

13. The students entered, each with *his* diploma. (Each is singular)

14. Will either of the boys bring *his* sister? (Either is singular)

15. No one has any idea what *his* mark will be. (no one is singular)

B. Have your teacher or some one in the class help you to correct these sentences. If you ask a classmate to assist you, be sure that you select some one who does excellent work and speaks and writes splendid English. Unless you can find such a person, ask your teacher to look over the work.

Problem XIV — Exercise 6

A.

1. I had not heard of *John's* being promoted. (Possessive case used with verbal noun " being promoted ")

2. No one would have thought of *your* coming now. (Possessive case used with verbal noun " coming ")

3. There is no use of *his* going to the office. (Possessive case used with verbal noun " going ")

4. She left without *my* knowing it. (Possessive case with verbal noun " knowing ")

5. There was no enjoyment in hearing *his* singing. (Possessive case used with verbal noun " singing ")

6. I do not like to think of *mother's* being so far away. (Possessive case used with verbal noun " being ")

7. There is no danger of *his* seeing us. (Possessive case used with verbal noun " seeing ")

8. The possibility of *his* going never occurred to us. (Possessive case used with verbal noun " going ")

9. Who ever heard of *their* paying a fine? (Possessive case used with verbal noun " paying ")

10. The idea of *father's* trying to buy a machine seemed impossible. (Possessive case used with verbal noun " trying ")

B. Have your teacher or some one in the class help you to correct these original sentences. Mistakes are often made in using the objective case with verbal nouns; consequently have some one who understands the work assist you.

Note: If you are studying Latin, you have learned or will learn about the gerund. The verbal noun " ing " is a gerund and is sometimes called by that name. We, however, shall call it a " verbal noun."

Problem XIV — Exercise 7

A.

1. No one may enter the gymnasium without *his* card. (Antecedent is in the singular number and of the common gender)

2. Who ever heard of *his* being a musician? (Possessive case used with verbal noun)

3. *Who* did he say the president of the organization is? (Subjective complement, nominative case)

4. Is that *she whom* you are looking for?
(she — subjective complement, nominative case
whom — object of preposition, objective case)
(Better — Is that she *for whom* you are looking?)

5. You have had as much experience as *I*. (Subject, nominative case)

6. The man *who* I believe is best fitted for the position is manager. (Subject, nominative case)

7. Send your address to the secretary or to *me*. (Object of preposition, objective case)

8. She is taller than *he*. (Subject, nominative case)

9. I know the man with *whom* you are talking. (Object of preposition, objective case)

10. The boy *whom* we paid was the one *who* brought the letter.

    (whom — object complement, objective case
    who — subject, nominative case)

11. My sister and *I* are going away. (Subject, nominative case; last in series; use personal pronoun)

12. When can you take *me* and my friend to the country? (Object complement, objective case)

13. Harry and John have not been here for a long time. (A subject should not be repeated)

14. A person likes to be free to express *his* ideas on a subject. (Antecedent is in singular number and of the common gender)

15. He hurt *himself* when he was getting Marian and *me* a drink.

    (himself — reflexive pronoun, as object complement
    me — indirect object, objective case)

16. *Mary's* playing is always enjoyed. (Possessive case with verbal noun)

17. Neither of the women will allow *her* children to play in the street. (Antecedent is singular and feminine)

18. You may tell *whomever* you meet. (Object complement, objective case)

19. No one regretted *his* knowing about the matter more than *I*.

> (his — possessive case with verbal noun
> I — subject of " did " understood)

20. *Who* do you think is the best architect in this city?
> (Subject, nominative case)

B. Have some one in the class help you correct these sentences.

Problem XV — Exercise 1

A.

Verb	Kind	Receiver of action
1. went	intransitive	
2. established	transitive	missions
3. was discovered	transitive	California
4. broke	intransitive	
5. waved	transitive	sword
uttered	transitive	command
could be heard	transitive	which
6. came	intransitive	
7. set	transitive	lamp
8. have sat	intransitive	
9. raise	transitive	window
10. rose	intransitive	
entered	intransitive	
11. awoke	intransitive	
waked	transitive	mother
12. has lain	intransitive	
13. set	transitive	books
14. sit	intransitive	
15. laid	transitive	blankets
16. has awaked	intransitive	
lay	transitive	sheets

17. wake	transitive	father
18. have sat	intransitive	
19. will lie	intransitive	
20. lies	intransitive	

B. Have your teacher or some one in the class help you to correct this part of the exercise. Be sure that you understand transitive and intransitive verbs before you go on to the next exercise.

Problem XV — Exercise 2

A.

Verb	Kind	Voice
1. gave	transitive	active
2. arrived	intransitive	
3. hired	transitive	active
rode	intransitive	
4. were seen	transitive	passive
lay	intransitive	
5. wore	transitive	active
6. had been dis- charged	transitive	passive
were allowed	transitive	passive
7. had been made	transitive	passive
sent	intransitive	
8. should be used	transitive	passive
9. was	intransitive	
10. nodded	transitive	active
smiled	intransitive	
11. will be	intransitive	
12. was influenced	transitive	passive
13. was involved	transitive	passive
14. was heard	transitive	passive
ran	intransitive	
15. was discussed	transitive	passive

B.

1. Orders for unmooring the ship *were given* by the captain.
3. Horses *were hired* by us.
4. We *saw* the whales at a distance as we lay in the harbor.
5. The appearance of a holiday *was worn* by everything.
6. When we *had discharged* our duties, they *allowed* us a few hours for amusement.
7. After we *had made* the arrangements, cousin George was *sent for* by us. (This is not the best way to express the thought.)
8. One *should* not *use* notes in debates.
10. His head *was nodded* by him.
12. That book *influenced* me greatly.
13. The last issue *involved* no principle.
14. When the children *heard* the noise, they *ran* out of the room.
15. The members of the club *discussed* a very important question.

C. Select some one who understands this work to help you correct this part of the exercise. Master each step before you go to the next.

Problem XV — Exercise 3

A.

1. I *saw* him yesterday.
2. He has *broken* his glasses.
3. He has *lain* there two hours.
4. Have you *forgotten* about the party?
5. He *began* to work last week.
6. How many glasses of water have you *drunk?*

7. The boy was not *drowned*.

8. After he had *lain* down, his mother entered the room.

9. I *came* to school early this morning.

10. They *did* their lessons well.

11. My brother *grew* too fast when he was little.

12. Have you *seen* him recently?

13. It was so cold that the milk was *frozen*.

14. I *ran* to school this morning.

15. She *drew* a beautiful picture.

16. Mother *laid* my books away.

17. She *lay* on the bed as she read.

18. Are those bottles *broken?*

19. He *threw* the ball a long distance.

20. The man *blew* the horn.

B.   Since the principal parts of the verb are given in the dictionary, it is not necessary to give them here. Be sure that you have written them correctly.

C.   Have your teacher or some excellent English student help you to correct these sentences.

Problem XV — Exercise 4

A.

1. The man *will take* his daughter away.

2. I *have done* my work now.

3. They *saw* us at the theater.

4. The children *had broken* the dish before I came.

5. When he comes, I *shall have gone* to the city.

6. The boys *had drunk* three bottles of milk before I could stop them.

7. The man *has lain* there all night.

8. Those flowers *grew* too rapidly.

9. I *shall sit* here until he comes.

10. The girls *have worn* those dresses since Christmas.
11. Before father came in, mother *had begun* to prepare the supper.
12. I *saw* those boys as they were hunting for the treasure.
13. The dog *has bitten* the child.
14. That skirt *shrank* in the washing.
15. The sun *has shone* all day.
16. She *will be frozen* before you can get there.
17. The girls *set* the table while father and mother rested.
18. Some boys *have waked* the little child.
19. That boy *has thrown* a fine ball.
20. The teacher *lay* down to rest.

B. Have your teacher help you to correct these sentences.

Problem XV — Exercise 5

A.

1. He *came* into the room just as I was leaving.
2. Some one *has broken* my new glass vase.
3. How much milk *had* you *drunk* before I came?
4. How many times do you think that bell *has rung?*
5. She *began* to take music lessons when she was very young.
6. They *had gone* when I arrived.
7. The teacher *saw* the boy close his book.
8. The choir *sang* a beautiful anthem at the beginning of the service.
9. *Has* she *lain* there long?
10. I *did* my work as well as I could.
11. The boys *ran* down the hall shouting and laughing.
12. That little dog *has run* up and down the street trying to find his master.

13. The frightened child *had gone* before we could talk with him.
14. I *saw* you, but you were too busy to see me.
15. You might *have drunk* when the others *drank*.

B. This is a very important assignment; for that reason have your teacher help you to correct it.

Problem XV — Exercise 6

A.

1. Each of the men *has come* to do his work.
2. *Were* you here yesterday?
3. He *is* not present today
4. Every pupil in this room *has done* his work alone.
5. The mob on the streets *has lost* its leader.
6. The boys and the girls *have seen* that play.
7. *Am* I not a help to you?
8. This automobile with all its equipment *sells* for one thousand dollars.
9. Either John or James *has* the book.
10. Every one of those pupils *wants* to succeed.
11. There *are* many boys and girls in this room.
12. Every one of the girls *likes* to go to camp.
13. Into the room *comes* each of the boys with a flag and a banner.
14. Neither of us *is* anxious to go again.
15. There *were* several men waiting in the office.
16. One of the inspectors *is coming* to see us today.
17. Do you know if any of the men or women *have seen* my books?
18. There *are* several questions that should be answered.
19. Everybody in that room *has written* the answers.
20. We *were* here on time.

B. Have your teacher help you to correct this original work.

Problem XV — Exercise 7

A.

	Mood	Reason
1.	Subjunctive	wish
2.	Subjunctive	condition contrary to fact
3.	Indicative	condition not contrary to fact
4.	Indicative	condition not contrary to fact
5.	Subjunctive	condition contrary to fact
6.	Indicative	condition not contrary to fact
7.	Subjunctive	condition contrary to fact
8.	Subjunctive	wish
9.	Subjunctive	condition contrary to fact
10.	Subjunctive	condition contrary to fact
11.	Subjunctive	condition contrary to fact
12.	Subjunctive	condition contrary to fact
13.	Subjunctive	wish
14.	Subjunctive	condition contrary to fact
15.	Subjunctive	wish

Note: In sentences 3, 4, and 6, the condition is not contrary to fact; therefore the verb is not in the subjunctive mood.

B. These sentences are very important. Have your teacher help you to correct them.

Problem XV — Exercise 8

A.

1. Infinitive phrase — " me *to show* him the flowers," object complement of " wanted " — present tense
me — objective case, subject of infinitive " to show "

him — objective case, indirect object of " to show "

2. Infinitive phrase — " Mary and me *to go* with them," object complement of " invited " — present tense

me — objective case, subject of infinitive

3. Infinitive phrase — " him and her *go* with us," object complement of " let " — present tense

her — objective case, subject of infinitive

4. Infinitive phrase — " *to see* whom when you went there," object complement of " did hope " — present tense

whom — objective case, object complement of " to see "

5. Infinitive phrase — " the winner *to be* him," object complement of " expected " — present tense

him — objective case, complement of infinitive " to be "

6. Infinitive phrase — " *to have eaten* the pie," object complement of " would like " — perfect tense

he — nominative case, subject of " would like "

B. Have your teacher help you to correct these sentences. Be sure that you have not split your infinitive by putting any word between the infinitive and its sign.

Problem XV — Exercise 9

A.

1.

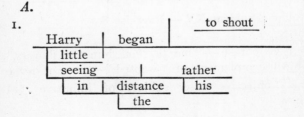

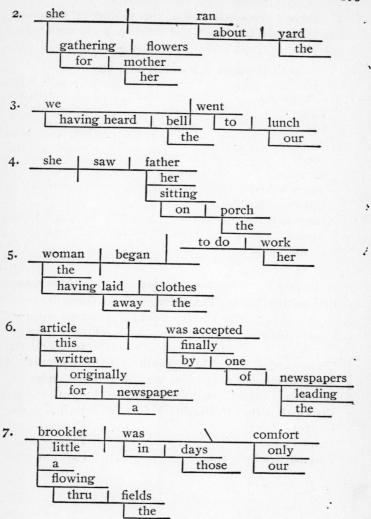

2. she | ran
   about | yard
   the
   gathering | flowers
   for | mother
   her

3. we | went
   having heard | bell
   the
   to | lunch
   our

4. she | saw | father
   her
   sitting
   on | porch
   the

5. woman | began
   the
   to do | work
   her
   having laid | clothes
   away | the

6. article | was accepted
   this | finally
   written | by | one
   originally | of | newspapers
   for | newspaper | leading
   a | the

7. brooklet | was | comfort
   little | in | days | only
   a | those | our
   flowing
   thru | fields
   the

B. Have your teacher help you to correct these sentences. Be sure that every participle is a modifier.

Problem XV — Exercise 10

A. Predicates	*Infinitives*	*Participles*
would like	to see	having read
had heard	going	stationed
do expect	to see	
goes	to hear	
do want	singing	
was wrecked	to signal	
had forgotten		
have seen		
were		
should study		

B. *goes*	*was wrecked*	*have seen*
1. Intransitive	1. Transitive	1. Transitive
2.	2. Passive voice	2. Active voice
3. Present tense	3. Past tense	3. Present perfect tense
4. Third person	4. Third person	4. First person
5. Singular number	5. Singular number	5. Plural number
6. Indicative mood	6. Indicative mood	6. Indicative mood
7. Principal parts	7. (Regular)	7. Principal parts
Present — go		Present — see
Past — went		Past — saw
Past participle — gone		Past participle — seen

were

1. Intransitive
2.
3. Past tense
4. First person

5. Singular number
6. Subjunctive mood
7. Principle parts
    Present — be
    Past — was
    Past participle — been

C.   *Infinitives.*

to see	object of " would like "
going	object of preposition " of "
to see	object of " do expect "
to hear	object of " do want "
singing	object of " to hear "
to signal	object of " had forgotten "

Participles.

having read	modifies " I "
stationed	modifies " man "

Problem XVI — Exercise 1

A.

1. *Were you* ever in San Francisco?
2. *Every one* of the pupils *is* doing excellent work.
3. The little *boy doesn't want* to go to bed.
4. There *were* two *books* lying on the library table.
5. *Each* of the men *works* for the same company.
6. *We were invited* to go to the theater.
7. The *jury was discharged* by the judge.
8. Every *pupil* who joins the class *expects* to work hard.
9. *Mr. Jones, Mr. Smith,* and *Mr. Brown were* the committee chosen to investigate the plan.
10. When *were you* at my house?
11. *Each* of them *seems* to be earnest.

12. There *are* only three *words* in that sentence.
13. The *furniture*, which consisted of a table, a couch, and two chairs, *was sold* at an auction.
14. A *basket* of apples *was put* on the table.
15. That wonderful *collection* of paintings *was sold* yesterday.
16. The *title* of the book *is* " The Just So Stories."
17. I thought *you were* at home.
18. A *boy* from each of the rooms *goes* to the office for announcements.
19. *Neither* the coat nor the hat *is* mine.
20. Each went home and not *one* of them *has referred* to the matter since.

B. Have your teacher or some one in the class look over these sentences. It would scarcely be wise for you to select some one who you found was not able to make the subjects and predicates of his sentences agree.

Problem XVI — Exercise 2

A.

1. Some one *has broken* that glass.
2. I *did* my lesson last night.
3. She *has* not *seen* him for years.
4. This morning I *ran* all the way to school.
5. The man *began* to tell us a story.
6. The little girl *has gone* home.
7. She *has torn* her dress.
8. The boys *did* their lessons quickly.
9. *Is* that chair *broken?*
10. How many glasses of milk *have* you *drunk?*
11. When I *came* into the building, I *saw* a most peculiar sight.

12. After I *had seen* her, I unexpectedly *saw* her husband.
13. *Has* the bell *rung?*
14. The men *did* their work too hurriedly.
15. *Have* you *begun* to read that essay?
16. The girl *has* already *sung* once, but she will sing again.
17. Although he *had gone* only a short distance, he was very tired.
18. I *saw* that play when I was a little girl.
19. No one *saw* them as they entered the building.
20. The child *did* a woman's work.

B. Have your teacher correct these sentences.

Problem XVI — Exercise 3

A.

1. How long has he *lain* there?
2. Will you *rise* and recite?
3. I *lay* on the couch last evening and slept until Henry *woke* (*waked*) me.
4. I was surprised to see him *lying* (*lie*) on the floor.
5. She has *laid* all those things away.
6. Around the table *sat* (*sit*) three men.
7. They *raised* (*raise*) the curtain.
8. To the left of us *lay* (*lies*) a beautiful farm.
9. They let the book *lie* on the grass all night.
10. The books were *lying* where we *laid* them.
11. I will *rise* and say what I think.
12. As the men *raised* the sail, the wind *rose*.
13. The poor old man was *sitting* on the grass, and near him *lay* a hungry dog.
14. When I *laid* my sewing away, I *lay* down to take a nap.

15. She *laid* her heavy burden on the ground and then *sat* down to rest.

16. Shall I *set* this basket on the table?

17. The tide has *risen* since we came here.

18. The city *lay* (*lies*) to the west of us.

19. Why do you *sit* there before you have *laid* your bundle down?

20. I was *lying* there when the little child came up to me, *laid* his hand on my face, and *waked* (*woke*) me.

B. Have your teacher help you to correct these original sentences. If there is some one in the class who you think understands the work so well that he always uses these words correctly, let him look over your sentences.

Problem XVI — Exercise 4

A.

1. I hope that we *shall* be friends. (Futurity)

2. He says that he *shall* be fifteen years old next week. (Futurity)

3. When *shall* you return to new York? (Futurity)

4. How *shall* we be able to find his house? (Futurity)

5. I *will* not trouble you. (Volition)

6. *Shall* I telephone the doctor? (Futurity)

7. They *shall* not go until their lessons are finished. (Volition)

8. You *will* surely fail if you do not study. (Futurity)

9. *Will* you go to the mountains with us? (Volition)

10. How soon *will* Henry leave? (Futurity)

11. *Will* they wait there until noon? (Futurity)

12. They *shall* see that I can succeed. (Volition)

13. Harry said that he *should* be glad to go with us. (Futurity)

14. *Shall* we take these magazines home? (Futurity)
15. Mother said that Harry *would* accept the position. (Futurity)
16. You *shall* wait here until I allow you to go. (Volition)
17. How much *will* you contribute to the fund? (Volition)
18. We *will* not go until he arrives. (Volition)
19. He says he *will* not read that book under any condition. (Volition)
20. When *shall* you be twenty years old? (Futurity)

B. Have your teacher look over these sentences. Be sure that you understand the correct use of *will* and *shall* before you go on to the next exercise, for this is very important work.

Problem XVI — Exercise 5

A.

1. If you *were* I, should you buy this hat? (Condition contrary to fact)
2. I wish that she *were* coming tonight. (Wish)
3. If she *were* not so proud, I should be glad to help her. (Condition contrary to fact)
4. I use her car as if it *were* my own. (Condition contrary to fact)
5. I wish I *were* going with you. (Wish)
6. If he *were* well, we should like to have him go on the fishing trip. (Condition contrary to fact)
7. He would come if he *were* asked. (Condition contrary to fact)
8. We wished he *were* there with us. (Condition contrary to fact — wish)

9. If he *were* here now, he would help us. (Condition contrary to fact)

10. If I *were* wealthy, I should try to be unselfish. (Condition contrary to fact)

B. Have your teacher or some one in the class help you to correct these sentences. Be sure that you have used the subjunctive forms of " be " that express a wish or a condition contrary to fact.

Problem XVI — Exercise 6

A.

1. I hope to use correct English some day.
2. She will try to work more conscientiously.
3. It is my aim to finish my course soon.
4. My mother told me never to fight.
5. We tried to rest quietly, but that was impossible.
6. Are you willing to contribute either money or time?
7. It is a good thing to sit quietly and think.
8. Do not attempt to jump across that stream.
9. I like to read my books silently.
10. He desired to purchase that ring secretly.
11. I had not thought of his coming before Christmas.
12. I hoped to see her.
13. I expect the visitor to be her.
14. The old lady does not like to be disturbed suddenly.
15. We had not thought of Jim's being responsible for the fire.

B–C. Have your teacher help you to correct these sentences. If there is some one in the class who is able to do this in such a way that you will be helped, go to him. Do not let any one do your work for you.

Problem XVI — Exercise 7

A–B. Have your teacher help you to correct these sentences.

C.
Correct sentences — 2, 4, 7, 8, 10
Incorrect sentences.

1. The participial phrase, " running down the street," is not placed near " I," the word it modifies.
3. The participial phrase, " standing on the mountain top," is not placed near " We," the word it modifies.
5. " Entering the attic," is a dangling participial phrase, for there is no word that it modifies.
6. " Having slept for only a few minutes," is a dangling participial phrase, for there is no word that it modifies.
9. The participial " coming home from school " is not placed near " I," the word it modifies.

Problem XVI — Exercise 8

A. Yesterday I *went* to see my grandmother. When I *arrived* there, she *asked* me to pick some cherries. I *was* glad to do this. I *got* the ladder and *climbed* to the top of the tree. Before I *knew* it, I *had* a quart of big red cherries for her. When I *showed* them to her, she *was* happy. So *was* I a little later, for she *made* them into a pie for me.

B. Have your teacher correct this paragraph. It should be absolutely perfect in every respect. Do not be satisfied with anything less than 100 per cent.

Problem XVI — Exercise 9

A.

1. You *ought not* to read so late at night. (*Ought* is not a participle and cannot be used with *had*.)
2. That poor little boy *was hurt*. (*Got* is not an auxiliary verb.)
3. She could *have gone*. (*Of* is not a verb.)
4. He *isn't* afraid of that engine. (*Ain't* is never used. It is not a contraction of *is not*.)
5. Mother, please *let* me have a dollar for my books. (*Let* means to allow.)
6. My father says I *may* go to the beach for a week. (*May* means to have permission.)
7. *Isn't* she a dear little child? (*Ain't* is never used. It is not a contraction of *is not*.)
8. I *can* do this work easily. (*Can* means to have ability.)
9. Mary *has* a beautiful new bookcase. (*Got* is not an auxiliary verb.)
10. You *ought not* to tease those little children. (*Ought* is not a participle and cannot be used with *had*.)
11. *May* I read this book, Miss Smith? (*May* means to have permission.)
12. Several men *were* burned when the tank burst. (*Got* is not an auxiliary verb.)
13. *Am I not* a member of the club. (*Ain't* is never used. It is not a contraction of *am not*.)
14. I *can* not go until I have finished my work. (*Can* means to be able.)
15. If she *had taken* the test, she *would have* passed. (*Of* is not a verb.)

16. Harry *has* a new suit of clothes. (*Got* is not an auxiliary verb.)

17. My teacher *will let* me do that for her. (*Let* means to allow.)

18. I suppose I *ought not* to talk in this way. (*Ought* is not a participle and cannot be used with *had*.)

19. *Isn't* he going to the picnic? (*Ain't* is never used. It is not a contraction of *is not*.)

20. *Am* I *not* a good student? (*Ain't* is never used. It is not a contraction of *am not*.)

B. Have your teacher correct these sentences.

Problem XVI — Exercise 10

A. Look over these sentences with some classmate who uses excellent English, or have your teacher correct them.

B.

1. *Weren't* you happy when you saw your mother? (Plural verb with " you ")

2. One of the boys in that club *is* very talented. (Singular subject " one " takes a singular verb)

3. There *are* a few blossoms on the trees. (Plural subject " blossoms " takes a plural verb)

4. Some one has *broken* that dish. (Past participle is used to form present perfect tense)

5. When a jury *hands* in a verdict, *it is* discharged immediately. (Collective noun with singular meaning takes a singular verb and singular pronoun)

6. Every one of the students *has* a reason for his choice. (Singular subject " every one " takes a singular verb)

7. They *laid* the carpet on the floor. (Past tense of transitive verb *lay*)

8. He expected her *to call*. (Present infinitive is used because the action of the infinitive takes place after the action of the predicate)

9. When *were* you in Chicago? (Plural verb with " you ")

10. I wish he *were* here now. (Condition contrary to fact takes the subjunctive mood)

11. When a person like you *believes* such a story, I am inclined to think it is true. (Singular subject " person " takes singular verb)

12. Any one that can remain calm at such a time *is* worthy of praise. (Singular subject " any one " takes singular verb)

13. They *lay* in the grass all night. (Past of intransitive verb *lie*)

14. A little girl, accompanied by her nurse and three friends, *has* just left. (Singular subject takes singular verb)

15. When they spoke of *my* being president, I was too surprised to say a word. (Verbal noun takes possessive modifier)

16. I will try never *to fail*. (Split infinitive is not correct English)

17. Each of them *is* trying to speak correct English. (Singular subject " each " takes singular verb)

18. *Will* you call for Mother this afternoon? (Volition is expected in the answer)

19. John, as well as James and Henry, *is* coming here for the holidays. (Singular subject " John " takes singular verb)

20. There is no danger of *his* running away. (Verbal noun takes possessive modifier)

21. If I *were* you, I should not buy so expensive a hat. (Condition contrary to fact takes the subjunctive mood)

22. I *will* do that whether she is here or not. (Volition)

23. The committee *holds* a meeting every Tuesday evening. (Collective noun with singular meaning takes a singular verb)

24. I had hoped *to see* him. (The action of the predicate precedes that of the infinitive)

25. *May* I go to the city, Mother? (" May " means to have permission)

26. Shall I *sit* here? (Intransitive verb)

27. The papers of every student *are* returned when they are corrected. (Subject " papers " is plural)

28. I did not think that I *should* enjoy the party, but mother said she *should*. (In the direct quotation " shall " is used)

29. That is one of the saddest stories that *has* ever been written. (Subject " that " is singular, for its antecedent " one " is singular)

30. Where *were* you when I called? (" You " takes plural verb)

31. When I was *lying* on the ground, Dash *lay* down beside me. (Forms of intransitive verb " lie ")

32. There she *lay* absolutely helpless. (Past tense of intransitive verb " lie ")

33. *Set* your basket down and then come and *sit* with me. (Forms of " sit " and " set ")

34. They began to come, and immediately I *had* to prepare dinner. (" Come " is past tense; therefore " had " must be the past tense)

35. He *doesn't* like to have his mother go away. (Singular subject takes singular verb)

36. What *shall* we do if we cannot find a garage? ("Shall" is generally used in the first person when a question is asked.)

37. There *seems* to be a doubt in your mind. (Singular subject "doubt" takes singular verb)

38. *Were* you at the concert yesterday? ("You" takes a plural verb)

39. She *ought not* to act so foolishly. ("Ought" is not a participle and cannot be used with "had")

40. Each pupil in this class *seems* to be studious. (Singular subject "each" takes singular verb)

41. My brother sat down and *told* me all about the party. ("Sat" is past tense; therefore "told" must be in the past tense)

42. If I *were* going, I should be glad. (Condition contrary to fact takes subjunctive mood)

43. *Will* you study French next year? (Volition is expected in the answer)

44. We hope *to be* at home soon. (Split infinitive is not allowed)

45. Poor old Towser! He has *lain* on the damp porch all night. (Past participle of "lie")

46. *Shall* I telephone you tomorrow? (Simple futurity; first person in questions use "shall")

47. She was hurt when the glass broke. ("Got" is not an auxiliary verb)

48. The idea of *John's* renting a machine had not occurred to us. (A verbal noun is modified by a possessive noun)

49. *May* I be excused to go to the game, Mr. Lane? ("May" means to have permission)

50. He said he *should be* glad to accept the invitation. (In the direct quotation "shall" was used)

51. She *did* her work well. (Past tense of " do ")
52. I will try *to get* my work done early. (The sign of the infinitive is " to," not " and ")
53. Mother will not *let* me go. (" Let " means to allow)
54. I *saw* them when they drove past in a big machine. (Past tense of " see ")
55. *Shall* you see him in the morning? (Simple futurity is expected in the answer)

Problem XVII — Exercise 1

Note: The sentences of the exercise are written correctly in the key. You will find the reasons by consulting the exercises and the problems indicated by the numbers. Be sure that you give the reason for every word.

1. Each of the boys *has* left *his* books at home.
   has — XV, 6 (This means Problem XV, Exercise 6)
   his — XIV, 5
2. The man *whom* you want is not here.
   whom — XIV, 4
3. Who ever heard of *John's* running for Governor!
   John's — XIV, 6
4. Tell *her* and *me* the story.
   her ⎱ XIII, 4; XIV, 1
   me ⎰
5. We *saw* the children playing in the water.
   saw — XV, 3
6. It is *I*.
   I — XIII, 3; XIV, 1
7. Is it *he who was* hurt when the boiler *burst?*
   he — XIII, 3; XIV, 1   was — XVI, 9
   who — XIV, 4   burst — XV, 3
8. They *sang* that song many times.
   sang — XV, 3

9. I *ran* into the house before I knew Mr. Jones was there.

   ran — XV, 3

10. I do not know *whom* to ask.

    whom — XIV, 4, XV, 8

11. I tried *to walk* quietly as I went up the stairs.

    to walk — XVI, 6

12. The little child fell into the water and was *drowned*.

    drowned — XV, 3

13. I intend to select the person *who* you think will be satisfactory.

    XIII, 3; XIV, 4

14. The jury *was* dismissed after *it* had given *its* verdict.

    was — XV, 6; XVI, 1

    it, its — XIII, 5

15. His report on electrical appliances, especially those used in homes, *was* very interesting.

    was — XV, 6; XVI, 1

16. She said that she *should* try to go.

    should — XIV, 4

17. *Whom* do you want to see?

    whom — XIII, 4; XIV, 4

18. When *were* you at my house?

    were — XV, 6; XVI, 1

19. Is that *she who* gave the interesting lecture?

    she — XIII, 3; XIV, 4

20. Please *lay* the books where they are supposed to *lie*.

    lay }
    lie } XV, 1, 3; XVI, 3

Note: If there is a question about any of these, be sure that it is answered before you to go the next exercise.

Problem XVII — Exercise 2

Note: The sentences of the exercise are written correctly in the Key. You will find the reasons by consulting the exercise and the problem indicated by the numbers.

1. *May* Mildred and *I* play with *those* children?
    may — XVI, 9
    I — XIII, 3; XIV, 1
    those — XIV, 3

2. I had never heard of *his* having traveled abroad.
    his — XIV, 6

3. I rewarded the child *who* I believe had done the best work.
    who — XIII, 3; XIV, 4

4. That tank has *burst*.
    burst — XV, 3

5. I do not know *who* he is.
    who — XIII, 3; XIV, 4

6. My sister and *I* like to read good books.
    I — XIII, 3; XIV, 1, 2, 3

7. *Let* me go with John and *her*.
    let — XVI, 9
    her — XIII, 4; XIV, 1; XV, 8

8. *Shall* I *set* the table?
    shall — XVI, 4
    set — XV, 3, 4; XVI, 3

9. If I *were* going, I should wear a heavy coat.
    were — XV, 7; XVI, 5

10. *Who* do you think that big man is?
    who — XIII, 3; XIV, 4

11. She *doesn't* know *who* you are.
    doesn't — XV, 6; XVI, 1
    who — XIII, 3; XIV, 4

12. I thought you *were* at home.
     were — XV, 6; XVI, 1

13. *Can* you give Mary and *me* a ride?
     can — XVI, 9
     me — XIII, 4; XIV, 1

14. Goodness! that is *he who* took the watch.
     he — XIII, 3; XIV, 1
     who — XIII, 3; XIV, 4

15. I expect the stranger to be *her.*
     her — XV, 8

16. *Shall* you come tomorrow?
     shall — XV, 4; XVI, 4

17. The boys *came* first; the men followed.
     came — XV, 4; XVI, 8

18. When the boys have *gone,* we *shall* do the work.
     gone — XV, 4; XVI, 2
     shall — XV, 4; XVI, 4

19. I *shall* fall unless one of you men *helps* me.
     shall — XV, 4; XVI, 4
     helps — XV, 4; XVI, 1

20. He expected *to win* the prize.
     to win — XVI, 6

Problem XVII — Exercise 3

Note: The correct sentences are written in the Key with the correct words italicized. You will find the reasons by consulting the exercise and the problem indicated by the numbers.

1. (*a*) If you *were I,* what should you do?
     were — XV, 7; XVI, 5
     I — XIII, 3; XIV, 1

2. (*b*) Was it *he* who bought the umbrella?

    he — XIII, 3; XIV, 1

3. (*a*) Did you hear about *his* asking for a copy of that book?

    his — XIV, 6

4. (*a*) To *whom shall* we send invitations?

    whom — XIII, 4; XIV, 4

    shall — XV, 4; XVI, 4

5. (*b*) I *shall* be glad to see *you* and your friend at my home Tuesday afternoon.

    shall — XV, 4; XVI, 4

    you — XIV, 2, 3

6. (*a*) I *saw* a funny sight today.

    saw — XV, 3, 4; XVI, 2

7. (*b*) Each of *those* boys *has* lost *his* locker key.

    those — XIV, 3

    has — XV, 6; XVI, 1

    his — XIV, 5

8. (*b*) Mary and *I* were so tired that we *lay* down to rest.

    I — XIII, 3; XIV, 3

    lay — XV, 3, 4; XVI, 3

9. (*a*) I will try *to do* my work carefully.

    to do — XVI, 6

10. (*a*) When he had finished his work, he *laid* his books away.

    laid — XV, 3, 4; XVI, 3

11. (*b*) Is there any danger of *his* coming tonight?

    his — XIV, 6

12. (*b*) John, the boy who sells fruit, *was* hurt today.

    (he) — XIV, 3

    was — XVI, 9

13. (*b*) Can you *teach* me how to speak correctly?

    (See note after group 13)

14. (*b*) Did you expect her to be *me?*
    me — XV, 8; XVI, 6

15. (*b*) Nothing can ever come between you and *me.*
    me — XIII, 4; XIV, 1

16. (*b*) He tried *to tell* me quietly where he had *laid* the book.
    to tell — XV, 8; XVI, 6
    laid — XV, 3; XVI, 3

17. (*a*) Where *were* you when I telephoned? Were you *lying* down?
    were — XV, 6; XVI, 1
    lying — XV, 1; XVI, 3

18. (*a*) When I *saw* her coming, I *ran* around the corner and into the house.
    saw ⎱ XV, 3, 4; XVI, 2
    ran ⎰

19. (*b*) Do you know *who* each of *those* boys *is?*
    who — XIII, 3; XIV, 4
    those — XIV, 3
    is — XV, 6; XVI, 1

20. (*a*) We looked as if we were ready to *lie* down and never *rise.*
    lie ⎱ XV, 3; XVI, 3
    rise ⎰

Problem XVII — Exercise 4

Note: The correct sentences are written in the Key with the correct words italicized. You will find the reasons by consulting the problem and the exercise indicated by the numbers.

1. (*a*) Have you heard of *his* being given the position of postmaster?
    his — XIV, 6

2. (b) She *doesn't* seem to want to go.
     doesn't — XV, 6; XVI, 1
3. (b) *We* boys like to go on fishing trips.
     we — XIV, 3
4. (b) If she *were* here, she would enjoy the new house.
     were — XV, 7; XVI, 5
5. (a) You *ought not* to let your mother work so hard.
     ought not — XVI, 9
6. (b) Each one of them *seems to be waiting* anxiously for an opportunity to speak.
     seems — XV, 6; XVI, 1
     to be waiting — XVI, 6
7. (b) Is it *I whom* you want to see?
     I — XIII, 3; XIV, 1
     whom — XIII, 4; XIV, 4
8. (b) When I had *laid* my bundles on the table, I *sat* down to rest.
     laid — XV, 3; XVI, 3
     sat — XV, 3; XVI, 3
9. (a) Have you *seen* her recently?
     seen — XV, 3, 4; XVI, 2
10. (b) Is it *he who* you think is coming?
     he — XIII, 3; XIV, 1
     who — XIII, 3; XIV, 4
11. (a) My friend and *I shall* call tomorrow.
     I — XIII, 3; XIV, 1, 3
     shall — XV, 4; XVI, 4
12. (a) She has not *drunk* any water for a week.
     drunk — XV, 3; XVI, 2
13. (b) I wish I *were* going with *those* boys.
     were — XV, 7; XVI, 5
     those — XIV, 3

14. (*b*) *Running down the street*, I finally caught my
hat.
XV, 9; XVI, 7

15. (*a*) I *awoke* suddenly and then ran to *wake* my
brother.
awoke — XV, 3; XVI, 3
wake — XV, 3; XVI, 3

16. (*b*) Listen to *his* playing. *Isn't* it beautiful!
his — XIV, 6
isn't — XVI, 9

17. (*b*) *Were* you glad when the team won?
were — XV, 6; XVI, 1

18. (*b*) How many of *those* dishes have you *broken?*
those — XIV, 3
broken — XV, 3; XVI, 2

19. (*b*) When can you send some groceries to her and
me?
me — XIII, 4; XIV, 1

20. (*a*) *Who* do you suppose the visitor is?
who — XIII, 3; XIV, 4

Problem XVII — Exercise 5

Note: The sentences are written correctly in the Key
and the words that were changed are italicized. The
reasons for the changes will be found by consulting the
problems and the exercises indicated by the numbers.

1. I was so sleepy that I *lay* down for an hour.
lay — XV, 3, 4; XVI, 3

2. *Will* you be here Monday?
will — XVI, 4

3. I *saw* a man *who* looked like my uncle.
saw — XV, 3, 4; XVI, 2
who — XIII, 3; XIV, 4

4. When I saw those boys help *themselves* to the refreshments, I ran to catch them.
   themselves — XIV, 2
5. Can you tell me *who* that man is?
   who — XIII, 3; XIV, 4
6. *Let* me go.
   let — XVI, 9
7. Do you think *we* boys would do such a thing?
   we — XIV, 3
8. No one among those people *wants* to give away everything *he owns*.
   wants — XV, 6; XVI, 1
   he — XIV, 5
   owns — XV, 6; XVI, 1
9. Some one called while you *were* away.
   were — XVI, 1
10. John and *I* asked *those* boys to go with us.
    I — XIII, 3; XIV, 3
    those — XIV, 3
11. *Doesn't* he sing beautifully!
    doesn't — XV, 6; XVI, 1
12. I am as old as *she,* but that is known only to you
    and *me*.
    she — XIII, 3; XIV, 1
    me — XIII, 4; XIV, 1
13. There *were* so many people in the hall that we were
    unable *to walk* easily.
    were — XV, 6; XVI, 1
    to walk — XVI, 6
14. If she *were* older, I think she could do the work
    easily.
    were — XV, 7; XVI, 5
15. Give Harry and *me* some money.
    me — XIII, 3; XIV, 1

16. Is it *she who* they think has the keys?
    she — XIII, 3; XIV, 1
    who — XIII, 3; XIV, 4

17. *May* we have these books for an hour?
    may — XVI, 9

18. My mother and *I* often read aloud in the evening.
    I — XIV, 2

19. Each of the rooms *was* painted white.
    was — XV, 6; XVI, 1

20. *You* and your friends are invited to spend the evening with my mother and *me*.
    you — XIV, 2
    me — XIII, 4; XIV, 1

Problem XVII — Exercise 6

Note: The sentences are written correctly in the Key and the words that were changed are italicized. The reasons for the changes will be found by consulting the problems and the exercises indicated by the numbers.

1. There *were* only two items that they didn't mention.
    were — XV, 6; XVI, 1

2. They must *have* been here while we *were* away.
    have — XVI, 9
    were — XV, 6; XVI, 1

3. Mr. Jones, who sings in our choir, has a beautiful voice.
    (he) — XIV, 3

4. Either Mrs. Hamilton or Mrs. Reed *is* intending to bring the ice cream.
    is — XIII, 1; XV, 6; XVI, 1

5. Uncle Joe brought Janet and *me* gifts from abroad.
    me — XJII, 4; XIV, 1

6. We *ought not* to leave grandma alone in the house.
    ought not — XVI, 9

7. I *will* never be so thoughtless again; of that I am certain.
    will — XV, 4; XVI, 4

8. He *did* his work hurriedly, for *he* and *I were* going away.
    did — XV, 3; XVI, 2
    he — XIII, 3; XIV, 1, 3
    I — XIII, 3; XIV, 1, 3

9. *Sit* down and talk with me.
    sit — XV, 3; XVI, 3

10. The little child was *lying* on the grass.
    lying — XV, 3; XVI, 3

11. He said that he *should* return as soon as possible.
    should — XVI, 4

12. I insist that the boys *shall* not interrupt the speaker.
    shall — XVI, 4

13. *May* Johnny play with Jim and *me?*
    may — XVI, 9
    me — XIII, 4; XIV, 1, 3

14. John *has* a new car *that* runs very easily.
    has — XVI, 9
    that — XIV, 4

15. Neither the boy nor the girl *was* ready to start.
    was — XV, 6; XVI, 1

16. I know one *whom* I shall ask, but it won't be *she.*
    whom — XIII, 4; XIV, 4
    she — XIII, 3; XIV, 1

17. No one *saw* them except *me.*
    saw — XV, 3, 4; XVI, 2
    me — XIII, 4; XIV, 1

18. John and *I* hoped *to see* Edgar when we *were* in
    Boston.
    I — XIV, 3
    to see — XVI, 6
    were — XV, 6; XVI, 1

19. Each of us *was* eager to hear the new organ.
    was — XV, 6; XVI, 1

20. My mother will not hear of *my* being out so late.
    my — XIV, 6

Problem XVIII — Exercise 1

A.	*Adjectives*	*Adverbs*
1.	new	there
2.	those little	seldom
3.	English	easily
4.	those orange	very rapidly
5.	best	
6.	red sweet	
7.	correct	really
8.	bad	
9.	closed	angrily
10.	sick	
11.	that good	very
12.	sweet	
13.	happy that business	very
14.	angry	

15. every	well
16.	correctly
17. hot	
18.	respectfully
19. brilliant	remarkably
20. sick	suddenly

B. Have your teacher or some one in the class help you to correct these sentences.

Problem XVIII — Exercise 2

A.

1. He's a *very* friendly man. (The adjective " friendly " must be modified by an adverb.)

2. I was *almost* as hungry as he. (" Almost " means " nearly.")

3. *That* lady has a camera. (An adverb cannot modify a noun.)

4. How *prettily* she dances! (The verb must be modified by an adverb.)

5. She was *nearly* dead when they found her. (The verb must be modified by an adverb.)

6. We visited a church that was *near-by*. (" Near-by " is an adverb and cannot modify a noun.)

7. Is *this* picture yours. (An adverb cannot modify a noun.)

8. She *surely* is a bright little child. (The verb must be modified by an adverb.)

9. He *almost* always helps his mother with the work. (" Almost " means " nearly.")

10. Have you been a *very* good boy? (The adjective " good " must be modified by an adverb.)

11. I *surely* wish I had that car. (The verb must be modified by an adverb.)

12. I am *nearly* exhausted. (The verb must be modified by an adverb.)

13. We can *almost* always find something to do to help others. ("Almost" means "nearly.")

14. A meeting was held in a *neighboring* hall. ("Nearby" is an adverb.)

15. He's *very* good to the children. (The adjective "good" must be modified by an adverb.)

16. I was *most* delighted to see my cousin. ("Most" means "in the highest degree.")

17. I am *almost* tired out. ("Almost" means "nearly.")

18. He is a *most* interesting speaker. ("Most" means "in the highest degree.")

19. I *surely* do like that book. (The verb must be modified by an adverb.)

20. Do you like to see a person dress *gaudily?* (The verb must be modified by an adverb.)

B. Have some one who understands the work help you correct these sentences.

Problem XVIII — Exercise 3

A.

Word	Kind	Degree
1. thoroughly	adverb	comparative
2. well	adverb	positive
3. scarcely	adverb	
dark	adjective	positive
4. thoughtful	adjective	comparative
5. taller	adjective	comparative
two	adjective	
6. best	adjective	superlative

7. largest	adjective	superlative
youngest	adjective	superlative
8. more	adjective	comparative
9. saddest	adjective	superlative
10. fast	adverb	positive
11. smaller	adjective	comparative
merrily	adverb	comparative
larger	adjective	comparative
12. very	adverb	
stern	adjective	positive
13. first	adjective	superlative
that	adjective	
14. sooner	adverb	comparative
15. beautiful	adjective	comparative
16. respectfully	adverb	comparative
17. last	adjective	superlative
18. nervous	adjective	comparative
19. well	adverb	positive
better	adverb	comparative
20. difficult	adjective	comparative

B. Have your teacher look over these sentences.

Problem XVIII — Exercise 4

A.

1. Which is the *better* book, " Rab and His Friends " or " The Call of the Wild? " (Comparative degree because two objects are compared)

2. Which is *taller*, John or Henry? (Comparative degree because two persons are compared)

3. She is the *liveliest* of all the girls. (Superlative degree because more than two persons are mentioned)

4. Who walked *farther*, you or Harry? (Comparative degree because two persons are mentioned)

5. Of her two children, John is the *stronger*. (Comparative degree because two persons are mentioned)

6. Which of the two children is *more* careful in his work? (Comparative degree because two persons are compared)

7. Which of your hands is the *cleaner?* (Comparative degree because two objects are compared)

8. Marian is the *older* of the two, is she not? (Comparative degree because two persons are compared)

9. Do you know who the *youngest* pupil in this school is? (Superlative degree because more than two people are compared)

10. That is the *funniest* joke in the paper. (Superlative degree because more than two objects are compared)

11. William is the *most* courteous of all the young men. (Superlative degree because more than two persons are compared)

12. Which of the two men is the *more* likely to be elected? (Comparative degree because two persons are compared)

13. Which is the *cheaper* way to Chicago, by the Canadian Pacific or by the Union Pacific? (Comparative degree because two objects are compared)

14. There is not much difference between the two boys except that John is the *taller*. (Comparative degree because two objects are compared)

15. Which is the *higher*, Mt. Ranier or Mt. Whitney? (Comparative degree because two objects are compared)

16. I shall buy the *less* expensive of those two coats, for I like it *better*. (Comparative degree because two objects are compared)

17. This room is *more* comfortable, for the other has no large windows. (Comparative degree because two objects are compared)
18. She is the *more* agreeable of the two sisters. (Comparative degree because two persons are compared)
19. That is the *loveliest* sight I have ever seen. (Superlative degree because more than two objects are compared)
20. I had several pencils, but I have lost the *best* one. (Superlative degree because more than two objects are compared)

B. Have your teacher help you to correct these sentences. If you know of some one in the class who uses adjectives and adverbs correctly, you may consult him.

Problem XVIII — Exercise 5

A.

1. *No* one ever told me about that accident.
2. *Never* give me any more of that medicine.
3. A person should *never* fight. (*No* one should ever fight.)
4. I can *hardly* hear you.
5. She had *but* three cents when I left the store.
6. I had *only* one.
7. I *don't* want any lunch.
8. I could *scarcely* hear a sound.
9. I *don't* think it will rain.
10. I *hardly* expected her to come.
11. I *never* can see anything that I want to see.
12. They *didn't* intend to stay so late.
13. Why *hasn't* he done any of those problems?
14. I *never* want him to come here again.

15. They had heard *only* one or two songs when the fire broke out.
16. *Haven't* you done any of your work yet?
17. I have *but* three pounds of flour.
18. You could *hardly* imagine a more discouraging talk.
19. *Won't* you ever speak to me again?
20. *Aren't* you ever going to stop?

B–C. Have some one whose spoken English is excellent help you to correct these sentences. Of course you will not select a person who is guilty of using double negatives in his speech.

Problem XVIII — Exercise 6

A. Have your teacher look over these sentences.

B.

1. He had seen her only once.
2. They had just entered the room when the girl fainted.
3. There are only two ways of securing good results.
4. Have you ever heard a wild cat scream?
5. They were nearly starved when the boat landed.
6. She almost lost her footing as she stepped on the narrow plank.
7. He remembered nearly all of the poem.
8. I also gave the old coat away. (I gave the old coat away also.)
9. I had only a few pennies.
10. We were so busy that we could write only a few lines to the family at home.
11. John merely asked him a civil question.
12. Also send me some bananas and oranges.
13. The old woman was quite exhausted from the heat.

14. When I was in the store yesterday, I saw only one bargain.
15. When shall we ever finish this work?
16. I can go shopping only on Monday.
17. I need only three dollars.
18. Harry had almost reached the top of the house when his mother saw him.
19. Do you remember ever to have been here before?
20. I saw him only once before.

Problem XVIII — Exercise 7

A.

1. He feels *bad*.   (Predicate adjective describes the subject)
2. How *sweet* that rose smells.   (Predicate adjective)
3. This maple sugar tastes *good*.   (Predicate adjective)
4. The child felt *bad*.   (Predicate adjective)
5. The old man looked *angry*.   (Predicate adjective)
6. This cherry tastes *bitter*.   (Predicate adjective)
7. That little baby looks *happy*.   (Predicate adjective)
8. How *sweet* that music sounds.   (Predicate adjective)
9. I can feel those keys *easily*.   (The verb is modified by an adverb that tells how.)
10. The old man looked at us *angrily*.   (The verb must be modified by an adverb.)
11. How *fragrant* that lily smells.   (Predicate adjective)
12. He has been looking *queer* for some time.   (Predicate adjective)
13. He becomes *noisier* as he grows older.   (Predicate adjective)
14. She feels *fine* tonight.   (Predicate adjective)
15. He treats the child very *gently*.   (The verb must be modified by an adverb.)

16. Those flowers grew *quickly*. (The verb must be modified by an adverb.)

17. He spoke very *uncharitably* about the woman. (The verb must be modified by an adverb.)

18. The air from the orange trees smells *sweet*. (Predicate adjective)

19. My little girl is feeling *well* this afternoon. (Predicate adjective)

20. The road felt *rough* to his bare feet. (Predicate adjective)

B. This work is very important and should be corrected by your teacher.

Problem XVIII — Exercise 8

A.

1. She looked *everywhere* for her hat. (No such word as " everywheres ")

2. My father is *somewhat* better. (The adjective must be modified by an adverb)

3. I gave some money to *a* beggar who was sitting on the street. (Indefinite article is used to point out an indefinite object)

4. *A* student of Latin can read French easily. (Indefinite article is used to point out an indefinite object)

5. I saw *a* dog and *a* boy running down the street. (The article must be placed before each noun when we wish to denote more than one person or thing)

6. *The* poet and his friend often sat under the maple tree. (Definite article used to point out a particular object)

7. Do you like *that* style of coats? ("Style" is singular and must be modified by a singular adjective)

8. Did you see *an* old woman as you entered the building? (Indefinite article used to point out an indefinite object)

9. My eyes feel *somewhat* better now. (The adjective must be modified by an adverb)

10. Some day we shall forget *the* trouble we have had. (Definite article used to point out a particular object)

11. I don't like *that* kind of people. ("Kind" is singular and must be modified by a singular adjective)

12. *The* secretary and *the* president were not able to attend the meeting. (Definite article used to point out a particular object)

13. *This* kind of melons is the sweetest. ("Kind" is singular and must be modified by a singular adjective)

14. I prefer *that* kind of melons. ("Kind" is singular and must be modified by a singular adjective)

15. I must have put my purse *somewhere* in this drawer. (No such word as "someplace")

16. To *a* studious person *that* kind of examples is not tiresome.

   (a — an indefinite article is used to point out an indefinite object)

   (that — "kind" is singular and must be modified by a singular adjective)

17. I wish I had *a* book to read. (Indefinite article is used to point out an indefinite object)

18. My brother wants *this* sort of stamps for his collection. ("Sort" is singular and must be modified by a singular adjective)

19. She will not read *that* kind of books. (" Kind " is singular and must be modified by a singular adjective)

20. Your child must be *somewhere* in this building. (No such words as " somewheres " or " someplace ")

B. Let some one in the class help you to correct these sentences.

Problem XVIII — Exercise 9

A.

1. Which do you like *better,* the beach or the mountains? (Comparative degree because two objects are compared)

2. People *almost* always like to play. (" Almost " means " nearly ")

3. He is the *fastest* runner on the team. (Superlative degree because more than two persons are compared)

4. Mildred is *more beautiful* than Mabel. (Adjectives of three syllables are compared by prefixing " more " and " most " to the positive)

5. It was a *real* pleasure to talk with her. (" Real " means " genuine ")

6. I *surely* am glad to see you. (The verb must be modified by an adverb)

7. *This* knife is sharp. (A noun cannot be modified by an adverb)

8. They were *nearly* dead when they were found. (" Nearly " means " almost ")

9. He spoke his piece *well*. (" Well " modifies the verb)

10. The girls looked *beautiful* in their pretty white dresses. (Predicate adjective)

11. Go *slowly*. ("Slowly" modifies the verb)
12. She doesn't like *that* kind of shoes. ("Kind" is singular and must be modified by a singular adjective)
13. That tree has grown *rapidly*. ("Rapidly" modifies the verb)
14. Henry is the *stronger* of the two. (Comparative degree because two persons are compared)
15. I want to go away *somewhere*. (No such word as "somewheres")
16. He hasn't *any* of my pencils. (Double negative is never allowed)
17. Are you *almost* ready to leave? ("Almost" means "nearly")
18. He studies *considerably* every night. ("Considerably" modifies the verb)
19. How *heavily* he walks. ("Heavily" modifies the verb)
20. I shall take three of *this* kind. ("Kind" is singular and must be modified by a singular adjective)

B. Ask your teacher or some one who is excellent in his English to help you to correct these sentences. Why did you select these particular points?

Problem XVIII — Exercise 10

1. (*a*) He *surely* does speak *well*. ("Surely" and "well" modify the verb)
2. (*b*) This machine goes very *slowly*. ("Slowly" modifies the verb)
3. (*b*) This *kind* is best. ("Kind" is singular and must be modified by a singular adjective)

4. (*a*) He is the *richest* man in the world. (An adjective of one syllable is compared by adding " er " and " est " to the positive)

5. (*b*) He has done his lesson *well*. (" Well " modifies the verb)

6. (*b*) She learns her lessons *quickly*. (" Quickly " modifies the verb)

7. (*b*) The milk in that bottle is *nearly* gone. (" Nearly " means " almost ")

8. (*a*) He is the *older* of the two. (Comparative degree because two persons are compared)

9. (*a*) I lost my book in the store *somewhere*. (No such word as " someplace ")

10. (*b*) You are doing *well* now. (" Well " modifies the verb)

11. (*a*) Which of the two boys should receive *more* credit? (Comparative degree because two persons are compared)

12. (*a*) The horse is the *most* intelligent of all animals. *Note:* In this sentence the horse is compared with all animals. For this reason the superlative degree is used. If we compare the horse with all *other* animals, we should say, " The horse is more intelligent than all other animals," for we are comparing two objects: (1) the horse and (2) all other animals. Although the second group contains many objects, it is considered as one group.

13. (*b*) We couldn't find the watch *anywhere*. (Two negatives in one sentence are not allowed)

14. (*a*) Do not look at us so *angrily*. (" Angrily " modifies the verb)

15. (*b*) He is a *very* good man. (" Real " means " genuine " and is an adjective)

16. (*b*) Which is the *taller,* you or your brother?
   (Comparative degree because two persons
   are compared)
17. (*b*) I *surely* will try to help the child. (" Surely ".
   modifies the verb)
18. (*b*) She is *more* considerate than all the other girls.
   (Comparative degree because two groups are
   compared: (1) the girl herself and (2) the
   group made up of other girls)
19. (*b*) I saw a man and *a* woman on the street. (The
   article must not be omitted when two persons
   are named)
20. (*b*) I am feeling *very well* today. (" Very " must.
   be used, for " real " means " genuine " and is
   an adjective. " Well " means to be " in good
   health ")

Problem XVIII — Exercise 11

1. Did you sleep *well* last night? (The adverb " well "
   modifies the verb)
2. The boat goes *very rapidly*. (Use " very " because
   " real " means " genuine." Use " rapidly " because
   it modifies the verb)
3. John *surely* does his work *well*. (The adverb
   " surely " modifies the verb. The adverb " well "
   modifies the verb)
4. She *hardly* noticed me. (Double negative is not
   allowed)
5. Please don't walk so *slowly*. (The adverb " slowly "
   modifies the verb)
6. I have just told Mary about the fire. (" Just ". must
   be placed next to the word it modifies)

7. Do you like *this* kind of ties? ("Kind" is singular and must be modified by a singular adjective)

8. She *almost* knocked me down. ("Almost" means "nearly")

9. Of the two Janet is *more* obliging. (Comparative degree because two persons are compared)

10. Which of you two girls can eat *more* candy than the other? (Comparative degree because two persons are compared)

11. How *beautiful* the sky looks tonight. ("Beautiful" is a predicate adjective)

12. (1) New York is *larger* than any *other* city in the United States, or
    (2) New York is the *largest* of *all* cities in the United States.
      (1) (Comparative degree because two groups are compared)
      (2) (Superlative degree because more than two objects are compared)

13. They had *only* one dollar between them. (Double negative is not allowed)

14. She is a *very* interesting person. ("Real" means "genuine" and is an adjective)

15. He looked guilty, but he never said anything to *anyone*. (Use "guilty" because it is a predicate adjective. Double negative is not allowed)

16. I feel *somewhat* better this afternoon. (The adverb "somewhat" modifies the adjective)

17. How *soft* that plush feels! (Predicate adjective)

18. I will try to be good every day. (Correct as it is)

19. You *could* hardly tell what the woman was saying. (Double negative is not allowed)

20. She *had* only one friend. (Double negative is not allowed)

Problem XIX — Exercise 1

A.

1. Why should there ever be any trouble *between* you and me?
2. Is any one *besides* your friend coming?
3. Where were you when you fell *off* the car.
4. We are waiting *for* James, who has just gone *into* the store.
5. He walked *into* the room without knocking.
6. She was angry *with* me.
7. Please go *into* that room.
8. Can you open this can *with* your knife?
9. Are you angry *with* me?
10. Do you know any one in this city *besides* me?
11. We went *into* the office.
12. This is different *from* what I expected to see.
13. She died *of* pneumonia.
14. *Among* the three men there was a friendly feeling.
15. He fell *into* the well.
16. They were waiting *for* the car.
17. May I sit *beside* you?
18. The Capitol is located *in* Washington.
19. The hat will be finished *within* an hour.
20. I correspond *with* many people.
21. Is there harmony *among* you three girls?
22. When we lost our money, I had to part *with* my jewelry.
23. The tramp was killed *by* the train.
24. When you are *in* Paris, buy me a new gown.
25. Mildred is different *from* me in many ways.
26. When I have an appointment with a person, I do not like to wait *for* him.

27. On the Fourth of July we hang the flag *out* the window.
28. She said she could not agree *to* the plan.
29. Johnny, don't put your head *out* the window.
30. Why are you angry *with* her?
31. He took it *off* the shelf and put it *into* the vase.
32. There will be five guests *besides* Aunt Anna.
33. Did you ever stop *at* the little town of Chester?
34. *Within* five minutes she was telling me the joke.
35. He is different *from* his brother in that he enjoys being in the mountains.
36. How can you agree *to* such a ridiculous plan?
37. Does my plan correspond *with* (to) yours?
38. He sat down *beside* me.
39. At that time Mr. Johnson was living *in* Buffalo.
40. I wish some one *besides* me could go to the store.

B.   Have your teacher help you correct these sentences.

Problem XIX — Exercise 2

A.

1. I took it off the table.
2. Where is she going?
3. Where is your hat?
4. She threw the paper out the window.
5. Why can't you sit opposite me?
6. Must you leave later?
7. Can you divide that line into two parts?
8. She wants you to speak to her.
9. When I got off the car, I saw Mr. Hamilton.
10. I shall be glad when the picnic ends.
11. A second passed, and then every one began to laugh.
12. I don't know where my book is.

13. I sat near my friend.
14. John, where is James going?
15. Why don't you ask him to come?
16. A certain rich man divided his money among the poor.
17. The little boy stood near the policeman.
18. Who sat opposite you at the banquet?
19. Mrs. Dow sat back of us.
20. I wish I knew where my purse is.

B. If any one in the class was guilty of using a redundant word, speak to him about it. Let him look over your list.

Problem XIX — Exercise 3

A.

1. It's *of* no use to talk about the affair.
2. When will he be *at* home?
3. My mother was born on the sixteenth of September.
4. Did you stay *at* home last night?
5. Why do you act *in* that way?
6. Did Columbus discover America *on* the fourteenth of October?
7. It's *of* no use to write to him.
8. Can you buy some rope *of* that size?
9. *In* the last year he made fifty thousand dollars.
10. Is it *of* any use to send them an invitation?
11. I wish you would not act *in* that way.
12. *In* the preceding summer I went to Alaska.
13. Try to buy some cloth *of* that weight.
14. He left *on* the sixth of August.
15. I shall stay *at* home all summer.

B. Have an excellent student look over these sentences with you.

Problem XIX — Exercise 4

A.

1. She bakes the bread *as if* she enjoyed the work.
2. John is not *so* strong *as* he was in the fall.
3. He acts *as if* he had lost his way.
4. I wish I could play *on* the piano as Mildred can.
5. *Either* be quiet *or* run outside to play.
6. He is not *so* tall as I am.
7. *Unless* I go now, I shall be late.
8. The boys are *as* studious *as* the girls.
9. He will go *either* to France *or* to Italy.
10. You will never be able to succeed *unless* you spend some effort.
11. The team did not play *so* well this year *as* it did last year.
12. That poor man can *neither* read *nor* write.
13. I cannot go *unless* you go with me.
14. It seems *as if* she is always busy.
15. I have not yet decided whether I shall go to college *or* stay in the city and work.
16. Mother bought not only a coat but *also* a hat.
17. I will spare neither money *nor* time to locate that boy.
18. I wish I could either play *or* sing.
19. This house looks just *as* it did ten years ago.
20. You are not *so* tired as she is.

B. Have some excellent student look over these sentences with you. If there is a doubt about any of them, consult your teacher.

Problem XIX — Exercise 5

A.

1. I read articles about Marconi and Edison, who are very interesting men.
2. Night descended on the silent forest, and Stephen heard the solemn cry of the owls, which frightened him exceedingly.
3. He looked pitifully at the stern face, but saw that he would receive but little sympathy from the Indian who had captured him.
4. When Bob awoke in the morning, he told his mother about his dream, which amused her very much.
5. The fire had recently been replenished with green wood, which made a dense smoke.
6. (The sentence is correct as it stands. Why?)
7. He bought some books about electricity, which were very interesting.
8. The old man looked about for some weapon, but he could find nothing better than his cane, which he seized.
9. (The sentence is correct as it stands. Why?)
10. I am trying to sell this property, which is located in the business district.
11. Mrs. Jones induced her husband to buy a house, which is located in a beautiful residential district.
12. Mr. Pearson, soon after his arrival at the hotel, went into a conference with Mr. Simmons, who told him the cause of the failure of the bank.
13. Mr. Houston said the lumber would be brought in boats, which the company owned.
14. The building, which has been carefully planned, will contain ten rooms.

15. The thermometer registered as high as ninety-five degrees, which was the highest point it has reached this year.

16. The exhibition, which was opened Saturday night, was one of the most elaborate ever attempted in the United States.

17. The manager of the factory investigated Mr. Vose, who was able to give much valuable information.

18. The athletes wished to have an opportunity to know the men who will have charge of selecting the team.

19. We had a good crop of wheat, which is valued at several million dollars.

20. The manager of the dry goods store has advertised for a floorwalker, who must have had at least five years' experience.

B. Have your teacher look over these sentences to see if they are written correctly.

Problem XIX — Exercise 6

1. The board is *behind* the door.
2. I won't go *unless* you go.
3. Can you get a pencil *of* her.
4. He is not *so* young as he seems.
5. Neither John *nor* Harry can go.
6. A person should never be angry *with* anyone.
7. *Within* two hours the house was completely ruined.
8. He doesn't play *as* John does.
9. The boys cannot go to the beach *unless* they do their work.
10. Do you know if John died *of* diphtheria.
11. I shall wait *for* you until two o'clock. If you do not come then, I shall go home.

12. She is different *from* her sister.
13. Who was that man sitting *beside* you?
14. Don't jump *into* the well.
15. It broke his heart to part *from* his sister.
16. I wish I felt *as* you do.
17. Please put it *on* the shelf.
18. There was a dispute *between* the two men.
19. Why did you sit *among* the boys on the team?
20. You act *as if* you are tired.

Problem XIX — Exercise 7

1. (*b*) Did you agree *with* Mr. Smith?

   (According to correct usage, we agree *with* a person)

2. (*b*) Did he sit *near* you?

   (" By " is redundant)

3. (*a*) The poor child fell off the roof.

   ("Of " is redundant)

4. (*b*) I do not like to have any one sit beside me when I am studying.

   (" Beside " means " by the side of ")

5. (*b*) When are you going *into* the school?

   (" Into " conveys the idea of motion)

6. (*b*) I have waited *for* him long enough. Why doesn't he come?

   (According to correct usage, we wait *for* a person when we expect him)

7. (*b*) Are you intending to leave *on* the tenth of this month?

   (Preposition must not be omitted)

8. (*b*) She never went *unless* her work was finished.

   (" Without " is a preposition; " unless " is a conjunction)

9. (*b*) I cannot divide this pie into three equal parts.
    ("Up" is redundant)

10. (*a*) When did you part *from* your sister?
    (According to correct usage, we part *from* a person)

11. (*b*) She looked *as if* she was very sad.
    ("Like" is never a conjunction)

12. (*b*) He died *of* influenza.
    (According to correct usage, a person dies *of* a disease)

13. (*b*) Why does she walk *in* that way?
    (The preposition must not be omitted)

14. (*a*) These sentences are not *so* hard as the others.
    (The correlatives are *not so — as*)

15. (*b*) Are you very different *from* your sister?
    (According to correct usage, a person is different *from* another person)

16. (*a*) I can be there *within* an hour.
    (According to correct usage, we say *within an hour*)

17. (*b*) Mother cannot go unless I do her work.
    ("Except" is never a conjunction)

18. (*b*) I'll try to get some money *of* my father.
    ("Off" is redundant)

19. (*b*) The party ended *with* refreshments.
    ("Up" is redundant)

20. (*b*) I wish you would not walk *on* the lawn.
    (According to correct usage, we say *on*)

Problem XIX — Exercise 8

1. Why do you look out the window so often?
    ("Of" is redundant)

2. My friends and I took a long hiking trip which we enjoyed very much.

   (" And " must connect words that have the same grammatical value)

3. Is any one *besides* you going?

   (" Besides " means " in addition to ")

4. I told him that it's *of* no use to try to influence Robert.

   (The preposition must not be omitted)

5. How long did you wait *for* John at the station?

   (According to correct usage, we wait *for* a person when we expect him)

6. My father is never angry *with* me.

   (According to correct usage, the expression is *angry with*)

7. I shall be going a little later.

   (" On " is redundant)

8. Please stay *at* home tonight with me.

   (The preposition must not be omitted)

9. The girls cannot go *unless* they have escorts.

   (" Without " is never a conjunction)

10. That carpet looks *as if* it had received hard usage.

    (" Like " is always a preposition, never a conjunction)

11. I can neither eat *nor* sleep.

    (According to correct usage, the correlatives are *neither — nor*)

12. Must I part *from* my mother?

    (According to correct usage, we part *from* a person)

13. When you go *into* the office, please telephone my sister.

    (" Into " conveys the idea of motion)

14. I can never leave *on* the first of September.
    (The preposition must not be omitted)

15. This building is not *so* large as the one we visited yesterday.
    (According to correct usage, the correlatives are *not so — as*)

16. Have the boys thrown their caps out the window?
    (" Of " is redundant)

17. Who took my book off the desk?
    (" Of " is redundant)

18. Her mother sat *behind* us.
    (According to correct usage, we must say " behind ")

19. Will you be *at* home tomorrow?
    (Preposition must not be omitted)

20. The teacher often sat among the pupils in the class.
    (" Among " denotes more than two)

Problem XX — Exercise 1

A.

Note: The sentences are written correctly in the key. You will find the reasons for each correction by consulting the problems and exercises indicated by the numbers.

1. The man, *who* I thought was a writer, asked Mary and *me* to buy some of his pictures.
    who — XIII, 3; XIV, 4
    me — XIII, 4; XIV, 1

2. Do you use *this* kind of pens?
    this — XVIII, 8

3. It is necessary for you and *me* to go now.
    me — XIII, 4; XIV, 1

4. If anyone disobeys the law, *he* should be punished.
   he — XIV, 5
5. *Doesn't* her child sleep *well?*
   doesn't — XV, 6; XVI, 1
   well — XVIII, 1
6. John is the better *swimmer* of the two, *isn't* he?
   better — XVIII, 3, 4
   isn't — XVI, 9
7. Every person that thinks *he* can do as *he* pleases will soon learn that this is impossible.
   he — XIV, 5
8. Harry and *I* like to sit before the fire and talk.
   I — XIII, 3; XIV, 3
9. I *could* scarcely believe what they had *just* told mother and *me.*
   could — XVIII, 5
   just — XVIII, 6
   me — XIII, 4; XIV, 1
10. *We* boys planned to go to the mountains.
    we — XIV, 3
11. I have resolved to save my money, *which* I shall need next year.
    which — XIV, 5
12. Was it *I whom* you sent for?
    (Better — Was it I for whom you sent?)
    I — XIII, 3; XIV, 1
    whom — XIII, 4; XIV, 1
13. If any one calls, tell *him* I shall be back soon.
    him — XIV, 5
14. Which of you two girls worked the *harder?*
    harder — XVIII, 3, 4
15. I shall be satisfied with *whomever* you choose.
    whomever — XIII, 4; XIV, 4

16. Must I divide my candy *among* all the children in the class?

up — XIX, 2

among — XIX, 1

17. That is the man *who* every one thought would be mayor.

who — XIII, 3; XIV, 4

18. *Isn't* she younger than *he?*

isn't — XVI, 9

he — XIII, 3; XIV, 1

19. Everyone is going except *her.*

her — XIII, 4; XIV, 1

20. There was no thought of *John's* winning the prize, for *we* boys knew that he *could* hardly write a sentence *correctly.*

John's — XIV, 6   could — XVIII, 5

we — XIV, 3   correctly — XVIII, 1

B.

1. When John and I returned to the front of the
   (1)
   house, we found that one of the windows had been
   (2)
   partially opened.

   (1) XI, 1

   (2) I, 3

2. One of the guests, a woman from New York, told
   (1)   (1)
   me she had never seen the poet before.
   (2)

   (1) VIII, 4

   (2) I, 3

3. Just send a letter, a post card, or note to this address, and you will receive the story of a great institution.

The words have superscript markers: "letter" (1), "card" (1), "dress" (2), "institution" (3).

(1) VIII, 5   (3) I, 3
(2) IX, 4

4. Inasmuch as all the instruction is carried on by mail, it makes no difference where you live.

"mail" (1), "live" (2).

(1) XI, 1   (2) I, 3

5. I have earned the money that I needed, and I know several women who want me to make more dresses for them.

"needed" (1), "for them" (2).

(1) IX, 4   (2) I, 3

6. Among the members of the class are housewives, mothers, business women, teachers, girls at home and in school, and girls in shops and stores and offices.

"housewives" (1), "mothers" (1), "teachers" (1), "girls at home" (1), "school" (1), "offices" (2).

(1) VIII, 5   (2) I, 3

7. As soon as we received our instructions, which came in separate envelopes, we read all about the interesting facts regarding our work.

"instructions" (1), "envelopes" (2), "work" (3).

(1) XI, 1   (3) I, 3
(2) XI, 2

8. The roomful of men stirred uncomfortably,$^{(1)}$ and one or two laughed awkwardly.$^{(2)}$
   (1) IX, 4
   (2) I, 3

9. She needed help desperately$^{(1)}$; she needed money and friends and a home.$^{(2)}$
   (1) IX, 7
   (2) I, 3

10. We are here,$^{(1)}$ you dear fellow,$^{(1)}$ because we know and appreciate the melancholy which comes over one when he is far from home.$^{(2)}$
    (1) VIII, 3
    (2) I, 3

11. The woman,$^{(1)}$ who was on the verge of crying,$^{(1)}$ checked herself and merely smiled at her accuser.$^{(2)}$
    (1) XI, 2
    (2) I, 3

12. Yes,$^{(1)}$ I will do that if you want me to,$^{(2)}$ mister.$^{(3)}$
    (1) VIII, 6
    (2) VIII, 3
    (3) I, 3

13. Why should he not be happy when justice and honor and fame had come to him?$^{(1)}$
    (1) I, 3

14. He paused on the threshold, for outside the door
    he heard a loud voice calling him.
    (1) IX, 4; page 342   (2) I, 3

15. There was no light in the alley; all the backs of the
    blocks around it were intensely dark.
    (1) IX, 6   (2) I, 3

16. A person, who called himself a sculptor, showed the
    audience some interesting paintings.
    (1) XI, 2
    (2) I, 3

17. Any person that will mistreat a little child is not
    really human.
    (1) I, 3; XI, 2

18. They often asked us where we were going, but we
    did not wish to tell them.
    (1) IX, 4   (2) I, 3

19. Did you see the balloon, John?
    (1) I, 3   (2) VIII, 3

20. Have you ever read the biography of Charles
    Dickens, the author of " David Copperfield " ?
    (1) VIII, 4
    (2) I, 3

Problem XX — Exercise 2

A.

Note: The sentences are written correctly in the key. You will find the reasons for each correction by consulting the problems and exercises indicated by the numbers.

1. I might *have* known that they *were* coming tonight.
    have — XVI, 9
    were — XV, 6; XVI, 1

2. My little boy is feeling *bad* today.
    bad — XVIII, 7

3. This paper is not numbered *correctly*.
    here — XVIII, 2
    correctly — XVIII, 1

4. Have you your purse with you?
    got — XVI, 9

5. How *quietly* she talks.
    quietly — XVIII, 1

6. What fun we could have if she *were* here.
    were — XV, 7; XVI, 5

7. I *had* but one dollar in my purse.
    had — XVIII, 5

8. Will you *sit* here *beside* me?
    sit — XV, 3; XVI, 3
    beside — XIX, 1

9. John is the *fastest* runner on the team, but I *don't* think he will be able to play.
    fastest — XVIII, 3, 4
    don't — XVIII, 5

10. How long *will* the play last?
    will — XV, 4; XVI, 4

11. The little boys *taught* him how to swim.
    taught — XVI, 9

12. I wish I could *lie* down for an hour.
    lie — XV, 3; XVI, 3
13. *May* I go to the park, mother?
    may — XVI, 9
14. I *saw* four men entering the store.
    saw — XV, 3; XVI, 2
15. I *ran* home last night as fast as I could go.
    ran — XV, 3; XVI, 2
16. I don't know what I *did* with my purse.
    did — XV, 3; XVI, 2
17. Some one has *broken* my ink bottle.
    broken — XV, 3; XVI, 2
18. Mr. Smith, with his wife and children, *is* taking a
    trip abroad.
    is — XV, 6; XVI, 1
19. Did he hurt himself *badly?*
    badly — XVIII, 1
20. I wish he *were* going to visit you and *her.*
    were — XV, 7; XVI, 5
    her — XIII, 3; XIV, 1

B.

1. He took a glance into the street behind him,[(1)] and
   when he saw nothing,[(2)] he turned and went into the
   café.[(3)]
   (1) IX, 4
   (2) XI, 1   (3) I, 3

2. He stood erect for a moment,[(1)] and then his glance
   fell upon the small child at his side.[(2)]
   (1) IX, 4   (2) I, 3

3. Even if they had recognized him,[1] would they let others know that he was in the city?[2]
   (1) XI, 1
   (2) I, 3

4. He will tell you the truth,[1] James.[2]
   (1) VIII, 3
   (2) I, 3

5. When Willie spoke,[1] his voice sounded as if it came from a weary and worn-out man.[2]
   (1) XI, 1
   (2) I, 3

6. Again a faint smile crept from under the chief's gray moustache,[1] and his eyes became earnest and appealing.[2]
   (1) IX, 4
   (2) I, 3

7. Well,[1] go out and see the game,[2] Willie;[3] but don't go down to meet the boat.[4]
   (1) VIII, 6   (3) IX, 7
   (2) VIII, 3   (4) I, 3

8. From my desk I could see the stern-faced man,[1] who was in charge of those poor hungry children.[2]
   (1) XI, 2
   (2) I, 3

9. As she thought of it later, she knew it was right for
(1)
her brother to go.
(2)

   (1) XI, 1
   (2) I, 3

10. Dearie, I do not blame you, but I would not do it
(1)   (2)
again.
(3)

   (1) VIII, 3   (3) I, 3
   (2) IX, 4

11. We entered the machine, which was upholstered in
(1)
gayly flowered cretonne, and sat down on the soft
(1)
cushions.
(2)

   (1) XI, 2
   (2) I, 3

12. We explored the ten-cent store, which had always
(1)
been the children's favorite store, and each bought
(2)
one little present.
(3)

   (1) XI, 2   (3) I, 3
   (2) XI, 2 ; IX, 4

13. Miss Glynn, a little, elderly, sweet-faced woman, stood
(1)   (2)   (2)   (1)
before the crowd of children.
(3)

   (1) VIII, 4   (3) I, 3
   (2) VIII, 5

14. Attracted by the display of pink and white cakes, we
(1)
had our lunch in a stuffy little restaurant.
(2)
(1) XVI, 7
(2) I, 3

15. The boys ordered what they liked, and every one
(1)
was supremely happy.
(2)
(1) IX, 4
(2) I, 3

16. When the girls said they wanted to go into the
principal department store of the village, the boys
(1)
rebelled most strenuously.
(2)
(1) XI, 1
(2) I, 3

17. We had dinner with Mr. Johnson, the senior mem-
(1)
ber of the firm.
(2)
(1) VIII, 4
(2) I, 3

18. I am going to town, and I wonder if you would like
(1)
to go with me.
(2)
(1) IX, 4   (2) I, 3

19. Lena sat down on the bed, which she had just
(1)
made, and breathed a sigh of relief.
(1)   (2)
(1) XI, 2   (2) I, 3

⁽¹⁾
20. Way up on the mountain side two old veterans, who

⁽¹⁾
have not spoken to each other for years, hold down

⁽²⁾
an old and forsaken mine.
(1) XI, 2   (2) I, 3

Problem XX — Exercise 3

A.

Note: The sentences are written correctly. You can find the reason for each change by consulting the problems and exercises indicated by the numbers.

1. Don't you *lie* down to rest every afternoon?
   lie — XV, 3; XVI, 3
2. Do you know where she is going?
   to — XIX, 2
3. It was *she* whom they wanted, but we *could* hardly hear what they *were* saying.
   she — XIII, 3; XIV, 1
   could — XVIII, 5
   were — XV, 6; XVI, 1
4. The days are much *warmer* now, and it is hard *to be* studying always.
   warmer — XVIII, 3, 4
   to be — XV, 8; XVI, 6
5. Each of the boys *was* studying so much that *he* did not hear the bell.
   was — XV, 6; XVI, 1
   he — XIV, 5
6. The matter *lies* entirely between you and *me*.
   lies — XV, 2, 3; XVI, 3
   me — XIII, 4; XIV, 1

7. The boys *rose* as the ladies entered.

     rose — XV, 3 ; XVI, 3

8. Reaching forward from where he sat, he laid his long, friendly hand upon the older man's shoulder.

     Phrase — XVI, 7

9. *He* and *I were* not expecting to hear of *father's* being elected.

     he — XIII, 3 ; XIV, 1, 3

     I — XIII, 3 ; XIV, 1

     were — XV, 6 ; XVI, 1

     father's — XIV, 6

10. He talked entirely of *himself* and of *his* going to New York.

     himself — XIV, 2, 3

     his — XIV, 6

11. I cannot study *unless* I have a better light.

     unless — XIX, 4

12. Have you ever eaten *that* kind of figs?

     that — XVIII, 8

13. I wish I *were* going with *those* boys.

     were — XV, 7 ; XVI, 8

     those — XIV, 3

14. *Has* each of the children *his* car-fare?

     has — XV, 6 ; XVI, 1

     his — XIV, 5

15. When we *were* going into the store, we *saw* a man and *a* woman standing near the door.

     were — XVI, 1

     saw — XV, 3 ; XVI, 2

     a — XVIII, 8

16. Who is the *younger,* John or James?

     younger — XVIII, 3, 4

17. Mother cannot go *unless* I help her.

     unless — XIX, 4

18. He *ought not* to expect her and *me* to do all of
    the work.
    ought — XVI, 9
    me — XIII, 4; XIV, 1
19. Nobody in this house does *anything* to help mother
    and *me*.
    anything — XVIII, 5
    me — XIII, 4; XIV, 1
20. We *saw* her while she *did* the work.
    saw — XV, 3; XVI, 2
    did — XV, 3; XVI, 2

B.

1. Lady, listen; that man is the one who took your
   (1)   (2)
   (3)
   purse.
   (1) VIII, 3   (3) I, 3
   (2) IX, 6

2. When a person like him decides to do a thing, he
                                              (1)
   usually does it.
           (2)
   (1) XI, 1   (2) I, 3

3. Now that you are here and have finished your
       (1)   (2)
   work, won't you stay and talk with us?
   (1) XI, 1   (2) I, 3

4. Oh, Mr. Jones, what are a few thousand dollars to a
   (1) (2)   (3)
   rich, grateful, and generous man like you?
       (4)   (4)   (5)
   (1) VIII, 6; VIII, 3   (4) VIII, 5
   (2) VIII, 2   (5) I. 3
   (3) VIII, 3

5. A certain softness was coming into the man's proud
   (1)
   face; something almost kindly was twinkling in
   (2)
   his eye.
   (1) IX, 6
   (2) I, 3

6. At first it hardly seemed that she had heard him, for
   (1)
   her mother held her attention so closely.
   (2)
   (1) IX, 5   (2) I, 3

7. As he passed along, a close observer might have
   (1)
   noticed the frown on his face.
   (2)
   (1) XI, 1   (2) I, 3

8. Well, John, we are out of luck today; but we will
   (1)   (2)   (3)
   make a success of this business yet.
   (4)
   (1) VIII, 6; VIII, 3   (3) IX, 7
   (2) VIII, 3   (4) I, 3

9. The elevator was not running at that time of
   night, and Mr. Thompson was forced to walk up
   (1)   (2)
   the dark stairway to the offices.
   (3)
   (1) IX, 4   (3) I, 3
   (2) VIII, 2

10. One thing is certain; I will not be here tomorrow
    (1)
    morning.
    (2)
    (1) IX, 6
    (2) I, 3

11. Although he did not yet know how dangerous the
    (1)
    situation was, he was not entirely unaware of his
    (2)
    danger.
    (1) XI, 1
    (2) I, 3

12. John pressed me hard for an immediate agree-
    (1)
    ment, but I would not yield; I had no faith in
    (2)
    (3)
    the man's account.
    (1) IX, 4   (3) I, 3
    (2) IX, 6

    (1)   (1)
13. Her suit, which she had wanted so much, was now
    (2)
    a source of trouble and annoyance to her.
    (1) XI, 2
    (2) I, 3

                                        (1)
14. Since it was at least eight miles to the Glen, the
    (2)
    station agent advised me to hire a taxi.
    (1) XI, 1
    (2) I, 3

    (1)   (1)
15. Fred's place, the store around the corner, was where
    (2)   (3)
    we went; and as we neared it, we could hear some
    (4)
    one talking loudly.
    (1) VIII, 4   (3) XI, 1
    (2) IX, 7   (4) I, 3

16. As Charley spoke, a vision flitted through his mind. ⁽¹⁾ ... ⁽²⁾
   (1) XI, 1
   (2) I, 3

17. In the company of Mr. Blimbery and Mr. McKay, fellow traders like himself, Jim had gone to the restaurant for lunch.
   (1) VIII, 2   (3) I, 3
   (2) VIII, 4

18. I'm interested in the story, John; I want to hear more of it.
   (1) VIII, 3   (3) I, 3
   (2) IX, 6

19. As the two men hurried toward the door, Charley rose and thrust back his chair.
   (1) XI, 1
   (2) I, 3

20. He had not been at the office that morning, nor had any one heard from him; but Charley knew what he was doing.
   (1) IX, 4   (3) I, 3
   (2) IX, 7

INDEX